To Meet and...

TO MEET
AND TO GREET

Faith with Faith

Kenneth Cragg

EPWORTH PRESS

ISBN 0 7162 0483 5

First published 1992
by Epworth Press
1 Central Buildings, Westminster, London SW1H 9NR

Phototypeset by Intype, London
and printed in Finland by
Werner Söderström Oy

How oft amid these flowing streets
Have I gone forward with the crowd and said
Unto myself: 'The face of everyone
That passes by me is a mystery.'
Thus have I look'd, nor ceas'd to look, oppress'd
By thoughts of what and whither, when and how.

William Wordsworth,
The Prelude, 6, 626–31

The spirit never shows
What terror would enthral the street
Could countenance disclose
The subterranean freight
The cellars of the soul.

Emily Dickinson,
Collected Poems, 1225

The thoughts of faith revolve
In troubled versions through the mind
And labour to resolve
In satisfactory kind
The enigmas of selves.

The singularity
Of each translates to common need
And sharp disparity
Demands a mutual heed
In searchings of the heart.

Contents

Preface

'I preached . . .' wrote the Welsh priest-poet, R. S. Thomas, 'but our eyes never met.' Was it the preaching status that prevented it? If so, and knowing that eyes should meet, the preaching was aware of its own lack, caught in the paradox of communication meant and foiled. All the large questions of meaning, authority, office, evasion, incomprehension, distance and otherness are in that summary of how it was between pulpit and pew. They only multiply when we move out of the chapel into the world, out of familiar culture into unfamiliar.

It is clear that academic theology has become increasingly busy with the problem of communication. 'Dialogue' has become a vogue word and books multiply. Assured 'divinity' gives way to 'religious studies'. Yet do 'eyes really meet' where religions respond, through their custodians, to their bewildering diversity?

The nine chapters of *To Meet and to Greet: Faith with Faith* are concerned to focus on aspects of the whole equation that need special emphasis. Among them is an urgent realism about the reproach of religions. Some faith dialogue seems to develop an air of self-congratulation, if not complacence. It makes us happy with ourselves, being so much better than fanatics. It is good that we should be conversing, but penitence needs to be paramount if we are to be honest with the histories that accuse us all. Religions need to be aware of themselves as often neither admirable nor desirable in the imprint they have left on history.

Such will to honest realism – not against the other, but about us all – also argues a livelier responsiveness to the secular mentality across the world. We need to measure the sharp unwantedness about dogma, tradition, ritual, which demonstrates itself in varying moods of irreligion present through all territories of faith. Eyes need to meet outside as well as around the sanctuaries.

Vital to these concerns there must be a meeting of hands to take up obligations to society, ecology and development which no faith can now monopolize. These are liabilities we have not understood if we do not see that they are shared. They will be reviewed here, not primarily in terms of sociology or economics, but rather in their claim on intellectual comprehension and religious motivation. This is why we must begin with a right sense of the cosmopolis we now inhabit with the age-long mystery of planetary wonder and the sordid realities of our misanthropy alongside the splendours of the human meaning.

Alertness to perennial crisis in our human-ness means a will to appreciate, by mutual discovery, what we legitimately possess in common. It may be only in the religious interrogation of our environment in nature and of ourselves in selfhood, rather than in the answers we hold as clues. Our eyes may meet in our searchings and there is much we can inter-possess in the imagery with which language and metaphor enable us to state it.

In that context it falls to each meeting, greeting faith to present the convictions by which it lives, to show cause why its distinctiveness is worthy of perpetuation, why it claims the right to be present and articulate in the human whole. This task can only be undertaken inwardly by each faith for itself, but always in a right attention to its own tensions and to the scruples that belong with authenticity. A Christian attempt to do this comes in the final chapter about the 'home' without which no meeting could occur. Non-entities do not converse.

Two matters are never far away from the will to meet. They have to do with the possibility of common prayer and with the vexed question of 'conversion'. The fact – and the limits – of common spirituality, its form and credentials, are discussed in Chapter 7. Chapter 8 aims to examine what 'conversion' ought to mean by setting our convertibility into the paradigm of redemptive love and asking what its realization means within the self and for community.

Nine chapters make no claim to comprehend the whole. They merely explore a theme indicated by Jesus, in the Sermon on the Mount, according to Matthew: 'If you salute your brethren only, what do you more than others?' (5.47). Jesus was there regretting the common Semitic practice of restricted greeting. In that tradition 'greeting', or one's 'peace', had an objective existence, passing over – as did the contrasted effectiveness of a curse – to rest upon the recipient person, house, or place. 'Your peace' Jesus ascribed to his disciples: 'my peace,' he said, 'I give you.' Just as the Jew shook off the dust of his feet on leaving an alien land in vigorous dissociation, so kindred and home were greeted with peace. 'The son of peace' is a familiar phrase in the Gospels, analogous to 'a son of the Torah', the one truly destined for the 'peace' offered and worthy to receive it. When offered by mistake to one not worthy, i.e. the stranger, peace should be withdrawn. Its integrity obtained only for those fitted to have it bestowed on them.

The precept 'Salute brethren only' was seen by Jesus as fit to be overridden by a new ethic. His peace would pass beyond the closed circle of clan and kin. To meet and greet faith with faith is to do likewise. Admittedly, the idea is radical. Malediction on each other is more the old tradition between beliefs. Hence the need to come away from what I playfully describe as Adamant Square and Cavil Row, having first noted that we live together in cosmopolis. Salutation, then, has much to overtake: greeting has to struggle with lingering suspicion of itself.

Knowing the hinterland of past enmity, alert to presently entrenched antipathies, 'peace' has need of deep resources. It moves in the elusiveness of religious meanings, the prejudices of long allegiance, the subtle temptations of what is institutional. If the peace of salutation is a healing peace, it must undertake the sicknesses; if a reconciling peace, it must monitor the enmities; if a ruling peace, it has to ride the disorders; if a divine peace, it must respond 'worthily of God' to the human predicament. Salutation has to be much more than the art of being peacable. It means an exercise of mind and will alive to its necessary perplexities but not daunted by them. The preaching that has a faith to commend must learn to 'let the eyes meet'.

For reasons of simplicity the only diacritical signs used are those that distinguish the glottal stop and the consonant 'Ain. Technical terms are briefly explained in the index. As an essay, not a treatise, the book does not carry a bibliography.

I

Cosmopolis

Space photography allows us to see our whole planet, a blue splendour in its solar orbit, and discern whole continents in the design of sea and land. The vision educates us into the mystery of earthly being. It condemns us for the grossness of our habitation of so fair a globe. A thing so majestic deserved a wiser tenancy than humans have contrived.

Imagination does well to know it so, if terrestrial romance, as the sight inspires it, is to be fused with honest realism. We possess a cosmos. But the very technology which presents it to our eyes spawns the 'sordid particulars' of exploitation, war and tragedy in which, if at all, 'the eternal design must appear'.[1] To see the earth as one and whole from space is to confess it one and in no way whole as the city of mankind, a habitat whose human history has contracted it into a single neighbourhood, drawing its races and communities into the suburbs of one metropolis. When, in the heyday of the Persian Safavids, Isfahan was their pride and joy, Cairo, they boasted, was 'one of its suburbs'.

Technology today has a similar pretension. It is not only that the spreading city is the symbol of this present time on every continent, it is also that mobility, communication and media information have compelled cultures and identities into a common history. Techniques have made cosmopolis actual and the sciences, natural and social, are set to monitor and control its fortunes. We live – all of us in some sense – this physical and human universalism. Privacies of every kind indeed persist. There are innumerable villages within the one cosmopolis, most of them haunts of anxiety and toil. But there is nothing, physical or economic, that divides which does not also inter-weave the life of any. The paradox which makes privation more self-aware, makes affluence more culpable. Cosmopolis as seen by astronauts is a visual wonder: as lived by the earthbound it is the realm of human crisis.

The purpose of these chapters is to study the relations of the religions of humankind within today's experience of these dimensions. Have they not claimed to hold the clues both to the meaning of the whole and the guidance of the parts? Are they not appointed custodians of the absolute? Do they not presume to preside, credally, directionally, ritually, over what human responsibility with the earth must know and do? Yet, in the flux of history, they have survived to seem discredited or simply bypassed by the very technology that most needs the discipline of right interpretation. Secularization has been for almost three centuries a gathering tide of agnosticism, of acceptance of a human autonomy as the only thing there is. Such God-forfeiting conclusion may be exultant in some quarters, fed by the very vices of the religions. In others it is wistful and regretful. For others again the sheer intoxication of scientific aspiration and competence, or the pervasive pressures of its pursuit, have left transcendent questions to the useless margins.

This recession in religious sensitivity must be wisely diagnosed, its sources and logic probed. We must see the will to be secular which figures so largely in modern reading of the human condition as a verdict against the faiths of the world *and* a quest somehow to satisfy what necessitated the verdict. In part it is an appeal for a worthier spirituality, in the yearning for which no religion should suppose it has monopoly.

In sounding out contemporary secularism we have also to study the reactions of the faiths to its demands. These are often taken as threat and menace calling for hostile re-assertion. Or they are seen as a purging corrective, a discipline of adversity which may be salutary. Either way, a further study has to be what the situation has done for the relations of religions with each other. In the last half century there has been a ground-swell of concern between them for encounter. 'Dialogue' has become a word in vogue. The secular scene, to be sure, is not the only cause of this development. Religions have long been in interior debate and have often shaped each other. Liaison about a common enemy is not a fair account of what is happening.

There are aspects of this inter-faith activity which tend to complacence or even self-congratulation. For some, tolerance becomes almost a faith itself, irresponsibly sanguine about the things that divide. It then deals superficially with issues that deserve more anxious scrutiny, perhaps more sceptical review. We do no justice to history when we propose to heal its hurts slightly. We need at all costs to avoid the condescension which sometimes attaches to easy invocations of 'the centre' and discountings of 'the circumference'. We need to know and feel the pain of inter-religion and beware lest we increase it. Our exchanges must be lifted into the mysterious wonder of that blue majesty on which we dwell. They must be down within the conflicts and perplexities which attend its human story.

(ii)

We do well to begin from this twin perspective of celestial brightness and terrestrial predicament, and assess the secular instinct as a rubric reading both. The universe, it argues, is simply there. Its bewildering immensity and unimaginable age veto all but anthropocentric significance. Earthboundness can yield no clue to vastness which cannot have credibly been engineered to eventuate in us. The absolute is an absolute silence. We are on our own. That conclusion, it is said, finds corroboration in the evident way in which all venture into meaning is a human enterprise.

Our sciences, our cosmology, our astronauts, wrest from the yielding silence whatever it is we know. Our knowledge, like our future, is man-contrived. If we are on our own on this stage of drama we are on our own in the action. Conclusion has to be avowedly secular in this entire sense. We must undertake what it entails without wish for consolation and without illusion of transcendent reference.

In this temper secularism is a puzzle to itself. For what it reads of 'man in the universe' has to negotiate with 'the universe in man'. All we know and attain may indeed be self-concerted, autonomous, but plainly we cannot think of it as self-derived. It is responsive to the given. It is moulding, shaping, experiencing, what it has received. It is, quite literally, within 'responsibility' not only as a capacity to relate and respond but as an onus resulting from what follows. Every human competence is a human liability. In having autonomy we are incurring obligation. Morally we recognize this in our awareness of society and the inter-play of power. Religion means that we recognize it in an inclusive context of time and meaning, the context of a given-ness which is not merely technical, physical, intellectual, within a realm we control, but also intentional, a realm of divine enterprise and magnanimity. The two realms coincide, or they could not be what they are. They are parted only in human interpretations, the one only empirical, the other full of faith.

It is the vocation of the faiths – when they are faithful[2] and not merely banal or angry – to possess and commend this reading of the world, but to do so in a careful sympathy with the secularity that is minded to distrust it. Such sympathy appreciates that much distrust comes from the excesses of religions, but on every count it is appropriate. The larger context may seem too good to be true. Or it may seem to be loved only in ignoring the tests and toils by which secular technology proceeds. 'Not believing in belief' is a condition believers need to understand.

It might be said that Buddhism practises this sympathy too well, at least in its Theravada form. It is ambivalent about the dominion which science claims and pursues. For willed 'dominion' we must look to the Semitic faiths. But Buddhism does begin in its own way with the anthropocentric situation. It starts from the human end and sees it as predicament and *dukkha*, or the suffering of transience.[3] The environment which deceives us into ventures of control and response is read as affording no abiding satisfaction. The self-hood that seeks must know it cannot find. The techniques it needs are those 'skills' of the Eightfold Path which take us towards the goal of 'non-self', in which the illusion of separate identity is at an end. The end is not 'extinction'. For, truly, there was no-thing to extinguish. But it is the effective negation of desire and, with it, the cessation of the 'me' that deludes and is deluded.

This mode or mood of anthropocentric reading of experience must come to its own terms with this teeming, circling globe in space which is its home. Its renunciation is inspired instead by what is lived upon it. Theravada Buddhism may well seem to those outside it a religion of profound dismay, yet it does have kinship with some of the less sanguine forms of secularity, which suspect secular activists of a blindness to their own absurdity. To these we must return. It is no doubt a human option. We *are* free to read a sort of 'not-meant-ness' into everything. Philosophy has never been exempt from that temptation. But is it churlish? Can we not 'have faith'? May we not reconcile ourselves positively to life, instead of negatively? Or, in metaphor, 'arrows of desire' require the bow-string drawn.[4] The world would seem to be inviting trust. To be 'in it' is to be 'at it'. To evade response is to make one. The womb, it would seem, invites the confidence with which the embryo replies. When we arrive we are instinctively possessed of air and hunger and we begin to discover personality, our own by dint of others'. Even our freedom to renounce this meant-ness only transpires within it, since meaning is inescapable. May it be that meaningless-ness is, in truth, self-induced? That the secular boredoms of contemporary literature, which we must examine later as aspects of cosmopolis, are nothing but our apathy?

Buddhism undertakes its version of the human meaning with a gallant compassion. On a different hypothesis its disciplines might be saluted and emulated by all. Once committed to the illusoriness of the self, it ministers to those it serves with a patience and care – and in the case of the Mahayana available grace – that any faith might covet to offer. But has its responsibility to the self engrossed it irresponsively to all else? What of the Semitic theisms and cosmopolis?

(iii)

They certainly take world and time as meant. They recognize a cosmos and read it as inclusively intended. This is the meaning of their doctrine of creation – a doctrine not primarily answering a question how? or when?, but rather why? Their scriptures are full of the theme of a creating 'word'. 'By the word of the Lord were the heavens made . . . He spake the word and they were made, and all the host of them by the breath of His mouth.' So the psalmists and the prophets. 'The word' is the issue of the will and executant of it. Within it is the impulse which says 'Let there be . . .' and there *is*. That divine *fiat* is equally the theme of the Qur'an, where 'the heavens and the earth' are a steady refrain in the ascription of 'lordship' to God.

It is understood as a lordship which invites a partnership from man, remits its creation to a 'deputy', to whose trust it is assigned as ploughman and vinedresser, as seaman and contriver. This is the 'dominion' of the Bible which the Qur'an calls *khilafah*. All technology is seen as its fulfilment. These scriptures never visually beheld 'the round world' they have interpreted as meant for human meanings. But the techniques which enable readers now to do so are the current fruit of their conviction about humanity as 'God's imperialist'.[5] By this light Adam was no Prometheus doomed to perpetual struggle with a futile and denied ambition. We are within a cosmos which yields our polis, a world which awaits our ordering will and mind.

It is necessary to believe so in order to know human perversities for what they are. These arise, these matter, not because we have autonomy but because we are defiant. The mastery we should receive as meant for gratitude we usurp as apt for lust and presumption. We then repudiate the servant-status which is the counterpart of our authority. Here, in all their long story, is the place of 'the law and the prophets'. Man the king is called to be man the priest, the celebrant within the dominion, the conscious artist of the divine praise. The task of prophethood is to acquaint humanity with that destiny and to summon to it. 'Hold by the reality of God and demand much of life' might be a bold phrasing of the conditional charter it prescribes with due warnings, as in the Qur'an, against heedlessness and all that contravenes a true creaturehood under God.

There are aspects of this acceptance-to-be which distort what we might call 'the trust of the trust', the doctrinal grounding of the human privilege. It has been the temptation of Semitic theism to see itself so much 'on behalf of God' that it has succumbed to being only on behalf of itself. The authority it had as a witness has been turned into an ultimacy it enjoyed in its own right. It has committed what some secular minds see as an annexation of God, whether in the name of peoplehood, or institution, or *jihād*. *Allāhu akbar* can become *Islāmu akbar* and what properly only serves God substitute for him by arrogating a status he never conferred in exceeding the one he has. To these presumptions we must turn in later chapters.

They have been a factor prompting to secularity. We recall Nietzsche's loaded question: 'Who among us would be a free-thinker were it not for the church?'[6] Yet, for all their compromise, the vision of the theisms as to humanity in this divine vocation abides. It does reverent justice to a sense of earth which space photography would seem to have confirmed at least for the imaginative among us. However, secularists remain unpersuaded. Their grounds are as varied as their reactions. Apart from the treacheries of religious institutions, the attitudes that want cosmopolis without religious faith may be said, for present purposes, to offer reasons of scientific origin, of radical despair, or of moral self-sufficiency. To consider these in sequence will be the right prelude to study of what is incurred because of them by religions moved to respond in terms of 'dialogue' with and between themselves.

(iv)

The first cluster of reasons has to do with the external success of the sciences. Technology is seen as the final arbiter. Its capacities are vindicated everywhere in the realms to which they can apply. Where they cannot, there is no other determinant on which we can correspondingly rely. The vagaries of human society and of the inner psyche may be to some degree solved by the scientific principle applied to them. But the human, the societal, the historical, are not susceptible, like the physical arena of the natural order and the chemistry of things, to skills of the technician. The latter continue to off-load on the human scene an ever-growing harvest of scientific discovery and ingenuity, for the manipulation of birth, the dissemination of information, the revolutionizing of patterns of living and even, in part, of thinking. But these still face, and even accentuate, the irrational in man and society, to which mere empiricism has no answer.

Scientific optimism can from time to time overlook this fact or remain so preoccupied with the technique-habit of mind and its ongoing promise as to ignore the hard evidence of its own limitations. Given those instincts, the appeal of religious faith is neutralized as lying outside what empiricism can approve. This form of secularity has often been linked with a theory of human development by which humanity has passed through stages of spiritual 'magic' to metaphysics and so finally on to a scientific materialism. We arrive at a humanism for which God is a relegated non-necessity. We attain to belief that, when out of its childhood, the world can never be other than secular. Some minds, however, having reached this conclusion experience misgivings about grown-up maturity.[7]

However, these misgivings are nothing like the radical despair of the second type of rejection of belief in God and the human as gifted to intelligible 'dominion' under God. The despair can sometimes put on a bold face and become brash or angry in remarking: 'I find it difficult to approve of God.' For Jewish, Christian and Muslim piety that sentiment may well be close to blasphemy. Is God to seek or need our approval? Or who are we to presume to give or withhold it? May the clay complain to the potter?

Yet clearly, such metaphor, though known to the prophets, hardly fits the faith about man. The problem of 'theodicy', of a 'justification of God', is inseparable from the biblical/Qura'nic version of man's essential dignity. He is other than will-less, malleable clay. Clay imagery belongs well with the body: it cannot fit the mind and heart. So the argument about our pain and tragedy must enter into God. 'Why thus?' was Job's agony, but only so because of his faith. That, indeed, in the very strength of theism. It takes the full measure of the mystery of evil and of wrong precisely in believing a good purposiveness behind all things.

No wonder, then, that questioning secularists turn their doubt about point and purpose into complaint about faith in God. Among them Colin Wilson writes:

> It seems to have struck no one that human beings are grossly exploited by God. We are expected to bear misfortune, to learn from experience . . . to offer thanksgiving for benefits received. Our role in every way is that of the slave and of the sycophant.[8]

Contemporary literature abounds with such de-theologizing of the world, extending that recession of the sense of God which technology releases and taking it into the inner experience of selfhood. The 'stream-of-consciousness' novel turns the self away from the large vocation to divine mystery into the enigma of individuation which so puzzles the Buddhist. T. S. Eliot's *The Wasteland*, with its strangely Buddhist undertones, became a symbol for numerous writers, Arab and Eastern as well as Western and white. Blacks, too, like James Baldwin, have wrestled with the heavy suspicion of meaninglessness and futility. The theme runs variously through the works of Albert Camus, Franz Kafka, Samuel Beckett, Virginia Wolff, Eugene Ionesco, Chinua Achebe, James Joyce, Richard Rive and many others.

The search for an authentic self, its definition under the threat of absurdity, and its rescue from the tyranny of poverty, oppression and conflict, burdens contemporary literature. Sometimes, as in the West Indian, Franz Fanon, it is violence in political resistance which gives the self release into meaning. Strife is not merely necessary for political liberation; it is the crux of emancipation from the colonized mind. Such inner 'liberation' via struggle for an outward one imprisons itself in the necessity of hatred. Mid- and late-century Palestinian poetry has been occupied with the same concerns. But Palestine differs from Algeria for which Fanon struggled. With Palestinian poets, the homelessness which resistance might solve has become instead a parable of the hopelessness which nothing can allay.[9]

Whatever the form or the context, languid or passionate, the self as its own 'experiment' dominates the literary scene. No inter-faith dialogue can be right which is not also dialogue here, as that which must engage them all. Buddhists and some Hindus are already there. For this is where they start. Theists are even more crucially there because of their confessed confidence in God and humankind. Some among them, not least in Islam, may well be minded to resist the issue, holding that God is unaccountable and conceding no need of theodicy. Yet so to react is to undermine their own convictions. Aspects of this hardness of heart, in Jew, Christian and Muslim, about God's inviolability and their own right to dogmatism will come in Chapter 2. It may serve us best here to look with the Qur'an into the question of any divine immunity from human question, and then to study the dubiety about theism in the writing of an eminent Egyptian Muslim who shares much Western pre-occupation with human futility. This will carry us forward to the third category of humanism without God.

(v)

The Qur'an from time to time uses the word *cala* ('upon'), which is the Arabic way of expressing 'liability'.

For example, Surah 6.12 says that God 'has written upon Himself mercy'. He has prescribed mercy as a duty, a law within his nature. This is a precious conviction, since broadly in Islam there is a sense of unaccountability about its theism. Humans cannot have, still less require, 'rights' on God. To think they could would somehow call omnipotence into question and, with it, divine disposal of all things, unless we believe the liability arises from within because of love and is, therefore, entirely free. Jews and Christians have likewise to cope with questions about divine arbitrariness.

However, for them all, it is clear that faith about creation, law and the sending of prophets, means that there are 'things of God' which genuinely turn on human consent. Obedience, gratitude, 'dominion' and much else are all divinely awaited as humanly willed. Plainly the willing may *not* fulfil the awaiting, since we are not automata. The issue matters to God. The divine-human situation is evidently relational. It is not 'one-way'. Given the ordering revelation, what is 'upon God' in this situation, seeing that – as the Qur'an well knows – human obduracy so often happens?

Islam would seem to say that then there is no further divine obligation, but judgment. The revelation and the guidance complete God's liability towards humanity. Here a crucial passage is Surah 4.165. After reference to noted prophets it continues: '. . . apostles, bearers of good tidings and warnings, so that mankind should have no possible case against God after the apostles – the God who is mighty and wise'. The saying 'no *hujjah* (plea, argument, excuse) against God', seeing that messengers have been sent, means exoneration of God when these are rejected. The Christian situation here is utterly contrasted. God undertakes liability, in Christ, going beyond injunction and prohibition into travail and redemption. But that is to anticipate. Islam believes in careful limits to divine liability for humanity.

The burden of this issue, either way, underlies the bitter reproach in the secularism I am reviewing. The question of God is inextricably bound up with the question of man. Those who find absurdity and enigma in the one must attribute it to the other. Their dismissal of

God, their grudge about theism, derive from experience of their human selves. The Jewish, Christian or Muslim case must meet them where they are. Hence their urgent meeting with each other and with Asian faithful who have long lived with another form of satiety and bewilderment in experience of themselves.

This twin theme of human dismay and divine interrogation was well broached by a writer from within Islam, the novelist Najib Mahfuz of Cairo, who worked in the Ministry of Religious Affairs. In his recent *Fountain and Tomb*, a character protests, in the context of a discussion about death:

> God does not relate to us and I cannot relate to Him. There is nothing but dead silence between us. I cannot explain the evil in life and do not understand the weaknesses and inadequacies of nature. I have always concluded that God – praise be to Him – has decided to leave us to our own devices.

Reproached for uttering what amounts to blasphemy, he continues:

> Belief in God demands belief in His lack of concern for our world, just as it implies that we are on our own.[10]

Chatter on the Nile, another story, coops up a cross-section of Cairenes in a moored house-boat. Within that parable, Mahfūz retails the confusions and inanities of their tedious, meandering conversation, as they compare notes about their boredom and frustration. Economic as well as personal ills are depicted here as elsewhere in Mahfuz' forty-year-long work in fiction.[11]

By far the boldest and most religious of his works is the long survey of the rise, time and ebb of three great 'prophets', Moses, Jesus and Muhammad. Their successive régimes within their quarters of the human city based on people-consciousness (Moses), gentle innocence (Jesus) and strong-arm power (Muhammad) avail only for a while, to be followed, after their demise, by return to sorry *status quo ante*, when their followers quarrel and their aura is forgotten. The theme is the failure of prophethood to achieve permanent amendment of life and the forlorn victimization of struggling humanity by thuggery and conflict.[12]

Meanwhile Gabalawi, the mountain-one (or 'God'), who allegedly has sent these 'prophets', is secreted mysteriously in his remote, wall-invested mansion from which he never emerges. His very existence is enigma. A grim episode suggests that he may have been killed by an intruder bent on investigating the puzzle that surrounds him. The 'God' in that demise is said, nevertheless, to approve the skills of a fourth, latter-day, figure who emerges to master nuclear fission and tragically bestow on the same vulgar men of power the ultimate weapon of terrorizing tyranny.[13]

Najib Mahfuz' absorbing and influential writing is proof that the burdens about human meaning and divine theodicy are in no way confined to Western 'wastelands'. They may be more difficult for Islam to accommodate, but they are surely present. The cosmopolis that is one in planetary beauty is one in its cargo of human awareness asking what their habitation means, or observing that 'the more the universe seems comprehensible, the more it also seems pointless'.[14]

Faiths in response to those demands are at differing times of their history and are differently minded in facing them. It is well to remember that Eastern reckoning with them is complicated by the Western form in which they are often clothed. There is always a sort of 'Western question' in the Arab, Indian and Asian mind, just as politically there was long an 'Eastern question' in Europe's relation to the Ottomans.[15] In coping with this psychological and spiritual complex of 'the other', it may be useful to invoke an intriguing passage in the Qur'an about 'the two easts and the two wests' (Surah 55.17). It has to do with the points in the horizon within which the rising and the setting suns move through the seasons. Poetically also, there are 'two easts' – the one the West sees as exotic, mystical, dreamy or fanatical, and the one that knows and shares all that makes the West sophisticated. Happily also there are two Wests, as capable in that sophistication of dreaming, suffering and yearning as any East. Aspects of this equation will be with us throughout these chapters.

I defer to Chapters 5 and 6 what we have confronted here. It remains to consider the third pattern of secularity, like the first in its dismissal of God and unlike the second in its greater equanimity and hopefulness as a studious humanism.

(vi)

It is the pattern of thought which might well be explored by asking, provocatively: Is God Christian? Is God Hindu? Is God Jewish? Is God Muslim? Absurd as the questions are, they nevertheless serve to focus how God is cast as the predicate of his custodian believers.

Impatient with these partisan advocates who conform God to their own advocacy, the secular humanist will make a disavowal of them the first requisite in any encounter with what might lie behind their theism. God must be rid of his institutionalized patrons, and allowed to be the symbol of a universal human capacity for moral responsibility, a human subjectivity to which there is no objective correlative. All human sense of God that the religions live by is simply the projection on to a 'beyond' of what is essentially within.

This view, which has no need to despair with the despairers, is plainly lethal to all religious structures, though it is far from being irreverent. It finds no warrant in appeals to revelation, nor in establishments of authority, nor in accredited channels of divine grace and wisdom. Since it is over these that so much religious controversy has revolved, moral secular humanism, making humanity the measure of the transcendent, obviously mutes them all. It contracts the 'God of Christianity', 'the God of Islam', into a human capacity for moral righteousness, for a responsibility that fulfils, by better human lights, what religions purport to undertake and have so often perverted.

It is a very subtle interrogation which this concept brings to the religious mind and to spiritual institutions of faith. It therefore belongs squarely with their dialogue, being at once a crucial foe and a candid friend. It takes over the functions of religions, does duty for them in underwriting love, reverence, mercy, compassion, hope and community. So doing, it purports to supply from within humanity just those sanctions, persuasions, impulses, which traditional devotion and divine worship were expected to inculcate and attain.

A leading source of this form of secularity was Ludwig Feuerbach (1804–1872) with his critique of religion as a false, illusory objectivity, since all that it authentically indicated was located within the human soul. His teaching is perhaps more appealingly savoured in the literary work of George Eliot, whose novels are pervaded by a deep moral sense of duty and whose whole quality might be summed up as 'dedication to "God" without God'. She found Christian clergy 'the most irresponsible of all talkers',[16] and thought herself emancipated from her evangelical Christian nurture. She believed she had turned 'faith' into a moral emotion, a commitment to humanity which was all the truer for *not* being entailed in dogma and church. Yet she could be patient with these for the sake of those who were not yet liberated from their confines. She wrote:

> I have too profound a conviction of the efficacy that lies in all sincere faith, and the spiritual blight that comes with no faith, to have any negative propagandism in me. I have lost all interest in mere antagonism to religious doctrines. I care only to know, if possible, the lasting meaning that lies in all religious doctrine.[17]

That 'lasting meaning' was a moral humanism, believing the universe to be purposive and humanity as self-sufficient.

There is much non-dogmatic humanism across the whole spectrum of modern religions. George Eliot has her parallel in Muslims like the eminent legist Asad Ali Asghar Fyzee of India, Muhammad al-Nuwaihy of Cairo, and Allah Bukhsh K. Brohi, Ambassador of Pakistan.[18] The Hindu mind lends itself readily to such reading of piety and ritual forms. There is much in political Zionism which understands Judaism in the same idiom, as a philosophy of humanity readily – if not desirably – detached from the régime of the synagogue. George Eliot, with her passion for Jewish romanticism and 'the Holy Land', would have been at home in secular Israel, the Palestinian anguish apart.[19]

All such will to secularity, in no way materialist and in no way trading bleakly with absurdity, puts at issue all that religions most strongly cherish while purporting to fulfil their social, moral role without them. It disputes their imagined monopoly of the spiritual realm and neutralizes many of their ancient conflicts. It asks, in effect, and disconcertingly, what 'being religious' truly is, means and presupposes. It reads cosmopolis in terms that dispense with faith-confessions.

An eloquent measure of its temper and logic in the West is Iris Murdoch's *The Sovereignty of Good* and her study of 'the idea of perfection, of 'God' and of 'good', and of the 'sovereignty' of 'good' over all else. She concludes:

> That human life has no external point or *telos* is a view as difficult to argue as its opposite, and I shall simply assert it. I can see no evidence to suggest that human life is not something self-contained . . . There is in my view no God in the traditional sense of that term: and the traditional sense is perhaps the only sense . . . Our destiny can be examined but it cannot be justified or totally explained. We are simply here . . . If there is any kind of sense or unity in human life, and the dream of it does not cease to haunt us, it is of some other kind and must be sought within a human experience that has nothing outside of itself.[20]

Yet it is not a lawless chaos in which we are alone. On the contrary, thanks to what *we* are in human-ness, it is the realm of 'the good', of right, of obligation, of compassion and of hope. There are every-where occasions for 'unselfing', in the apprehension of beauty and the arts, in mastering mathematics and language, in being truthful, humble and value-revering. This means *not* 'returning surrep-titiously to the self with consolations of self-pity, resentment, fantasy and despair'.[21] All is 'duty' in a living context realistically acknow-ledged.

There is much that, by one definition, is deeply 'religious' in such 'sovereignty of good', honestly attained. It is present across all cultures, as an understanding of cosmopolis. But it will not be saying *Allāhu akbar*, 'God is love', 'Hear, O Israel', 'Lord, Krishna'. It has by-passed Torah, Bible, Gita, and all scriptures, unless these can be read in its light.

Clearly, the heirs of all these 'revelations' have to take stock of this well-meaning supersession of them. The careful theist is left with many questions. Let us concede that life *is* 'self-contained', in respect of the egocentric situation in which we all exist. But if we think this 'privatizes' what 'the self contains', we have called in question what selfhood might embrace. Iris Murdoch admits to be preferring an option – which is not to dispose of the abiding option the other way. What may be read, according to Feuerbach, as a subjectivity wrongly objectified, may equally well be a veritable objectivity subjectively experienced. Meaning has certainly 'to be sought within human experience', but what may be found there *may* be such as *not* to leave us 'on our own'.

It is significant that writers like George Eliot stayed wistful in their humanism for visions they had known before. They embraced it to compensate for a vacancy that still remained. That may leave ground for questioning their decision. If there is that 'beyond us which is for us' we may not limit 'its' initiatives in revelation and grace – though if we believe we receive them we must be humble with the authority we believe them to confer.

In sum, response to secularity in all its forms requires of believing faiths a radical willingness for integrity and gentleness. It also requires them to be patient and perceptive among themselves. Stridency does not well suit either the terrestrial beauty of the cosmos or the precarious polis which it bears.

(vii)

It is often assumed in inter-faith circles that the ecumenical movement for *Christian* unity may be guide and precedent for some conjectural *religious* unity. There is no reason why greeting should not run through the entire human polis. Nor should the term 'ecumenical' serve only for inter-church activity. For the Greek behind the word means the whole inhabited earth, the human cosmos.

But 'not saluting brethren only' is more taxing than fraternal greeting. Or is it? The belief-and-claim problems may be deeper and wider, but the asperities which have occurred in inter-Christian relations could hardly be exceeded in inter-faith ones. It is the domestic tension which often brings the sharpest strain.

There is one practitioner of interior Christian greeting who had ample cause for enmity and abjured it, and who therefore can well be our mentor about any 'wider ecumenism', namely Richard Baxter (1615–1691), the Puritan Pastor of Kidderminster. His *Self-Review*, in which he took stock of 'soul experience' and 'heart occurrences', traces a growth in perception through, and only through, a growth in forbearance. In his earlier writings he found only 'the footsteps of my unfurnished mind'.

I knew not (then) how impatient divines were of being contradicted, nor how it could stir up all their powers to defend what they have once said . . . In controversies it is fierce opposition which is the bellows to kindle a resisting zeal.[22]

He saw that there were 'many distempers of the mind to be removed' and preferred to 'be a martyr for love than for any other article of the Christian creed'.[23] His conclusion, returning to a 'fire' metaphor', was that:

> Every degree of knowledge tendeth to more, and every known truth befriendeth others and like fire tendeth to the spreading of our knowledge to all neighbour-truths that are intelligible . . . When half is unknown the other half is not half-known.

'Acquaint yourself,' he advised his reader,

> . . . with healing truths . . . Be sure that you see the true state of the controversy and distinguish all that is merely verbal from that which is material . . . Bear with those that Christ will bear with: especially learn the master-duty of self-denial. For it is self that is the greatest enemy to Catholicism.[24]

'Catholicism', in his Puritan vocabulary, meant 'wholeness'.

What of such mature wisdom, it might be asked, outside 'what Christ will bear with' (if there are any such)? It may be urged that Baxter was unaware of inter-faith. But he wrote of 'heathen' and Muslims, and about 'having some more reason than I knew of before to think that God's dealing with such is much unknown to us'.[25] We will see in the next chapter the need to reproduce his like in the wider fields we frequent today.

Christians have to face what they mean by the indispensability of Christ. It can never mean indifference to others. For that would negate ever-open grace. It cannot mean apathy. What, then, should it entail? For many it means caution lest the distinctive truth be clouded or withheld. The decision of Archbishop Michael Ramsey to hold aloof from the World Congress of Faiths in the 1960s was a case in point. He did not attend an all-faiths service in the West London Synagogue despite a warm invitation. He suspected the idea of making 'religion', as it were, 'a unifying slogan'. It was not the right denominator on which to act. He approved of giving

practical expression to reverence for all faiths without the implication that all 'irreligion' was false and all 'religion' desirable.[26] His
restraint was motivated by his sense of the need to ensure that
Christian faith was not compromised by superficial associations outside itself.

Yet wise caution has within it a logic to take it further. As I have
earlier argued, deference to unbelief, and a sense religions ought to
have of their own discredit, themselves take us into inter-relation-
ship. The wrongs of religion are, to a degree, common property –
sloth, pride, prejudice, cruelty, strife, evasiveness and callousness
in face of wrong. These have often been induced in religions by the
very form of the histories lived between them. Inter-responsibility
leads further to diagnosis of why it should be so and, more urgently
still, to where and how faiths can find penitence and cleansing. The
nature of the human situation does not allow separate security.
Caution, therefore, needs to be joined with frankness but may well
not conduce to it.

In this context, there is also a danger of ambivalence. In *Nostra
Aetate*, the Second Vatican Council acknowledged the final goal of
religions as one and characterized 'the various religions' as being
where 'men looked for answers to . . . profound mysteries of the
human condition'. The relevant secretariat for 'Relations with Non-
Christians' is now named 'Pontifical Council for Dialogue with Other
Religions', thus discontinuing the negative, and perhaps derogatory,
descriptive 'non-Christian'.[27] The recent Draft Catechism from
Rome, however, writes in quite emphatic terms about the sole truth
of Christian revelation and the authority of the church. With other
faiths, too, it often seems that the will to relate is inwardly hedged
about by the will to reserve. There are still forbidden enquiries and,
as a cynic might say 'The apostolic church exists to congratulate
itself on its own apostolicity.' Is it not precisely in forcing upon us
all this awareness of the measure of our inward immunities that
our task and vocation are really understood? How inclusive such
immunities in bastions can be is the study of Chapter 2.

(viii)

Through all the themes and issues cosmopolis entails for the faiths
of mankind is the fact that, however they respond, there runs

through all contemporary things an inescapable universalism. It is within what conjoins us all in contemporary humanity that we have to handle what diversifies us in nations, creeds, races and cultures. In a world urgent for community are faiths only to continue to divide? Peace and war, human rights, market forces – unlicensed or controlled, ecology and the future, health, food, water and population, structures of finance and the zones of poverty – all these are dimensions of religion, its liability and interrogation. They are the context in which relationships arise. Pluralism has to answer to all that unifies.

But though it unifies it is not even-handed. Some it exalts and others it makes vulnerable. As we must study in Chapter 8, religious diversity is never likely to give way to one religious supremacy. Most cultures are effectively characterized, if not dominated, by a broadly determining faith. We talk too glibly about 'multi-faith societies'. Every identity tends to be self-preserving, its memory long and its self-possession sensitive. The question, therefore, presses whether the broadly determining religion within any identity should not be seen as primarily liable and responsible for the life of that society. May one faith be a proxy-custodian of the transcendent, tolerantly, on behalf of the other faiths as well? Chapter 8 will take the question further.

In so much of Asia actuality makes it so, tolerance or not. Pakistan was created to denote and to determine the authority of Islam for nationhood. The contrasted ideal of Nehru-style secularity in India is currently under threat from a Hinduism wishing to be for India what Islam is for Pakistan and drawing Hindu logic from the example. Judaism is, if uneasily, the religious norm of Zionism, just as Zionism has its own zealous custody of Judaism. Even in the most secularized Western societies there is a case for letting a traditional faith act as the chief mentor of moral and social issues. This need be in no way to the exclusion of minority faith-reference but simply a circumstance of history. If chief mentorship is seen as a privilege and is rightly pursued, the preponderant religion can in fact ensure space and potential for minority faiths. It will help also to obviate the sort of ghettoizing of minorities which might otherwise prevail.

It is a high ideal, and some minorities, not least Jewish ones, would prefer a pluralist society in which *all* religions are minority faiths. No one faith, on this 'secular' view, should be allowed to claim majority status, whatever the numerical proportions of religious allegiance. To be true, a pluralism must see all as co-equals, whether as citizens or as believers. This view would like to think that all traditions were comparably vulnerable. But it has to be asked whether all minorities are ready in good faith to live within pluralism.

However this issue is resolved, the vocation of each will be a crucial aspect of their dialogue and bears on many aspects of law, culture, civics, ethics and social norms. If 'to live is to let live', the living has to be self-critical and tuned to co-existence. On that score each faith has to be its own assessor.

For Christians, in their assessment, is there, perhaps, a principle in Paul's words to his readers in Rome: 'Receive one another as Christ also received us, to the glory of God' (15.7). To be sure, he is writing to fellow Christians. Paul would be the first to insist that 'Christ receives us' on the condition of faith. But, for Christian imitation of Christ, may it obtain also in 'reception' of outsiders? For faith was not initially present in Christ's readiness for us in grace. He 'received us' in openness to search, in penitence, in sincerity, in unworthiness as he knew it in us well enough. The faith he finally required he was patient to evoke. He was often found countermanding disciples who were otherwise minded. Radical in his claim, he was gentle in his compassion. If we are to relate beyond ourselves as Christ relates to us, we will need to share his mind. Our way with his truth will turn on how we perceive its way within ourselves.

On either count perceptions have greatly differed, as the next chapter must review.

2

From Adamant Square and Cavil Row

(i)

The insignia of Swissair is a white cross on a red ground. It appears on the tail assembly of its planes. When, in 1984, it was granted, alone but for Air France, the right to ply in and out of Riyadh, the capital of Saudi Arabia, the state desired the company to remove or conceal its insignia. Swissair explained that it could not repaint its planes every time they flew to Riyadh, nor could it reserve aircraft solely for such flying. After negotiation a compromise was reached. Swissair would always be in and out in hours of darkness and its pilots would be instructed to extinguish the tail lights on approach and while grounded. The Swiss were likewise required to hide the cross at their embassy.

To such lengths can the will to exclusion go. To be sure symbols are important and emotive. But all humans make the sign of the cross when arms are outstretched in gestures of weariness or embrace. We are all physically a horizontal across a perpendicular. It is hard to build or devise architecture which does not contain the offending sign. The Saudi flag flies unhindered everywhere in war and peace, bearing the very *Shahadah*, or confession of Islamic faith.

In that same Riyadh there is an extensive campus to house all foreign embassies. It is generously equipped with computerized underground water-piping to ensure graceful lawns and tree-lined shade. It has a costly sports complex and every up-to-date amenity. But it contains no churches. Foreign faiths are not supposed to pray on Saudi soil. Perhaps it is assumed that 'infidels' do not pray at

all, or that they should be left to be secular in order to confirm
Islamic verdicts on their culture.

Happily, in the neighbouring emirates of Abu Dhabi and Dubai
there are churches standing on ground expressly donated for them
by the emirs. Muslim attitudes are not all hostile. Moreover, rulers
have to take account of their own extremists and it has long been
an Islamic assumption that tolerance of non-Muslims should not
obtain in the sacred territory of 'the peninsula of the Arabs'.

All faiths, if variously, have to face this impulse to prejudice. If
we are to meet, we must come out of Adamant Square and leave
Cavil Row behind. Yet 'impregnable hardness' and the habit of
'finding fault unfairly' ('adamant' and 'cavil') have often characterized the attitudes of religions to each other. There is within us all
a will to partiality. We hold what is our own and, holding it, we
are ourselves. There is a strong tie between the two sides of identity,
believers and belief, just as alleged 'unbelief' denominates other
people. The Canaanites, to Joshua, were both other tribes and other
gods. The term 'heathen' covered both. They were in double part
'alien'.

Faiths tend to cherish this 'standpoint-boundness' – if we may
borrow a German term. It should be no surprise that it is so. If
faith is believed to be in trust with what is final and ultimate, it can
hardly be indifferently its custodian. Nor can custody of its truth
be at peace about change. For loyalty, continuity, tradition and
fidelity are built into its psyche. It must 'hold' 'through all generations', as the loved biblical phrase runs.[1] Meister Eckhart observed
that 'there is no greater obstacle to God than time', meaning that
flux for ever calls in question the eternal. Faiths are always alert,
by their very quality, to tasks of preservation which are, inevitably,
tasks of relation to time's inexorable motion. To adopt the Spanish
motto *Antes Muerto que Mudado*, 'Better dead than changed', at least
grimly indicates what the alternatives are. The past is always vital
to the present of religions. Yet how to control the sequence is their
perennial problem, since 'to live is necessarily to outlive'.

This situation of being instinctively retentive weighs heavily on
the relationships between them. They fear to be accused of conform-
ing to passing climates of opinion, of yielding to the very mentalities
they should challenge and instruct. They are under urge to retain
their own criteria of truth, and their authority is minded to reserve

these from comparison or question. 'Adamant' and 'square' are apt
descriptives of the retentive instinct of all religions – retentive of
followers, certainly, but equally of beliefs, rituals and codes.

(ii)

Admittedly they conceive and contrive their exclusivism in different
forms. But there are none that do, or can, make entire tolerance
their claim. Entire tolerance is bogus. For intolerance is, by definition, intolerable. It is sometimes held that the Semitic theisms are
the masters of assertiveness. 'God has spoken', 'You shall be my
people', 'God was in Christ', 'Muhammad is the apostle of God',
Allahu akbar. How adamant these can be and how they may be
allowed – in Richard Baxter's phrase – to 'befriend' other truths are
matters we have to explore. Asian faiths are no less absolute for
their own stance, no less exclusive of the Semitic theisms than these
are of them.

> The silence of the extraordinary faces – the great smiles, huge and
> subtle: filled with every possibility, questioning nothing, knowing
> everything, rejecting nothing, the peace which has seen through
> every question without trying to discredit anyone or anything,
> nothing refuted, nothing established.[2]

Thomas Merton in Sri Lanka in his *Asian Journal* captures the
enigma of the great Buddha images, bathed in serenity. But can
they be tolerant of Job? Or do they disqualify his passionate religious
travail? There is much to be said for serenity – depending on how
you reached it. But there is clearly a great intolerance here. It will
not live with the Hebrew psalmist crying: 'Rise, O God, maintain
your own cause', 'Say something on your behalf' (Psalm 74.22).
For there is no 'cause', and no 'something' needing to be said except
the vacuity of the request.

Yet the images of serenity with 'nothing refuted, nothing estab-
lished', are much to be desired where so many raucous voices are
presuming to do on God's behalf what the psalmist wanted only
divinely done. There may be a difference between Buddhist and
theist in the temper of the mutual exclusiveness: there is none in
the fact of it. Buddhism and aspects of Hinduism may be said to

endorse a plural world, but hardly on terms that accommodate the meaningfulness of history and the significance of personality to which Semitic theisms are committed. They comprehend all truths only by evacuating them of what others hold them to contain.

This equal, if contrasted, exclusivism among faiths turns squarely on the status and concept of sacred scriptures. Almost all faiths possess this most crucial of the elements of religion. All give central allegiance to documents of revelation or illumination to which they are bound and by which they are defined. The sacred page is their court of appeal, the oracle by which they are controlled. Its place is sacrosanct. It is the map of identity. There can be no inter-faith dialogue which is not also inter-scriptural negotiation.

Yet it is precisely sacred writings which seem least amenable to inter-relation. That depends, as we must see, on how we receive them. But, by their very nature, and the deference they inspire, they predispose their peoples to awed compliance. By their durability through time they conduce to static submissiveness and help to seal the generations in steady sequence of affection and submission. They tend, if we allow them, to foster a partisanship about truth, to institutionalize a sort of rivalry of readerships and, therefore, a competition of authorities. They stand between us all as, at once, our separate guardians and our agenda of concern. They raise the vital issues and yet avail to pre-determine them.

(iii)

Scriptures which may be highly contrasted in their contents are thus comparable in their role in the faiths. The *Dharmapada* serves the Buddhist, *Sruti* or 'God-breathed' scriptures the Hindu. Judaism lives by the Torah and the Writings, Christians by the Bible, Muslims by the Qur'an, Sikhs by the Granths. Even smaller sects and communities are mysteriously scripturized. These are all, to their heirs and adherents, 'lively oracles'.

In many quarters the pressures reviewed in Chapter 1 have stimulated even sharper attitudes of assertion and dogmatism around Holy Books, enlisting them yet more zealously in the defence of faith and the contest against all that is perceived as threat and malice in contemporary society. 'The Bible says' becomes, in these circles, the sufficient answer to all doubts or arguments. Comparably, 'the

Qur'an says' will suffice the Muslim. The disciplines of Buddhism, with the will to a serene scepticism and the abeyance of world-commitment, may instil a gentler textual difference. But the *Dharma* is still the absolute arbiter, the Buddha's 'Teaching' the determinant of truth, of truth to be attained, that is, and not simply read or quoted.

The Semitic 'peoples of their books' in their submission to them have many features in common. Though their scriptures are essentially welded into history and emerge within events or within retrospect upon them, the text is widely taken as somehow the *obiter dicta*, the very speech, of God. A Jewish attitude may serve here as typical of Christian and Muslim also in 'how to read'. *Tanakh*, or scripture, is seen by orthodox Rabbis as divine communication to man.

> Torah is not speech which happens to be written down . . . but is essentially a piece of writing . . . Revelation is originally and primarily writing, a text with no linguistic defects.[3]

As such, it may connect with history, but the true exegete is not a historian of, for example, the Exodus. It is what God has caused to be inscribed about the Exodus which signifies. 'Scripture' thus 'loses its context . . . and is true and valid without any contextual constraints'.[4] All historical relativism is thus avoided by accepting the text as the very enunciation of God, verily perceived by the eyes in its written actuality. Some writers call this view 'meta-linguistic'. The vehicle of God is the Hebrew writing.

There is a comparable theme in the Islamic reception of the Qur'an, and the same desire to detach it from empirical constraints. The Qur'an is understood, syllable by syllable, as God's utterance orally conveyed to Muhammad and written down as such. Entirely faithful transcribing in calligraphy, and scrupulously faithful rendering vocally, are thus mandatory for the Hebrew and Muslim mind. For the latter, 'slips of the tongue' on Muhammad's part are understood as Satanically contrived and divinely prevented, or – if unwittingly occurring then – over-ridden.[5] The scriptural text has to be inerrant by divine guarantee. Only so is the deep religious concern for the inviolable and the infallible duly satisfied. These are very much the 'premises' on Adamant Square.

It is crucial, however, to ask as a matter of integrity, not to say of dialogue, whether in truth it can be so, least of all in respect of the Christian scriptures where the absolutist instinct has been no less present. Some Christian appeal to the Bible has been as literalist as any, resting the entire structure of the faith on the letter of the text as 'God's word'. This compels us to ask whether revelation is, or ever could be, stenographic. We need a long patience to reach a right and credible 'scripture-mindedness', with its implications for our understanding of God, of what prophethood means, and of how revelation might be assumed to 'present credentials'. That third implication goes to the heart of the religious estimate of the human mind. Over each of them a crude literalism rides roughshod.

(iv)

So doing, it fails to persuade. Reverent readership soon discovers that the Bible narratives – the Exodus, the Exile and all before and after – are a wonderful distillation of event and experience, of history learned in memory and transmitted as conviction. All is a long process of apprehension in which oral tradition, transmission, authorship and editorial mediation played their part. It is not that myth is historicized but that history is mythicized, mediated in the meanings to which it gave rise.[6] The 'inspiration' which ensured the text was not the making of human passivity vocal or prophets automata-pens. Rather it was the engaging of whole personalities, with their minds and hearts, even their dialects, to be creatively employed by a divine agency that willed their understanding but only within their own liability for it and with it. The Old Testament can be well understood in no other way, broad as the areas are which this understanding leaves to reading response and reading obligation. There is in the Qur'an a similar interplay between text and situation.

Despite the traditional Muslim view of the Qur'an as directly dictated from above, its whole incidence within the Prophet's biography, or *Sirah*, locates the entire scripture in the *asbab al-nuzul*, or 'occasions of revelation'. These are not seen as the 'cause' of the text, but only as its setting. The cause is the divine will to speak. Nevertheless what is said relates to incidents in the context to which exegesis has to attend. Indeed the situations actually necessitate what the content affords as, for example, the frequent references to what Muhammad's opponents were saying about him and his message. To these he was given the response to make. Thus the very textual form is historical. Muhammad can hardly have been impassive when confronting, as he resolutely did, the antagonism, nor turned into total passivity while transmitting the retort to denigration. As the Qur'an reminds him: 'It has been sent down (the technical term for *wahy* or 'inspiration' from God) upon your heart' (26.194, cf. 2.97). The heart is not the lips.

Some Muslims recognize that it is imperative to acknowledge a vital personal role for Muhammad in the reception of the Qur'an.[7] To do so in no way undermines an intelligent faith in his being genuinely a recipient: it simply understands recipience in living terms where divine action in *wahy* does not over-ride or disparage human powers but recruits and heightens them. We need not suppose that the more a scripture is divine the less it is human, that the more it is God's the less it is a man's.

Yet classical Islam supposes the contrary, moved by an inveterate religious desire for absolute certitude. This the Islamic mind believes itself to possess by virtue of its faith that its final scripture is channelled infallibly through an illiterate medium with an eloquence defying all human explanation and, therefore, indisputably from God alone. The vexed question of Muhammad's literacy need not detain us here.[8] It is surely saner, and textually more fitting, to see him as a totally recruited self in prophethood rather than as a cypher, an unconscious conduit of flowing words.[9]

Wise Qur'an readership has, then, to wrestle with a living text via an exegesis moving with the contents perceptively. The range of event-experience is narrower than in the Hebrew Scriptures, but the principle is, broadly, the same. In the Qur'an God is addressing Muhammad, and Muhammad alone: in the Bible humanity is frequently addressing God. The sense of the revelatory is differently perceived. But in neither, properly understood, is there a substance we properly receive in passive credulity. Engage we must – with mind and feeling. This means that no scriptures truly fulfil their role in faith if supposed to do so infallibly. Nor indeed could they have been brought into being that way. Revelation, wherever we believe it to reside in scriptures, is surely transactional, where divine

initiative and human recognition inter-act. If that must be true of
how scriptures eventuate, it must be decisive for how they are read.

We must include the *Sruti* scriptures of the Hindu world in that
same conclusion. For comparable beliefs about their genesis in poet
and sage are evident. But it is in the Christian scriptures that
the principle of the transactional between God and man is most
profoundly present. Indeed, it is hard to see how the New Testament could ever have been mistaken by infallibilizers or seduced
by them. Its Gospels and Epistles are so bonded into event-experience. The Jesus-story is received by faith as the Christ-event: that
reception inspires the telling of the story. The principle in the
Old Testament of remembered event and assimilated meaning is
reproduced. Both demand a readership which appreciates its character as what happened and what what happened meant, and neither
without the other.

As such they are no oracle mediated through unconscious pens
or audited by unalerted ears. Their inspired sufficiency can truly be
received as such, but only by a willingness to engage with issues of
transmission, formation and interpretation. The Christian Gospels
do not commend their credentials to sleeping partners. 'Lively
oracles of God' require lively readers whose liveliness resorts with
queries, doubts, debate and scrutiny – all the concomitants of faith.

It is likewise with the Epistles. How, the Muslim is moved to
ask, can apostolic correspondence from Asia to Rome, or from
Rome to Philippi, constitute 'revelation'? For 'revelation' only
'comes down' from heaven, and is never horizontal, man to man.
The answer is that divine inspiration in them is set within the actual
nurture of the nascent church into its own meaning via the counsel
and mind of apostolic leadership. As sacred literature, it comes only
out of vital issues and yields for the ongoing future lively precedents
from which later generations may derive their own responsible
expression of faith and worship. Such literature cannot be read as
a slavish blueprint which needs and awaits no intelligence. New
Testament authority is not some telephone directory with listings
which engage no thought and need no circumspection. It demands
intelligent engagement with all the factors, the data, and vitality
that went to its making. The Christian scriptures are not documents
which give themselves to readers asking merely to be told and
having no mind for mental travail.

And then there is the fact of the canon. The writings acquired their status by decision of the community. That decision did not endow them with their quality: it recognized it. But the recognition was necessary. The mind of the church accredited the mind of the scriptures. There were candidates for inclusion which did not achieve it. Those that did cannot well be read as if they were not still meant for the careful reckoning they were once held to have deserved. The very closure of the canon means that its contents have to be taken with a readiness for all relevant questions and ongoing faithful possession.

(v)

If that is the sound case properly made for scriptures, why, it may be asked, are they so far and so often viewed as oracles, unquestioned and absolute? Fundamentalisms, old and new, insist on their being read with scant enquiry as to what 'it says' can mean when ascribed to a text. Behind the will to have it, without need of insight, lies a whole complex of anxiety. Adamant Square is where it is safe to be. Elsewhere is slippery slope. We must know where we stand, lest we lose our bearings and forfeit our comfort. Unease about inter-faith can itself feed these fears. What is distinctive may be obscured. Syncretism is a suspect danger. Or there are texts which seem to demand that we be absolute on their behalf.[10] The fact that other faith-people seem threatening with their rival absolutes stimulates an enmity. We sense the kindling of controversy and fear to be receptive, lest we fail to be loyal in what becomes a crisis of confidence.

Behind this, whatever the faith in question, we need to consider a whole dimension of anxiety in the 'adamant' mentality. It is the hidden perplexity about the nature of trust. How and why can we be confident of our own confidence? What is it that can rightly undergird 'Verily, verily', and Amen, 'it *is* so'? How can we have any confidence in greeting at all? Can the 'relative' really belong with the 'religious', the ultimate with the plural? Unless we face this deep issue in liberty, anxiety, if not cowardice, will keep us adamant.

How, we ask, can we be in the position of deciding for a faith when it is that from which we propose to take 'faith' itself? Surely we must receive it, from beyond, from due authority, from the given-ness of 'revelation', from right heritage? Can any of us presume to do anything but accept these? Accept them is what most believers do. The cynic would say that we believe as we do by accident of birth. The devout say they receive what comes to them as valid truth, authentic by lights of book, or church, or teaching, or inheritance. These are then tribunals which are not themselves on trial. They are sacrosanct. We do not have to ask for their credentials. They are taken as read before we start. Such is 'fundamentalism'. Its security has great satisfaction.

But once it occurs to us that question might be right we are out from our 'dogmatic slumbers'. Afraid, we may quickly retreat into them, or otherwise, we will have to start beginning to believe in a new way. We will realize, once we are thus alerted, that our simple acceptance of 'the authority' (whatever it be) thanks to our awakening *does* become itself an issue. Then our decision to defer to it – for actual decision it must now be – is something we now go behind to ask why we did so. This we did not do before. Once we see the situation for what it is, we realize that we must take responsibility in respect of that for which we did not wish, hitherto, to be responsible, namely faith. John Henry Newman wrote of yearning to come to the end of need for what he called 'private judgment', the obligation to 'adopt' a faith. He thought he found an end to 'private judgement' by 'submitting' to the infallible church. Yet that very decision, enclosing all else, was itself a 'judgment' privately made. Why not, then, also subject to steady openness and ripe review?[11] It appears that, unless we are to be always passive, faith has to be responsible for itself, and liable for its integrity inclusively.

This is the vocation that acknowledgment of actual pluralism underlines. To accept it is the surest way out of Adamant Square. To receive it joyfully does not mean that we shall have no dependable faith. Nor will it mean that what we arrive at will be some 'faith in faith' which we have contrived. Quite the contrary: the real, the authentic, the divine, the eternal, will still be our quest and our experience. Christian convictions by these lights we leave to Chapter 9. We shall be in the way of that truth which makes mind and heart free, and of the love which casts out fear. Part of the task of dialogue will be to see, and make to be seen, how this destiny to undertake responsibility for truth faces every system, every structure, of religion. It addresses equally the Buddhist dogma of withdrawal from assured selfhood, the Judaic conviction of divinely decreed exceptional status within humanity, the Muslim confidence in finality from God, the Christian assurance in Christ that 'God is love'. Without the willingness to liability for more than mere assertion in respect of our beliefs and loves, the world has the right to surmise that we purvey mere 'confidence tricks' or are ourselves the dupes of them.

(vi)

Examples of how this will to responsible, as distinct from blind, faith might relate to faith-relationships will be offered in Chapter 5. It is evident that not all believers are alert or conversant enough with their heritage to be responsible in these terms. Inter-faith imposes its own prerequisites that, for many, are far to seek. Birth, for many, remains the determining factor. What, therefore, of parentage, infancy, childhood and nurture in the economy of the faiths?

All, by their own lights, are tenacious for their children and the due inheritance of belief. In the Judaic tradition birth from a Jewish mother is itself the continuity of Jewishness, whatever the problematics of 'the renegade Jew'. Jewish writers have often pointed out how 'Christians have to become', whereas 'Jews already are'.[12] Status by birth for Jewry ensures diligent and loving nurture within the strong traditions of the family and the Sabbath and the *Bar Mitzvah*. Buddhists and Hindus rejoice to afford some of their children for the vocation of the monk, whose contemplative poverty serves the wider society in betokening the truth of 'transience' and the 'nonself'.

Based on Surah 30.30 of the Qur'an, Islam holds the doctrine that *all* human birth is into, and for, a humanness which Islam fully defines and expresses. On this count it is parenthood which diverts offspring into other faith. Islam is 'the nature on which God shaped (lit. natured) man'.[13] This underlies the Islamic concept of apostasy, by which Islam is, in effect, a faith one is not free to leave, though that 'non-freedom' operates only if one wishes to leave. Islam is, of course, as rigorous as any in its inculcation of Islam, reinforced by the great effectiveness of solidarity and the rhythm of prayer and alms, with the incidence of *Ramadan* and pilgrimage.

In some areas of Christianity, not least in modern times, there is a greater exploratory freedom, though in others the tradition is of strong inculcation and indoctrination. Where confirmation is separated from baptism and deferred to years of adequate perception, the coast is clear for personal assessment of truth and discipleship. The option, however, is within the givens of inheritance and commendation. There can be no intelligent abeyance of guidance. One does not assume that in education into mathematics, science, or history, or art, the young are left to reach their own conclusions. So also in faith. Christian baptism commits parents to a Christian nurture and to an ordering of the home in its ethos. But it awaits the free maturing faith of the growing adolescent for the pledge to find its own inward fulfilment, its translation into discipleship.[14] The situation is perhaps well captured in II Timothy 3.15: 'From early childhood you have known the holy scriptures which are able to make you wise unto salvation, through faith in Christ Jesus.' Timothy, half-Jew, half-Greek, had initiation, but it left room for his own achieving of decision, his own acceptance of meaning. One is not 'enabled to be wise' by a process of indoctrination. Such liberty of their youth, if faiths can allow it, is a vital factor in their greeting. Only responsible ways to faith, in the 'nurture realm', can leave hope of responsible discourse between faiths in the wider world. The self-critical can best serve the inter-critical.

It may be fair to ask how the Jewish and Islamic 'theologies of birth,' fit into the whole biblical/Quranic doctrine of creation and the sacramental nature of intercourse, birth and parenthood which it affirms. In the Jewish case there would seem to be a favouritism of progeny where birth ensures holy peoplehood in one context and not in all others. The Islamic view makes non-Muslim parentage the villains of the piece, the diverters from a naturally true being to a perverse one. Yet within the *khilafah*, or 'dominion', begetting is given equally to all races.[15] Would it be truer to think of *all* births as equally into an adventure of truth-discovery, without discrimination, not *pro* for some and *con* for others?

That question apart, it is clear that the issues of nurture, education, heritage and domestic parent/child relationships are a vital area of inter-faith responsibility. How do we rightly, how wrongly, relate faith-conviction and family ties? How do we manage education within diversity and reconcile it with the claims of faith-identity where, in the young, it is most in process? What of schools and colleges in greeting?

(vii)

Those questions return in Chapters 7 and 8. Meanwhile what of credentials by which faith must assess itself before it may commend itself? As I argued, all make acts of truth-recognition, or believe they do. I asked how they have confidence in doing so. I suggest that the criterion should be the depth of their perception of life, how adequate to 'the mystery of things', how honest in its measure of humanity. All faiths, unless they are inarticulate, are self-assessed. They are not self-generated. They are responsive to per-ceived reality, but by what terms of reference?

Here is the nub of the problem attending on their wide diversity, their deep disparity in criteria and in conclusion. The appeal to 'revelation' as in Semitic faiths, or to 'illumination' as in Asian faiths, is similarly beset by a dilemma. We say of the truth or light in these: 'Yes, this is it: we have found it. We make it ours.' If, in this way, we acknowledge and submit, we are adopting the answer as the one for us. Yet, doing so, are we not implying, by this capacity to recognize, that we know already what we should be looking for? If so, do we need it anyway? Is not the ability to identify it a kind of knowledge already in hand?

This has long been the sceptic's angle. Revelation rests on itself. Religious belief is really self-contained. It may help faiths wisely to converse if they are all, East and West, revelations or illuminations, alert to this common situation about their ground of confidence.

There is no need for despair. Truth, we come to realize, can only be self-commending, awaiting recognition. To have it 'out of the blue', in disconnection with ourselves – as implied in our dilemma – would mean not only its irrelevance but its total non-entity in 'no man's land'. Like love, truth is always reciprocal to mind: it is 'there' precisely in being received. To have it happen is not to invent it. Truth can be identified only in being by its very nature identifiable.

This confidence about it, however, still leaves us with the question of credentials. What of our differing acts of cognizance, our respective confidence in what we have come to hold? The Buddha through the *dharma* or 'teaching' has persuaded the *sangha* or 'community of monks' of the *anatta* in which 'un-selfing' is the proper goal of human experience in quest for the *nirvana* of 'non-being'. The Torah has assured its people of their distinctive status and all the unique privileges and demands of 'Hear, O Israel'. Islam has disciplined Muslim into the Oneness of God and the final, ultimate prophethood of Muhammad through the divine mandatedness of the holy *shari'ah*. Christians have, in wide diversity of comprehension, found the clue to God, in power, love and wisdom, via the significance to them of Jesus as the Christ. All faiths, and the sects within them or against them, have a faith *imprimatur* on a faith text, a validation of what for them is valid, authenticating its own authenticity.

This situation is not capable of reconciliation. The attempt to unify would only reveal explicit schism. Plurality has to be acknowledged to be there. But a right perception of it can make us think differently about staying on Adamant Square.

For Adamant Square is a total exclusivism, albeit in the same human world. To move to a facile inclusiveness would obviously discredit all sincerities by confusing what they earnestly differentiate. The need is neither entire inclusiveness nor rigorous exclusivism. Nor is it some reconception, too sophisticated to be viable in life. Surely what greeting has to mean is a curbing by each of a rigorous retentiveness of what they have within them for the sake of a referring into all. Cherished doctrines do exclusify themselves in part: they concede they are not shared. They must persist. So their custodians require. But, in being held in wise retentiveness, they can also interpenetrate with faith elsewhere. Faiths in their integrity unforfeited can thus make respective acts of cognizance toward one another. The end of that road may not be granted to our sight. Its beginnings certainly are. The Christian is no stranger to the Buddhist perception that the self is the crux of the human crisis. The Jew knows well the dimension of suffering and tragic redemption which the Christian sets at the heart of an understanding of God. The Hindu is deeply acquainted with the devotion to the One which inspires both Christian contemplative and Muslim sufi-saint. The Christian recognizes with joy the centrality of peoplehood to God explicit in Judaic faith if only to de-ethnicize its range and make it accessible to all by faith alone. The mystery of incorporation is gratefully retained.

In these and numerous other ways inter-penetrations of meaning are the stuff of greeting. Subtle inter-relatedness is present in our very controversies. The task is to reduce the inter-controversial on behalf of the inter-responsive. This will not forfeit our distinctive witnessing, but rather conduce it to greater relevance. Wherever we rightly exclusify in loyalty to what we find necessary in truth we also inclusify through relationship the reasons for doing so.

Surely it is only thus that we can hope to arrive at all. For in the long legacies we have all accumulated there is much suspicion. Incorrigible aggression only confirms and entrenches it. Even good intentions may be misread. In his travels in Sicily in 1184 CE the diarist of journeys, Ibn Jubayr, came to Palermo. There,

> We travelled along a road like a market, so populous it was, with men coming and going. Groups of Christians that met us themselves uttered the first greetings and treated us with courtesy. We observed in their attitude and insinuating address towards the Muslims that which would offer temptation to ignorant souls. May God in his power and bounty preserve from seducement the people of Muhammad.[16]

In our day such reactions are still likely. Only a true intention can surmount them. It requires a will to comprehend, to sympathize, to inter-relate, and to do so not only person-to-person but tenet-to-tenet, as cherished by either. The more fiercely we are custodians the less wisely are we communicators. This does not mean that antagonism may not be latent in what is between us: it is that the things in which it lurks be transacted in gentle forbearance. Otherwise there is neither point nor worth in what divides, nor merit in its handling.

(viii)

The reverse of that principle brings us to Cavil Row, which leads to and from Adamant Square. Denigration and the negative stance have often characterized what happens between faiths. In sour relationships all have to protest against distortions and cry: 'That is not what we hold.' We are all, of course, responsible in some measure for how we are perceived. Exoneration by disavowal of the characterization may be unconvincing, if we have not faced that in us which has prompted about us what we regard as travesty. It may be that others of our persuasion do exhibit it. We must take liability for unmalicious misconceptions. Perhaps we, or some of us, have occasioned them. There is also the onus on all idealizers of religions to be honest about what they cannot well shrug off, as well as open to the self-correction it demands. More of this in the following chapter.

Misreadings of others which are wilful and tendentious abound in our mutual histories. Faiths have often consorted with calumny. The Jewish community through history has most tragically suffered at the hands of Christian defamation. In some senses, the Qur'an itself proceeds with an animus against the Judaeo-Christian tradition, with misreading of what that tradition purports to say. Given the emotions present there is large occasion to misrepresent, unconsciously or otherwise. Zionism in its embattled experience may readily regard all anti-Zionism as anti-Semitic and thereby absolve Zionism completely. Examples are on every hand. Correcting and disowning them is a basic aspect of the obligation we have to each other.

In all this, as Henry Thoreau observed in *Walden*: 'Our buckets, as it were, grate together in the same well.'[17] Fine erudition may not always transcend the tangle. Thus the eminent Hebrew philosopher, Martin Buber, finds in Christianity only credence for a credo as the meaning of 'faith', whereas in the Judaic tradition 'faith' is fidelity, abiding trust in God. The one seeks a private salvation, the other stands in perennial corporate relation with God.[18] His *Two Types of Faith* betrays a bias. It calls for correction, not reproach. Jacob Neusner, likewise, sustains a spirited *confessio fidei* of Judaism within an animus in respect of Christianity. He decries the whole idea of a Judaeo-Christian tradition. The two, he insists, are totally different religions, they 'stand for different people, talking about different things to different people'. 'Judaism does not find itself required to answer questions in the way Christians choose to pose them.' He complains about a 'fundamental (Christian) inner-directedness', while writing sharply from within his own:

> We Jews maintain the Torah of our Rabbi Moses . . . (which)
> bears no relationship whatsoever to any other revelation that God
> may have had in mind. We are no relic, nor are we the stubborn
> and incorrigible heirs of a mere denial. We bear the living faith,
> the Torah of the One true God . . . So is the faith of Israel, God's
> first love.[19]

Christian history has only itself to blame if the ardour here, in all
its passion, is ready to overlook the bond of the creator God and
the Messianic hope, without whom, without which, the faith Neusner would segregate could never have found birth at Jewish hands.
Buckets are indeed grating in the same well.

If these are noble, even anguished, other examples of tension are
trivial and feeble. Yahya ibn Adi in his *Tract on Divine Unity* noted
that Christians could not count because 'with them, one is three
and three is one'. Or Christian critics have alleged that Islam is not
consistently 'unitarian' because the Qur'an frequently uses the plural
pronoun 'We' of God.[20] Christians charged that Muhammad was a
prophet of whom there was no foretelling. These only aroused
Muslims to find it, thus widening controversy and ignoring the deep
questions of authenticity. There are endless minutiae of Christian
ill-will with the Qur'an or Muslim ill-will with the New Testament
which can muddy the waters of genuine converse with their cavil-
lings.

Relations inter-faith may be superficialized in other ways. Buddhists frequently claim with justice that Christians insist on applying
their own category of 'salvation' without appreciating how Buddhist
thinking has already disavowed it. Christians deplore Buddhist
'extinction' and do not reckon with the Buddhist sense of how there
'is' 'no-thing' to extinguish. On a Buddhist count, doctrines of
anatvamada, or 'no-soul', and of *Nirvana* do make a structure in
which 'salvation' is sought and found. It is not 'salvation' in the
sense that Christians understand. We are reduced to cavilling if we
do not take the measure of each other.

Some Buddhists can well reciprocate by decrying the illusion of
Christian rejection of their illusion.[21] Competing 'illusions', whether
of self or no-self, end only in confusion. They are ready ground for
residents on Cavil Row. To stay with them is tedious. Only the
large-hearted can suffice.

(ix)

But have we not, thus far in this chapter, been eluding the ultimate 'truth-question'? Is this not the question which prompts all concern for the exclusive view of religious truth and, therefore, makes all so-called 'fundamentalisms' entrench themselves? Are we not over-looking error and falsehood? Do these not belong to the situation? Forbearance and sympathy are good, but do they suit all that is at issue? Is not Adamant Square the sound place to be? Are we confus-ing the spirit of our relationships for the substance? Can the latter always be conciliatory? What of the cutting edge of truth?

The questions deserve response – in part here, in part in Chapter 8. Each faith has to respond for itself. Only a Christian discussion can be made here. It falls into two parts. The one is how Christian truth relates outside itself: the other is how it understands its will for comprehension.

We have seen in Chapter 1 that there is a *de facto* pluralism. Numerous faiths exist. Adherents belong. Credentials differ. Tra-ditions persist. We cannot singularize religion. This means the acceptance of diversity. Within the constituent faiths in this diver-sity 'truths' obtain – for their people, their custodians, their faithful. This is the actual 'truth-for' situation which we must differentiate from the 'truth-of' question as to the many disparate patterns of believing and belonging. Some thinking stops at multiple 'truths-for', affirming that there is no other sort of 'truth', seeing in 'people holding it' the only sense that can be given to enquiry about 'truth'.

Christians need to go beyond that resolution of the truth-question. 'Truth-of' must remain an issue within 'truths-for'. That still leaves us with a 'belief-faith' situation in the other parties.

There is need for caution here both ways against the rigid and the facile. When the eminent theologian, Hans Küng, going by invitation to Teheran in 1985, said that 'Islam was a path of sal-vation' and wrote of the Qur'an as having 'obvious power as the Word of God for the faithful' and as being 'an effective word of the all-forgiving and merciful God for believing Muslims',[22] he was making a 'truth-for' verdict. 'For' is carefully used twice. But, Küng goes further, saluting the Qur'an as 'effectively' a word of divine forgiveness. Yet the Qur'an plainly disavows the principle concern-ing forgiveness which Christians believe is enshrined in the love that 'bears wrong' and only so doing 'bears it away' – the love and the principle being together present, representatively and divinely, in the cross of Jesus. That cross, however, the Qur'an strongly denies, whether as historical fact, or spiritual reality, or divine grace at work in the way necessary to the human situation. Further, the Qur'an repeatedly excludes the redemptive principle by its reiterated word that 'no burden-bearer bears any burden but his own'.[23] If that is as it would seem to be, then is 'truth-for' here consonant with 'truth-of' as to the cross?

Perhaps the question cannot be answered. Some would say it should not be pressed. Be that as it may, the situation illustrates what attaches to many other points at stake between the Christian and the other faiths. Gratitude and reverence for all honest 'truths-for' would seem to belong, for the Christian, with a continuing sense of obligation about 'truth-of' in every case. How is that obligation to conduct itself in the context of the many 'truths-for', with their grounds and consequences?

(x)

At least it is clear that there is seldom a total contrast between the content of actually held 'truths' across the religions, and the 'truths-of' Christian faith as internally known – in so far as there is consensus about them, which is a large proviso. There is almost always some kinship, some affinity, some shared dimension. The Christian need think nothing alien. The very controversies arise in the context of agreed convictions, congruent hopes, or simply shared yearnings. This being so, there is always a ministry of meaning which receives as well as gives and which interprets by help of what it finds.

The ultimate question in seeking, however painfully, to pass from 'truths-for' Buddhists, Hindus, Jews, Muslims and others on all counts, to 'truth-of' 'God in Christ' must be whether that task should fulfil itself by the thrust of Christian authority or by the appeal of Christian content. Does it move by the *diktat* of a claim or the sharing of its heart? For some, 'Thus says the Lord' is the right address, the gospel with its status, the church with its mandate. Then the other 'authority' is fit to be dislodged, deprecated, denied. The challenge is squared. 'By this sign conquer.'

The appeal of the content is the desirable alternative. It aligns

with Paul's favoured word about 'commending' (Romans 5.8; II
Corinthians 4.2). For 'commending' anticipates already, in the
other, a capacity to respond. It does not see other believing as all
antipathy but as part ally. It takes account of how blinded all minds
and souls can be. It does not underestimate the revolutionary side
of its intention. It 'stands at the door and knocks'. Admission is
sought by consent from within, which the knocking is designed to
gain. It does not see its word as liable to be received by proclaiming
its prestige, but by persuasion of its quality.

When a Christian 'truth-of' is present in those terms, the vexing
question of authority no longer presses. Authorities tangle and quarrel: witness conveys. This does not mean that the issue of authority
is resolved; it is simply in abeyance in order that the thing which
authority is on behalf of may avail. To see it that way coincides
effectively with the *de facto* pluralism which we have seen to be
inescapable. Some issues are best undertaken, not head-on, but by
setting them in a larger context in which they are not solved but
contained. The question, between faiths, as to final truth, is one of
them.

That conclusion is not at the expense of honesty.

3

To Common Honesty

(i)

According to Moishe Halpern, there is a Yiddish prayer which reads: 'Help me, O God, to spit upon the world, and on You and on myself.'[1] Spittle in some cultures has a therapeutic power. Not so here. The plea has a thoroughly Yiddish irony, a down-to-earth grimness, meant to shock and to amuse. 'The world, God and the self', in that order. It is the third that concerns us here – the self-reproach of one who is evidently a praying man, praying in very forthright terms.

We may assume that few who engage in current inter-faith relations would be liable to make petition in such vulgar language. Indeed, it is precisely the air of complacency and self-congratulation that attaches to dialogue which has to be called into radical correction. It is easy to approve and to admire tolerant and conciliatory gestures, so perverse and hateful are the legacies of enmity and strife. Yet enthusiasm needs to be watchful against subtle satisfactions which ignore how accusing of all religions honesty must be. Hence the task of this and the following chapter. 'Is not religion a cloak,' asked that lively realist, Dean Jonathan Swift, 'and honesty a pair of shoes worn out in the dirt?'[2] Our duty to one another is first a healing contempt for aspects of ourselves.

This is the reversal of the usual stance. What faiths have traditionally incriminated is the other party. Buddhism has reproaches for Hinduism, having developed out of it. The long Jewish indictment of Christians' behaviour has been tragically deserved. Antipathy in reverse is born of the malice which kindles it. Perhaps the wry humour of the Yiddish prayer is simply echoing the treatment the

long-suffering receive, if we recall Shylock's bitter words about
those who 'spit upon his Jewish gaberdine'.[3] Christians have had
long emotions of resentment about Islam. Tensions with them, and
with Jews, are close to the surface in the Qur'an itself, and the
Muslims have not been slow to live in them, given the sanction of
their own scripture.[4]

There is something in every situation which makes accusation
interact with vindication either way. By dint of framing external
charges one exonerates oneself, or at least diverts attention from
one's own liability. To be accused is to reach for rebuttal. For all
their holy themes, religions are no exception. Rather, their very
custodianship of the transcendent lends to all their verdicts, pro
and con, a warrant that can make these bold and rancorous. The
more reason, then, for faiths first to take into themselves the adverse
reckoning they have been disposed to reach about others. This is
no less necessary when they begin to practice and pursue the arts
of converse and of hope. It is these very arts which require them
to start by ceasing only to admire themselves.

Moishe Halpern's Yiddish prayer includes the praying mind
within the mock he makes of 'the world and God'. Religions belong
with such impatience, or at least with the riddle that provokes it.
To complain that we might well believe in God if we did not have
to relate him to the world is familiar enough. We have earlier noted
the sharp issue of theodicy, or 'the justification of God'. Then 'on
myself' has to be added, not as some inclusive bitterness, but as
knowing that the answer – if there is one – involves me also. I have
to do with however God is to 'be justified'. 'O wretched man that
I am,' was Paul's cry (Romans 7.24). Without it, 'O wretched world'
will be only petulance or boredom. 'And on myself' becomes, in
the solidarity of great religions, 'and upon ourselves'. It is this
dimension of honest self-knowledge within the households of faith
that this chapter must assess, leading in the next to the due penitence which must follow. Only so can dialogue find its way in truth.

(ii)

There is one immediate reflection. It is often thought in some
Christian circles opposed to dialogue and to inter-faith relations,
whether intellectual or practical, that such ventures have missed,

or deliberately ignored, what we may call 'the sin factor'. All seems
sweetness and light. We exude good will and forthwith solve all
problems. What, they ask, of the New Testament warning about
'blinded minds' and 'hatred of the light'? Has our quest for actual
or potential compatibilities and values obscured what calls to be
seen as error or 'hardness of heart'? Do not 'men love darkness
rather than light because their deeds are evil' (John 3.19) and
religions connive in making it so? Then, in truth, we owe each
other more than courtesy, if dialogue is not to evade the hardest
part of its reckoning.

The questions are serious and have troubled many. We must not
refuse them. The suspicion that religious acts are ways of escaping
from moral obligation is as old as the Hebrew prophets. 'Bring no
more vain oblations, cease to do evil, learn to do well,' cried Isaiah
(1.13, 16, 17), echoed by Amos and Jeremiah and many others in
their time and place. Karl Barth, reacting against the guilt of
German churches, insisted that the divine righteousness is perpetu-
ally at odds with human religiosity. Liberation theologians claim
that speculative theology is guilty evasion of divine demands. The
God who is debated in academia and honoured in wealthy sanctuaries is only truly to be known and found in active compassion down
among the poor.[5] In the real world it must be a hollow thing merely
to have religions cultivate good manners.

Yet, in going beyond these and shedding all complacency, we
must reckon with a vast complexity. Religions differ in their capacity
for moral self-criticism which, in its effective forms, has to be self-
generated. Furthermore, we have to avoid at all costs identifying
'the sin factor' with others unilaterally or associating it causally
only with their doctrines. Doctrines and concepts certainly generate
attitudes, and attitudes breed evils. No creeds, however, are exempt,
no philosophies immune. It is important, at one and the same time,
to be realistic about the culpability of *homo religiosus* and multilateral
in our register of it. In point is the inscription on the Memorial
Tablet to Jonathan Swift, in St Patrick's Cathedral, Dublin:

Here lies the body of Jonathan Swift, where savage indignation
can no longer lacerate his heart.

More generally, indignation lacerates only the culprits elsewhere.

Honest dialogue, then, has to take mutual stock of evils that beset
us all. Hypocrisies and hypocrites are everywhere. Saintliness enjoys
no single copyright. But, in accepting a mutual honesty, we have
also to explore how the set of our beliefs, the accents of our faiths,
acknowledge, handle or even foster these perversities in us all. Then
we do not simply associate 'blinded minds' and 'hardened hearts'
with any faith but our own. Rather, we must together seek to
know what it is about each of us, doctrinally defined and ritually
expressed, which serves to harden our own hearts, to condone our
wrongs, and dispose us to pride, or sloth, or enmity, or prejudice.
This is not to plead that dialogue should become some contrived
mutual confessional. It is to ask the inward questions that educate
us to penitence.

(iii)

When we appreciate, separately or together, how subtly evil inter-
penetrates religious thought and structure, we face two underlying
factors that call for careful study if honesty is to be intelligent. They
belong to all religious histories. They are like two sides of the same
coin. The first is the fact that religions can well be characterized as
encounters with evil, but with evil differently construed. In their
grappling with it they fulfill their genius distinctively. The second
is the fact – discernible in their story – of how their reckoning with
evil involves them, for its own sake, in instinctive attitudes to which
other 'evil' attaches, directly or indirectly. If we are to reach a
common honesty, we must wrestle with both sides of this equation.
When 'Satan is being cast out' an element contrives to remain.
There is something inconclusive about his defeat.

To think it so does not impugn faith in divine revelation, or
ultimate illumination. Nor does it doom us to some final dualism. It
is part of the living dialectic of truth which dialogue must patiently
explore, remembering the words of the seventeenth-century English
Quaker, Isaac Pennington:

> All truth is shadow except the last truth. But all truth is substance
> in its place, though it be but a shadow in another place. And the
> shadow is a true shadow, as the substance is a true substance.[6]

For many in Buddhism, broadly read, the evil lies in time and mortality, in the illusion of human desire which these both seem to invite and essentially deny. That sense of an implicit enigma in the experience of life, given transience and decay and death, leads further to the identification of evil in the *tanha*, or drive, of acquisitiveness and ambition. If this is to be atrophied, 'made to not be', by abnegation, then the ultimate evil will be the unreadiness to have it so, the refusal to concede this 'truth' of things. Conversely the 'good' for which such Asian religion strives is 'self-transcendence' into the bliss of non-being via the 'skills' of the Buddha's Eightfold Path, or in some Hindu patterns of karmic law and 'disinterestedness' in due outworking of the way to final escape from it.

There are indeed evils of pain and frustration, of unequal fates and burdens in the mortal world. But in this Asian 'management of evil' – if we may so speak – are there not great, sad forfeitures of potential good? Does not an evil of atrophy, listlessness, even churlishness, creep into the postures of admirable self-denial? Is the Satan of cupidity, of lust and violence, and sordid ambition, cast out only by surrender to a meaninglessness of time or a doubt of living personhood? Or does meaning return in the silence that does not ask?

The issue stands – and it stands between us, the nub of all our converse, East and West. The good is bought at a price. Desirable emancipation (the term is ironical) is attained with an abeyance of being, hardly to be desired. Or being persists in praiseworthy virtues of devotion and peace, perhaps voiding history of significant challenge to more than quietism and withdrawal, or its service only by exemplifying these.

What do we perceive to be the evil to which the genius of Hebraic religion responds? It is hard to discern categorically all the factors of event, experience and long interpretation which lie within its meanings. But clearly its response, or at least its shape, has to do with the relevance of a peculiar status. The 'chosen people' concept is a summation of vocation. Was it 'the house of bondage', in fact or in memory, which furnished the clue of 'enmity to us' as the key to the human scene? What lay behind that enmity could be nobly undertaken by a special destiny which, by first guaranteeing its own survival, could see itself as a benediction wherewith to bless all mankind, always on condition that the exceptionality persist.

This Jewish sense of the tribal, ethnic meaning of history was rooted in the triangle of people, land and memory. These are, of course, universal denominators of mankind, the who, where and whence of all nations. In the Hebraic tradition they became the material of 'covenant' and 'election', as 'peoplehood' was sanctified at Sinai, territorially possessed of 'the land of Canaan', and caused to inherit, via chronicle and prophet, the identity only memory can cherish and fulfil. Hence the tenacity of obedience to Torah, of territorial sovereignty, of Davidic monarchy and Solomonic Temple, and the paradoxical travail of Exile. Then, centuries on, Judaism undertook the conservation of Moses and the prophets in the fidelity of the synagogue and the treasury of the Talmud. The unique status of Jewry, crucial to its self-understanding, outlived the trauma of the Jewish origins of Christianity and lives resilient in all its forms against adversity and oppression.

Its exceptionalizing of itself is always seen as resolutely instrumental. In Abraham 'all the nations of the earth' will 'bless themselves' or 'be blessed'. Precisely for that reason election can never be shared or foregone. It is by its nature inalienable and, therefore, querulous about others who must be differentiated. Judaism implies the potential consecration of any nationhood by its deep hallowing of the natural order. In Noachid terms it concedes a covenant status about all human soil and harvest, land and people. It retains its Sinai copyright, but acknowledges 'righteous Gentiles'. The evil of the world is countered in the concept of Torah, of guidance under God. 'In God is my salvation.' 'The glory of Israel' is 'light to the nations'. 'Blessed be the Lord God of Israel who has visited and redeemed his people.' The songs have their proprietors: but appreciation can be universal.

Here in things Judaic are large and enduring responses to the fact of evil. 'The law of the Lord..an undefiled law, converting the soul . . .' Judaic prayers and longings have become the heritage of all mankind, to guide all feet into a way of peace. The world is a world of divine initiatives, of significant history, of transcendent intention and reference, of genuine human meaning, a place of final hope and critical destiny.

Yet, in 'casting out the evil' which all these resist and surmount, things Judaic have incurred dimensions sadly liable to evil. Exceptionality can be true and positive as an interior conviction: what when it is absolute as a solitary 'election'? To be sure, 'the godly of all nations inherit the world to come'. That Jewish dictum is honestly meant. Yet it is heard condescendingly. Is there not, as it must seem to the uncircumcised, a hint of inferiorization in lacking the unique status before God? The burden of this question, as we must see, was undoubtedly a vital factor in the appeal of Christianity as an open 'covenant'. It persists painfully in the use made of it in contemporary Zionism. That new 'openness', for which 'there was neither Jew nor Greek', believed it inherited all that was authentic about nationhood as vocation and about fidelity to God, but it saw these as universal possibilities for all identities of mankind. If they are not so, then have the nations no identity before God and in his purposes except as survivors with Noah?[7] Do they never overtake not having been at Sinai?

But the largest fear of ambiguity in the great positives of Hebrew faith springs from what others have done with the covenant form in which they come. Why is antisemitism so foul and so cruel and so unique a thing, unparalleled in the whole history of human enmities? Is its uniqueness responsive to the very uniqueness of Jewry, as if the hating world could not tolerate a 'one and only'? Is it the story of Joseph and his brothers writ large? They did not have the specially favoured mother. Some of them sprang from 'handmaids'. Joseph's pretensions made them jealous, criminally so, but yet understandably with all their sheaves-in-dream bowing down to him. Can there be only coincidence in the fact that the world's most tragically persecuted people are the world's most self-consciously 'chosen' one? The conjecture in no way exonerates the haters: it does interrogate the chosen status. Evil has certainly attended upon its good.

Other nations have aspired to be 'chosen' in their own right. The ambition has often defiled their history. 'The chosen people' must be 'one and only'. The status needs to be outwardly acknowledged as well as inwardly cherished. Its being is to be perceived; otherwise it feels uneasy. Much tragedy has flowed from this complex, the more sadly in that the emotions of mother milk, mother land and mother tongue, from which all identities derive, belong equally to all and call for the same gratitude, the same discipline and the same hallowing. Judaism strains inter-faith relations by the very form of its supreme contribution to them.

(iv)

In its identifying and casting out of 'Satan' Islam, too, raises formidable problems for all who would relate positively with it. Study of them must take us back to prophethood which, with the unity of God, is its most vital tenet. Prophethood encountered evil by virtue of its own witness to truth. Throughout the Semitic tradition the great prophets drew upon themselves the anger and perversity of the world that they addressed. Being spokesmen on behalf of God's righteousness and faithfully reminding mankind of its claims, they became, like butts in an archery, the target of the enmity which rejected those claims and resisted God's righteousness. They were called upon to suffer the consequences of their fidelity, in an evil world, to their given word.

This travail was a steady feature of prophethood in the Hebraic scene – witness Jeremiah and 'the suffering servant' of Isaiah (chs. 40ff.). We meet the same situation in the ministry of Jesus. It is there, emphatically, in the career of Muhammad in the Qur'an. His 'word' of the sovereignty of God and its repudiation of idolatry was at once confronted by the hostility of the pagan *Haram*, or sacred shrine, in Muhammad's native Mecca. Its custodians feared for their vested interests of trade and pilgrimage. They saw Muhammad as an upstart, a disturber of their tradition, an import from an alien source. A major segment of the Qur'an is occupied with this encounter, Muhammad being inspired with its contents in response to the context of Meccan resistance, ridicule and persecution.[8]

Unlike Buddhism, Islam, then, identified and incriminated the evil of the world, not in transience and the drive of the illusory self, but in the plural worship, the distorted notions, the wilful obduracy, of Muhammad's people in their pagan 'ignorance'.[9] These are the symptoms of a *zulm*, a wrongness, of a *dalal*, an astray-ness, of benighted mankind. His preaching is the touchstone by which the world learns its need of light and of pardon, and, most of all, of structured discipline in *taqwa*, or piety.

As in this way the foil of evil prophethood in Islam faced the implicit question of how the 'word' was to succeed, how the evil obduracy was to be overcome. For the unity and rule of God could not be an ambiguous issue, left for ever inconclusive. How so would it be final revelation and proper truth?

Plainly, in the Quranic 'trial-situation', it did not verbally succeed. Converts to the word were relatively few and did not swing
society into line. Hence the basic decision of Muhammad's prophethood, after thirteen years of sustained *balagh* (as the term is) or
'message-bringing', for the invocation of power. This was achieved
by the sequel to the emigration to Medina. There the steady building
up of an alternative centre during eight years ensured the appropriate divine victory and the effective establishment of Islam. The
prophet-preaching was vindicated by the prophet-armed: by the one
God's will was known, by the other it was achieved.

The mind of Islam has been permanently defined by this history,
making it the most politically assured of religions. It holds no
philosophy of force for its own sake: it approves force 'in the path
of God'. For other monotheists who recognized its power in political
terms, it had a tolerant covenant of protection. Over its own members its 'law of apostasy' ensures that personal departure from within
it amounts to a kind of treason which cannot be allowed.[10] Its will
to power is at once its vindication of God – who is thereby duly
worshipped – and the vindication of its truth as something both
affirmed as to meaning and achieved as social, political fact within
the *Ummah* and the *Dawlah*, the 'nation' and the 'state' of Islam.

Here again, as elsewhere, though differently, the way in which
the faith responds to evil holds within it the evil its very pattern
has incurred. In 'casting out Satan' this way, an evil problematic
still persists. It resides in the very success itself. Establishments of
truth-and-power contain conformists who are unpersuaded, adherents who are still their old selves. As noted in the previous chapter,
Muhammad was warned how 'Satan cast' unmeant things into the
speech of prophets which needed to be 'unsaid'. There were also
'unmeant things' in the quality of an allegiance which only prudence
brought.

It is here that honesty from outside Islam must relate with Muslims in a common sincerity. It has to ask whether the assurance,
so characteristic of Islam, has adequately measured how perverse
humanity can be even within a system of conceded truth and a
context of enforced conformity. Has its 'management of evil' via
final revelation, devout habituation, strong solidarity and the political order sufficed the human situation? Or are there remainders of
evil about which we must look more radically to God and more

urgently for society? The questions are only fair if we clarify, in genuine mutuality, the reasons why they come insistently to the Christian mind.

(v)

For the ministry of Jesus participated squarely in that same experience of opposition and malignity which we have seen to characterize both the Judaic and the Qur'anic scene. Indeed, in Christian understanding, that obduracy against Jesus on the part of his constituency gathered into a climax which faith came to identify as 'the sin of the world'. A variety of factors from Messianic precedent and spiritual discernment contributed to that verdict. But it was eloquent of the conviction that, in the rejection of Jesus – and with him of the Beatitudes and the gentle parables of prodigals and publicans – human wrongness had dramatically showed its hand. The Christian conscience has ever since been dominated by the resulting sense of how evil humanity can be. Deliverance from evil, as in the Lord's Prayer, has thus become its constant yearning. The crucifixion of Jesus has always been the source and spur of its realism, its measure of how radical human need must be seen to be.

'The sin of the world', patently, could not be understood quantitatively. Enormities of every kind have abounded before and since. There was nothing occasional, then, about crucifixions, nor since by different means. 'The sin of the world' was there qualitatively. Jews and Romans were not uniquely charged with it. By historical perception it appertained to humanity at large. It has remained for Christians the measure of 'the sin factor' in the world. It is, therefore, at the heart of what a common honesty from outside Christian faith must engage with in relating to it.

Jewry sees it as grossly over-loading what can be credibly assigned to one single, historical event. They may allow that experience, on the part of the Christian community, was expressed in this interpretation, just as 'mythicization' entered into Jewish comprehension of the Exodus as definitive of themselves. Does not the New Testament itself witness to this parallel when Paul writes of 'Christ our Passover . . .' (I Corinthians 5.7)? As such, perhaps it may be allowed to Christians, but by no persuasion otherwise. Jewry has, more intimately and more horrifically, its own bitter measures of 'the sin of the world'. Let Jesus be a heroic, yet forlorn, Jewish figure, too far and too extravagantly possessed by Christians.

Thoughtful Muslims, for their part, see well enough the approximate parallel between Jesus in Galilee/Jerusalem and Muhammad in Mecca/Medina, in respect, that is, of the common factor of loyal messengership and human opposition leading to the prophet's danger and potential tragedy at the hands of evil men. To be sure, there *was* something almost like Gethsemane at the nadir of Muhammad's fortunes in Mecca and in Ta'if.[11] But there the parallel ends. The contrast in what ensued was total.

Jesus read hostility to his word and person as vocation into suffering and the way to its redemption. He spoke of 'the cup my Father has given me' (John 18.11). The evil had not been dissuaded by the message given. The message faithfully given had only evoked the greater enmity. What then, of an invocation of force so that the will of God, at stake in the message and in the mission which brought it might not go by default?

Here Muslims are inclined to think that no forceful option was available to Jesus in the Roman context, as it feasibly was to Muhammad in the Meccan setting. This circumstance, if such it be, was part of the greater finality granted to Islam. For lack of comparable 'success', Jesus was vindicated by heavenly rapture, so that his pursuers were thwarted of their victory and he divinely assured of his. Christians do not read what eventuated in the climax of Jesus' danger in those terms. They see his readiness to suffer as the crux of a world's forgiveness, as we must more fully explore in Chapter 9. They see evil only overcome by being suffered for. Any other response either entrenches it by retaliation or condones it by evasion. Jesus allowed neither option. In that free decision Christians read the expression of 'the mind of God'. It is the meaning and the measure of what they call Jesus' 'Sonship to the Father'. They believe that the cross, expressing the wrongness of the world as being willed against Jesus, also embodies the divine answer to that wrongness in the grace it defines. 'Father, forgive them: they do not know what they are doing.' When our penitence aligns us with those meanings, we know this forgiveness for our own.

There are some aspects of Hinduism, and, indeed, of Shi'ah Islam, which allow themselves to grasp these Christian meanings, at least as 'shadow'. For rigorous Buddhists they can only be questioned as staying within the illusion of personhood and the misreading of the evil to which it leads. Most Muslims will want to call all into total question as being, in fact, far less effective in the human scene than the robust and practical 'management of evil' in the force factor of Islam.[12]

There the inter-faith issues rest. The plea here is not to resolve them but honestly to concede what they are and not to ignore them in platitude or obscure them in polemic. But have we been right and wise in locating the crux between religions in this realm of evil and its 'management'? Answer takes us further into what honesty has to undertake.

(vi)

Perhaps none other than Plato can help us towards it. In his *Politeia*, in 429 BCE, he described 'the perfect righteous man' who would be 'the world's deliverer' as one

> . . . who, without doing any wrong, may assume the appearances of the grossest injustice. Yea! who shall be scourged, fettered, tortured, deprived of his eyes, and after having endured all possible sufferings, be fastened to a post – he must restore again the beginning and the prototype of righteousness.[13]

Plato, of course, had no predisposition for a Christian viewpoint. He comes uncannily near to the heart of one. For only if we have a full measure of what evil means shall we have a right measure of how good avails. This is no pessimism, no macabre preoccupation with guilt. We must know the worst if we would know what masters it. Hebrew Messianism has something of this realism in its anxiety lest Messiah be identified prematurely so that evil postdates his alleged achievement.[14] For if it does, and we think of 'post-dating' chronologically,[15] then 'he' is discredited. But, Hebraic reckonings apart, and returning to Plato, it seems clear that ultimate good and the ultimate suffering will belong together, the world and humanity being as we know them in our honesty. Such is the nature of redemption.

It is precisely here that dialogue has to call itself to genuine realism. Honesty about ourselves has to be an honesty with ourselves

and so between ourselves. We have to set our inter-faith relationships in these dimensions precisely because it is where religions are,
by their very nature and by their very temptations.

It is evident on all hands that religions are gross offenders against
their own lights. Chapter 4 must deal with how this is so historically.
Our present concern is with the inner factors. 'Who will guard the
guardians?' has long been a troubling question for society and politics. It is no less urgent for the proprietors of the divine, the
placemen of the transcendent. For that, in all their variety, is what
religions through their accredited mentors are set to be. It is having
this role which tempts them into what one psalm named 'presumptuous sins' (Psalm 19.13). When another psalm called upon God to
'say something on his own behalf' (Psalm 74.22), was it perhaps
out of despair, as we saw earlier, that many loud voices were doing
so for him? At all events, to be 'on behalf of God' is to be the more
in danger of being on behalf of ourselves.

Sometimes the most telling reflections on this theme come understandably from outside faith-allegiance. That it should be so is no
surprise. There has been a large service to religion in our time from
humanist spectators who are not of the faithful. Already, in Chapter
1, we have learned from their relevance.

Notable among them is Albert Camus (1913–1960). His subtle
novel *The Fall* exposes the labyrinthine self-deception to which
religious meanings are prone. 'I am inclined,' his central character
concludes, 'to see religion . . . as a huge laundering venture,' an
exercise in self-exoneration which by its nature can never succeed.
'I deny the good intention . . . With me there is no giving of
absolution or blessing.'[16] Man is incorrigibly self-deluding in his
quest to be right. Jean-Baptiste Clamence, the 'judge-penitent' in
the story, knows – when he knows himself – that there are always
ulterior motives. His role as a judge gives him the habit of external
condemnation and so a guise of self-esteem. The self within him is
as tortuous as the canals of Amsterdam where he operates, turning
round upon themselves. His pride is challenged when he evades any
action to rescue a woman prostitute, whose 'fall' into a canal to
drown he is aware of at a distance. Now he has a radical charge
with which to accuse himself. Her 'fall' is his 'fall' from the conceit
of innocence and his self-preening self.

The rare will to honesty, however, becomes itself a snare. His incipient penitence brings him new ground for self-esteem. 'Look at me beating my breast.'[17] He congratulates himself that he is capable of feeling accused. How then should we conclude? 'In order to cease being a doubtful case does one have to cease being at all?'

> One.. practised the profession of penitent to be able to end up as a judge . . . The portrait I hold out to my contemporaries becomes a mirror . . . We are odd wretched creatures and, if we merely look back over our lives, there is no lack of occasions to amaze and scandalize ourselves.[18]

The terse incisiveness of Camus' writing makes it the more telling as a portrayal of the ambivalence that waits on all religion. It is a predicament from which no faith in 'chosen' status can have us immune. Indeed such conviction may only aggravate the condition. It is a perception which will not be countered by forcible establishment of régimes of faith-power. For these will only serve to foster the self-satisfaction in which they must indulge. We need to learn to live without being vindicated, in situations where penitence is all.

Yet that same penitence harbours a possible conceit. There is about evil, as the Danish philosopher, Sören Kierkegaard, perceived, a kind of potentially endless regression. Humility becomes an occasion for pride, seeing it compares well with ostentation and arrogance. So pride waits upon it – the pride of being humble. Catching myself in this snare, I disown and break free. I am *not* proud of the fact that I am humble. Here again, with better reason still, the trap awaits me. Detecting the further subtlety, I disavow my pride in not being proud of my humility.

This endless regression can only be escaped by penitence absolute and by the gift of grace and humour. But penitence absolute is that of which systems are not capable. Systems of dogma, law, ritual and code are structures of communal pride. They find accusation uncongenial because it undermines their security, their guardianship, their status on behalf of the unconditioned mystery of God or the transcendent. There is, therefore, always cause for pause in their affirmations, their symbols and their claims. It is evident that this sense of things has to be close to the business of their dialogue. Without it, how could they be aware of one another?

Buddhist discipline of the Eightfold Path has perceived this situation in its accent on right-mindedness, insight and meditation. These, on whatever premises about the self, can well be the quest of all, but they do not escape the dilemma of the self within them. The silent cell in the *Sangha* will be as liable to proper satisfaction as the rhetoric of the pulpit in the church. The very abeyance of desire, pursued as a 'skill' one cultivates, reaches for its own 'desire' therein. Like figures casting shadows in the sun, we cannot be ourselves in escape or absence from the selves we are. Whatever we will to be, or not to be, we transact within our being. Thus the impulse of penitence will bring us closer together than the logic of debate.

(vii)

For it is evident that religions are, in some sense, corporate selves. They have long history, interior cohesion and conscious identity. However well we heed what is legitimate in Wilfred Cantwell Smith's dictum that faith only exists in persons so that, for example, there is no such thing as 'Hinduism' but only 'Hindus,' there remains in fact the real solidarity of what others still call 'the faiths'.[19] They have their pride, their *amour propre*. They have acquired enormous vested interest in their continuity and their status. They possess long memories and enjoy the sanction of high prestige. Their scriptures anchor them to norms and rubrics of fidelity. Within themselves their sanctions seem impregnable. Moreover, their 'guardians' – rabbis, priests, scholars, officiants – have a deep stake in immunity from radical change or challenge. In every sense they are selves with ample potential to be 'selfish'.

Furthermore, corporate selves readily thrive on adversarial roles. Penitence is never prominent within controversy. Indeed, honesty is liable to be the first casualty of 'the strife of tongues'. The case has to be made, the opposition disqualified, the issue resolved in favour of the one and not the other. It is wiser, then, not to arouse communal self-will but rather to persuade all to self-interrogation, in which we may reach different perceptions of each other.

This in no way signals the absence of issues between us. They exist around what we have to be penitent about. We will study in the next chapter how doctrines develop their own self-interests just as hierarchies do. We have first to get beyond the pride of these if we are to grapple with their substance. Otherwise debate may well only confirm their entrenched character. It is sometimes loosely said that 'religions together' have simply to make the several identities 'better' – 'better Buddhists', 'better Muslims', 'better Jews', 'better Christians', 'better agnostics'.

The notion is superficially attractive only as long as the 'betterment' is unexamined and unspecified. By some criteria the 'better' Muslim admires the Ayatullah Khomeini, the 'better' Jew Rabbi Kahane. The 'better' Christian will bask in alignment with Mother Teresa, ignoring the Christianity of apartheid and of the IRA who are not excommunicated. Faiths, of course, can only be left to adjudge their own 'betterment', its why and whence and whither. But we have duties to each other, if dialogue means anything, in recognizing and realizing what is meant and needed. The necessary diagnosis, moreover, extends far into what we have done to each other when 'our buckets tangled in the same well'. Would it not, in fact, be a negation of dialogue if we thought the definition of the 'better anything' could be unilateral or private? This is not to question interior authority in each faith over its own *semper reformanda*. It is to say that the criteria are not sole property, nor the issue a separate concern. Further, the self-esteem resulting from the 'betterment' may itself become a handicap to larger truth.

(viii)

In urging common honesty and discovering its urgency, do we imply in all the foregoing a sort of ultimate despair? If religion is given to 'laundering itself' and there can be no corporate expression of faith immune from inner unworthiness, are we left to cynicism? Do we opt for a Swiftian distaste for all manifestations of belief, a Sartrean *nausea* about humanity at large? If we perceive, with John Bunyan's Pilgrim, that 'there is a way to Hell from the very gate of Heaven', then what of any enterprise of meeting? Do we meet and greet in a blind alley, a hopeless *cul-de-sac*?

The conclusion in no way follows. *Corruptio optimi pessima*. What we have studied is the other side of the claim of integrity, the battle for sincerity. It is the misanthrope who concludes that sincerity is unattainable, that the sincere man is simply deceived by his own propaganda – as some sociology alleges. The intention that can accuse and suspect itself is the intention that wills to be honest. Good will has to be its own censor – as it can be – unless we are to decline into total apathy. Life by its nature requires us to decide and leaves us with the onus of deciding aright. It invites us to that critique of one another, for love and truth's sake, which begins within a due critique of ourselves.

In such open relationships there is always that which we can retrieve even from dispute. Study of it we defer to chapter 5. In Christopher Fry's *The Dark is Light Enough*, the reply 'Weep for what you can' answers the disdain which boasts of being readier to 'weep for stags and partridges' than broken men.[20] The principle is sound. 'Weep for what you can' commiseration is always right. 'Rejoice with those who rejoice.' There are positives in every situation between faiths that we can identify and share, yearnings we can understand and weep with. Quarrel with the basic philosophy of Buddhism need not distance us from the relevance of the Buddhist quest to every other onus in selfhood. Puzzlement about the justice of Judaic 'chosen-ness' does not deny us right to share in the hope and the anguish of the Hebrew psalmist or discern the divine pathos within prophetic suffering. Likewise the Muslim's inveterate disavowal of Christ's Incarnation as Christians hold it to be need not deter him from its measure of divine power and mercy. For, duly understood, it is not a compromise of the divine greatness and glory but rather their evidence in grace. Correspondingly, a Christian's distance from the pattern of the post-Hijrah Muhammad need not exclude participation in the Qur'an's celebration of the dignity of man within the sacramental order of the natural world. The awe the Bhagavad Gita teaches in the presence of divine mystery and the ineffable wonder need not be alien to those who do not, and could not, belong with Hindus.

Such mutual participations do not compromise, nor – rightly judged – do they obscure, issues. They are the reverential aspects of mutual honesty, an honesty that refuses to be deterred by habitual antipathy or ingrained suspicion. The sense of them, furthermore, actually enables the judgments we may be required to bring. For it ensures that these will not be based on sheer avoidance, nor on deliberate ill-will, nor on insensitive prejudice. What remains between us in greeting will be the truer and the surer for being transacted there. To say that 'honesty is the best policy' is to risk its being merely politic, and then the honesty becomes itself suspect. Rather, honesty is readiness for truth and a condition of its discernment. It has its first fruit in penitence. Awaiting it are mutual discoveries.

4

And Active Penitence

Without due self-esteem no faith can exist. Yet the long drama that religious history presents cries out for comprehensive penitence. The business of this chapter is to ask how faiths can be serious with themselves not only in their thought of being right but in their evidence of being wrong. With what must penitence deal? What must it require?

At the heart of the Jewish liturgy came the annual Day of Atonement, a will to radical self-interrogation by 'the people of God'. In the presence of the divine holiness the nation was summoned to know itself and to atone. When Martin Luther in Wittenberg in 1517 circulated his Ninety-Five Theses the first of them said:

Our Lord and Master Jesus Christ . . . intended that the whole life of believers should be penitence.

In the Muslim's Qur'an comes the repeated call for *Istighfar*, or the 'seeking of forgiveness' from God in respect of all that has offended the divine law in human dealings in Islam.[1] The Buddhist Eightfold Path demands careful introspection as a constant habit of mind. The motive and content of behaviour must be interrogated and reproved. In thus assessing what is present the Buddhist judges what is past. Penitence in some sense would seem to need to be 'the whole life of believers', the first thesis for them all.

This has to be so, in as much as religions claim to be the mentors of all else, in trust with all that is ultimate and categorical. They cannot well themselves be exempt from their own meanings. All have at heart some kind of 'immaculate conception', whether 'the light of the Buddha', or the pure majesty of Lord Krishna, or 'the Book in which there is nothing dubious' (Surah 2.2). These, and their counterparts elsewhere, are such as to brook no trifling. Living by finalities, faiths exercise a mastery. By the same token they are its subjects.

Penitence, it might be said, is concern with that paradox. Enjoying sacred warrant, they have to admit themselves at fault. That which sacralizes all has to accuse itself. To hold what is believed to be inviolate does not make the holders thereby innocent. It is necessary for those who think they have the truth to perceive themselves to be untrue. Frequently the Qur'an calls for its faithful to be 'sincere before God in their religion'. It is therefore evident that they may not be.[2] By their very impetus, religious breed their own default. Their temptations are inseparable from their vocation, the more so in that they can always plead the mandate of heavenly vision or invoke the alibi of divine favour. Truth claims undo themselves by the very form they take and rituals play false with the meanings they intend.

(ii)

Religions find it difficult to come to terms with their own guilt. They are adept at exoneration. They vary widely in their capacity to question their own identity. One of the potentialities of dialogue is that it might promote the process. Contact certainly makes each more alive to its own image and may encourage them to admire it less and search it more. The will to vindication, however, is always strong. Dialogue, especially when affected sharply by political factors, may well excite it more. Yet to be comprehensively responsible for the image is vital to integrity, not least because anxiety about it can also be corrupting.

To have the theme of penitence take us in this way into study of the image faiths present to the world suggests that we go to a painful prayer in the Hebrew psalms. Occurring often, it breaths a concern that is characteristically Jewish. In Psalm 69.6 we find it: 'Let not those that seek thee be confounded through me.' Judaic faith bound theology and identity together in its conviction about 'God and his people'. Therefore, how the world saw Jewry was always relevant to how the world understood God via his pre-occupation with 'his people'.

Is not this situation in some sense also universal? It is always important for 'the faithful' to be rightly seen if 'the faith' is not to be misconstrued. The psalmist was very aware of a watching world, of himself as a sort of test-case about God. He was alive to himself as a potential source of 'mis-information'. This, at all costs, he wanted to prevent.

If we defer the things which, in his case, were really at stake, we see how apposite to greeting the parallel is. Religions are constantly decrying alleged misreadings of themselves. Assessed by outsiders they will be moved to say: 'This is a traversty of what we are.' The point is one I have conceded earlier. All have the right to disown what they say they are not, to correct what they claim is distorted image-ing.

There is much need here for patience. Such disowning has to answer to avowing. All faiths have interior quarrels. They occur in all belief systems. Versions of Judaism have been wryly said to be as numerous as Jews themselves. Muslim Mustafa differs from Muslim Hasan. So it is with Christians, Hindus, Sikhs, Buddhists and also sects of every sort. Indeed sects are the progeny of this situation. They consist by the capacity of religions to crumble into fragments in the definition of faith and the management of community and in the definition of who they *really* are.

These struggles can be ugly. The point here is that they occur. There is a very religious necessity about them. Practice *did* have to be accused of being unworthy of profession. Doctrine *did* need to be challenged for its own distortions. Why should perception of failure be often so tardy? And why often so acrimonious? At times, no doubt, there *is* wilful calumny from outside. Some misreadings are deliberately hostile and malicious. Yet even wilful enmity has to find what it can accuse. Inner acts of self-betrayal play into its hands. Why are these not self-correcting? How could faiths be so lacking in alertness to what disfigured them until critics came along from outside? The principle 'by their fruits you will know them' applies for every kind of fruiting, whether it be sound or otherwise.

In all the confusions of image awareness, defensive or penitent within, well-meant or ill-meant from without, it is important to plead for warm human rapport. In verdicts about faiths do the parties need to be always proprietors, or partisans, defending set positions? Is there hope of searching what is at issue without the mask of *parti pris*? Where all is programmed to serve ulterior ends the humanity is compromised which should obtain between each and all. Due witness has to be concerned with others for their own sake as fellow mortals, 'bound in the bundle of life'. Only so can relationships surmount the temptation to falsity within.

(iii)

We return to the Psalmist in 69.6. He was clearly in great straits, 'sinking in deep waters' and close to despair. He feared that the sight of him in his trouble would present a scandal to the world that might disprove the whole thesis about his people as 'the chosen of God'.[3] He was wrestling, Job-like, with the mystery of suffering and evidence of how insoluble it was. Plainly there was a link between any vindication of God and vindication of him. So it is, comparably, with the religions. They are evidence to vet, pro and con, whatever it is they have to say about the mystery they interpret. The Psalmist knew himself to be proxy for God in respect of any justification of belief.

It was for God's sake he had undergone persecution and been reduced to anguish of soul. He sensed he could become the occasion of cynicism, what today would be secularism, callous or wistful, through the conclusions observers would draw from the picture he presented. Depending on how the evidence was read, he could be taken for proof of indifferent deity, discredited worship, or impenetrable enigma. He himself, as believer, doubter, agonizer, was at the heart of everything, the puzzling referent of his faith. His anguish about truth was a struggle within himself.

Here, then, in his prayer, is the very crux of dialogue with the world and between faiths. The Psalmist in his plea stands in for the Muslim in his mosque, the monk in his cell, the Sufi in his *zawiya*, the devotee in his saffron robe, the theologian on his rostrum. The evidentiality of truth is with the credibility of truth-bearers and truth-wrestlers. They are the living crisis of their religion, and – as with the Psalmist – the private meaning is in public view, whether of good or ill report.

'Let not those who seek thee be confounded through me' – the prayer takes us to the heart of whatever 'thee' may mean, however 'me' is lived. And how 'confounding' religions can be! In the Psalmist's case the fear was that onlookers might be discouraged by the sight of his distress, undeceived about any credence he deserved. It is not generally so with comfortable faiths or their establishments. They are 'confounding', rather, for their dark crimes and futile follies, more rarely for puzzled travail over grief and shame. History is eloquent of the doubt-creating quality of religious belief and ritual. All the centuries have seen minds made sceptical and spirits desolated by the manifestations of religion.

There have been no unambiguous 'ages of faith'. Today the greeting must sometimes be 'A plague on all your houses!' from those who deplore the pretensions, the crudities and the hypocrisies of adherents of religions. To cry with the poet 'Mock on, Voltaire' may sound defiant in reply, but on its own showing is no real dissuasive.

(iv)

It is daunting and, after Chapter 3, perhaps unnecessary to attempt here any catalogue of religions at their worst, or to note how faith-protection is prone to obscurantism and the sanctities of piety are prone to impatience with other schools of reverence. Or how faiths have abetted the passions of nationalism and the greed of economic interests. Passive acquiescence in unrighteousness has inveigled faith into disproof of its claims. Some religious decisions about the mysteries of the world have fostered a cruel churlishness in the presence of them. Dogmas ride roughshod over the yearnings and perceptions of the heart. Theories of fatedness under karmic law have atrophied the will to live and care, to attain a common humanity. Or assurance about divine 'compassion' is married to hard rigorism in the confession of it. Beliefs as to divine omnipotence have sustained callous alliance with its irresistibility. Advocacies of faith are stultified by the poverty of their intelligence or the compromises of their practice. We have always to wonder how much worse religions might have been but for the restraints of gentler agnosticism within them or outside.

The Psalmist with whom we have been communing was at least

aware that he was a potential scandal to the world. Faiths so often have been indifferent to how and why they might be doubted. Reproach is massive. Some apologiae aggravate it further. From the Milvian Bridge and Constantine via the Crusaders and the sack of Constantinople in 1204, to the Inquisition, the Thirty Years' War, the Christian ledger is long defiled. The Jewish mind lives with the unforgettability of the Holocaust as the supreme indictment of humanity at large and of Christians in particular. That guilt-complex defies all resolution. The churches in Hitler's Europe are seen by the sternest prosecutors as heirs to a tradition of antisemitism they grimly failed to recognize as their guilt, still less to surmount by their courage.[4] Jewish reckoning with the horrors of the Holocaust has nevertheless to see them within the human whole both as to their antecedents and their meaning.[5]

The white man in his new continent post-Columbus has never fully honoured a single treaty made with Amerindians in the USA and Canada. 'Bury my heart at wounded knee' is not, therefore, merely a song about a place: it is a lament within a continent where religious faith readily assumed the right to possess in the terms of the New England poet: 'The land was ours before we were the land's'.[6] History records, but readily forgets, the terrible toll of the slave trade. Time accumulates genocides, whether in Germany or Armenia, Africa or the Far Pacific, land-borne or sea-borne. Faiths participate in the guilt of them, whether in concentrated violence or in the long, slow, silent, relentless privation of the unremembered poor, the unsung victims of the strong.

Much human suffering lies at the door of the caste system. A lively social conscience has to ask whether justice and compassion are best served by the 'dis-passion' of religious philosophies and their dis-interest in the content of actual history. Is the real evil of collective structures answered in the quest for liberation from the alleged 'evil' of personal individuation? Western theologians, for their part, are sometimes found tilting, quixotically, at windmills in neglect or urgent business in the social order and the economic scene. Christian evangelists become besotted with the fascination of market-place criteria and succumb to the patterns of crude salesman-ship, as in the advertisers' world. The blandishments of power or the comforts of ease quieten the conscience which faith should alarm and arouse, and truth-seekers are the more dismayed.

Wrongs that religion either blesses or ignores oppress the deprived in every part of cosmopolis – the poor and powerless, women, the un-privileged – while church and mosque and temple offer a pre-occupied worship.

Or the faith-deterring aspects of the religions lie in the range and bitterness of their inner rivalries, the rivalries on which they brood and feed. The sects in Lebanon and Ulster demonstrate how deeply rancour can implant itself. The creation of Pakistan in the middle of this century in the name of separate Islamic statehood entailed enormous human cost. Rejecting readings of Islam which welcomed all-India unity,[7] Muslim self-sufficiency in Pakistani form endangered continuing Islam in India and afforded to Hindu opinion the equal logic of a Hindu mastery in its own Indian house which the ideal of common citizenship may not always be able to resist. The pre-partition complexities, to be sure, were enormous. Post-partition history has hardly improved upon their legacy.

Indictment of the religions can never be complete. There are always extenuating factors, or at least a will to plead them. What matters is the capacity to know accusation for what it is. The familiar phrase *confessio fidei* has so widely and so grimly to read *corruptio fidei*. The reproach of faiths is written deeply in histories by which they are accused.

(v)

There is one other aspect of the guilt equation to consider before we pass to the basic question as to what penitence can mean and do. It relates to the vexed issue of religious leadership, the vested interests it acquires and the near tyrannies it may institutionalize.

All faiths, of necessity, have their human 'authorities' – clergy, rabbis, mullahs, monks, guides, scholars, and the rest, in a wide variety of roles. They, more than lowlier folk, have more urgent reason to pray the Psalmist's prayer: 'Let not those who seek Thee be confounded through us.' 'Offices' of learning, roles in rituals, *Fatwas* or judicial verdicts about faith and conduct – all are indispensable in religious life. The flux of time and the sequence of generations means ever-renewed tutelage and management of heritage. Scriptures also presuppose interpreters, readers, exegetes and scribes.

On every count and in every faith there is always an ambiguity between being in trust and being in control, within religious structures. At best the relationship of master to seeker is delicate; at worst there is the tyranny of Dostoevsky's Grand Inquisitor, deciding the limits within which believing should be regulated. Authority needs a right prestige. Yet prestige can grievously corrupt authority. Nowhere perhaps is the dilemma better captured than in the directive of a pastoral letter in the New Testament, 'Let no one despise you' (Titus 2.15), set alongside the truth about the Messiah whom Titus served which tells that 'he was despised' (Isaiah 53.3).

Perhaps the sages and the *Bodhisattvas* of the Buddhist world are the least offenders in the cares of mentorship. For the goal of the disciple is for each soul to reach uniquely. The teacher can only instil and train a skill in which no other can be proxy. The pupil becomes his own initiate. Even so, the master's role is paramount, his mastery of the relationship complete. In unworthy hands the techniques of Asian faiths may degenerate into a charlatanry where the devotee may be as captive as any infallibilist elsewhere. If, in fact, the self was meant and made for selfhood, then the techniques of a discipline to have it not so, however admirable in their sincerity, will be an exercise in constraint, a potential occasion of religious bondage. In the great Hindu classic, the Bhagavad Gita, the anxieties of Arjuna are over-ruled by Lord Krishna, in guise as his charioteer, against what may well have been his own better judgment.[8]

It is the Semitic theisms which, in their different ways, are most open to the suspicion of misused authority in the things of faith. In Islam the forms of religious leadership differ sharply between the Sunni and the Shi'ah communities. The former depend upon consensus within the 'house of Islam' as the sphere within which secure interpretation of the sacred law may be found. This *ijma'* (literally 'converging' or 'agreeing') rests on an old tradition of the Prophet that 'his people would never agree on an error'. It operates only in 'non-repugnancy' to the Qur'an itself and the tradition and the principle of 'analogy', these being the three primary 'sources', to which *Ijma'* is the fourth. However, this reliance on the mind of the community does not mean that any individual Muslim can pontificate. 'Consensus' requires *Ijtihad* or 'enterprise' to initiate and concert it. The 'door' of *Ijtihad*, as it is called, is traditionally open only to the experts who are skilled in all the minutiae of Qur'an interpretation, of tradition, and its 'criticism'.

Twentieth-century thinkers within Islam have had to struggle hard to 'open' the 'door' to wider circles of expertise so that devout surgeons, engineers, financiers – in whose world so many areas fall which cry out for law and guidance – might participate as well as, or in the place of, grammarians, pundits and '*ulama*' from Al-Azhar or Deoband.[9] Such laicization of Islam's self-definition is strongly resisted by timid or entrenched opinion on the part of those who want to retain a stranglehold on how Islam is interpreted and its sacred law understood.

It follows that at least for enquiring minds there continues something actually or potentially oppressive about the forms of Islamic nurture, not least where these continue focussed on routine recitation of the Qur'an to the neglect of free entrustment with its meanings. Though via technology and the patterns of the contemporary scene there has been a considerable change in the communal status and prestige of the learned in the Islamic sciences, they still wield much power over the Muslim masses. Popular emotion aroused by political factors plays into their hands, or into the hands of those who are more absolute than they within extremist sects. Even where state-controlled, the mosque preacher can still be a potent force in the schooling and grooming of a submissive mentality. A self-interrogating religious leadership in Islam does not readily emerge in the current scene or labours under heavy deterrents from many sources. Religious authority is the more suspect when it does not pause to consider that it should be other than it is. Those over whom it presides have then no escape from the same assumption and are restricted in mental 'enterprising' of their own.

Religious inculcation has a different feel in Shi'ah Islam, where the Ayatollahs stand in for the absent Imams in whose mysterious status the once-for-all revelatory truth of Islam is enshrined. 'Consensus' does not obtain here, but the esoteric wisdom of the 'spiritual heirs' of the Prophet through whom the exegesis of the Qur'an is mediated. Leadership is thus a more mystical property than in Sunni Islam and the emotions explicit in Shi'ah Islam, centering upon the memory of the immaculate 'people of the house' of Muhammad (Surah 33.33), make religious nurture both vivid and definitive. For the most part, it is left to outsiders to interrogate its oppressiveness.

Christian history has its own heavy toll on human freedom, its own tally of oppression of the mind. Sunni Islam prides itself that it has no 'clergy'. The point is fairly made. Its scholars and mullahs in no way infringe the role of the individual in the ritual prayer and the other rites of the faith. Every Muslim is self-sufficient in the things of devotion and piety. On official scholarship there has to be reliance; of mediation there is none. By contrast, the sacramental forms of Christianity are exclusive to the clergy, with some exceptions. The forms and rationale of such authority differ crucially and have been the long and bitter occasion of inter-Christian debate and schism. Our only concern here, within our theme of penitence, is with the temptation to oppression and perhaps conceit that waits on Christian sacramentalism. There is much that is hard to discern with certainty about the emergence of exclusive priesthood, beyond the New Testament, from within the apostolic legacy of faith and ministry. The first sense of 'apostolic' had to do with 'having companied with Jesus' – a status which by its very nature could not be bequeathed. Necessary roles of leadership ensued to successors, in respect of validating the credentials of much travelling Christians enjoying and receiving hospitality in a dangerous world. To these came further the tasks of ensuring due continuity of 'the Word' and of duly accredited ministry.

But when the 'elder' presiding over the eucharist in the name of all present came to assume the category of the 'priest' from sources in the Hebraic tradition, 'hierarchical' claims developed (from the Greek *hiereus*), and 'priest ruling' (hierarchy) followed via such writers as Cyprian (200–258 CE). The story is long and obscure. The telling is not my obligation here; only the consequent temptations are. Exclusive functions develop potential lordship, not always or everywhere effectively corrected by the doctrine of a 'universal priesthood of all believers'. Was the official exercise of such 'priesthood' by 'priests' alone on behalf of all a matter of 'order' and 'seemliness' and 'ministry', or was it, rather, a question of doctrine about an exclusivity for reasons beyond those of 'order'? In the latter case, it could readily become an indispensable channel of grace, a perquisite of those who held it and who would be tempted to endow their possession of it with vested interests of their own.

That way lay the actual tyranny against which Christian history has had to strive for so long. As with John Keble, in his famous Assize Sermon in 1833, the 'interests' of that 'priestly standing' could entail the defending of the long scandal of oppressive Irish bishoprics subsisting by exactions from a peasantry who had no love for them. The example is random and the occasion complex. There is much to be repented of in Rome, Constantinople, Canterbury and – in its own ethos – Geneva from the incubus of clericalism. Their offence against the liberty of grace and the magnanimity of truth cannot be in doubt. Without a lively instinct for our dispensability in the things of God we cannot well possess or exercise the dignities we believe he has bestowed upon us or the sacramental agencies with which we hold ourselves entrusted. That the instinct has often been criminally lacking in the story of all Christendom is the clue to its indictment and the demand for its penitence.

(vi)

If all the foregoing is rightly read as onus on the religions for self-doubt and accusation, what hope of response could it expect? What, if anything, could penitence achieve? Is it a category which can apply across the wide diversity of religious systems and structures? Penitence looks as problematic as the term 'salvation' which some Christians have applied to inter-faith discourse, in neglect of how disparate the content of the term can be.[10] Can it be at the centre of what we owe to each other?

There is point in such hesitation. Yet penitence is only taking ourselves seriously in a sceptical way: it is the art of suspecting ourselves. Much 'taking seriously' on the part of faith is aggressive, controversial, superiorizing, self-congratulatory. It tends to inward admiration and outward denigration, in postures that are either complacent or imperceptive. Genuine penitence is the other way. It denies itself the luxury of favourable comparison. It begins at home, but it is alert to the world as holding much against it.

Penitence lets the questions penetrate. It ceases to be evasive and so diminishes the distances that separate. It forgoes the cult of innocence which is so often the habit of external accusation and polemic.

This, it may be said, is to ask of religions precisely what is least congenial to their instincts. For they do not take well to being in the wrong, which is itself an urgent reason why they should. Whatever their instincts, they are – on some count or other – presumably allies of the good.

It is hard to come by any agreed philosophy of sin. The faiths of far Asia will always differ from the faiths of near Asia about the nature of evil. However far apart the theories, the sense of being unworthy can always apply. There can be meeting across disputed explanations.

Penitence – if we are theists – is a kind of inclusive apology to God. It is the acknowledgement of past or present wrong as the condition of a right present and future. It does not allow evil to be the final verdict on a situation, as would be so if penitence were absent. It is the heart of any release from sequential wrong, in contrast to the hardness of heart which leaves evil in control.

But we are not all theists. What of scepticism within the karmic law of caste as to the possibility of a break in the entail of moral consequences and the inexorable sequence of evil? The thought of any liberating penitence has heavy odds against it. Yet not if we can think of a certain solidarity in which initiatives to defy *karma* could be taken within shared humanity, thus breaking any severely individual working of the karmic law.[11] The factor of vicarious suffering, of redeeming forgiveness, undertaking to 'bear the evil', means that there *is* a break in the sequence of deed and guilt and fate. It is just such inter-human undertaking of each other's wrongs that forgiveness embodies and penitence receives, a penitence truly reciprocal to the forgiveness it awaits. Then the act of penitence makes space for hope. Given such change in the heart, there is no longer bare fated-ness. The karmic law is over-ridden by a law of love. Penitence suspends its operation.

(vii)

Can the faiths, in their dialogue, comprehend the human vocation to live in corporate penitence in order to give and receive the forgiveness which penitence accepts? The question obviously reaches far into the turmoils of contemporary politics and society. Is it feasible to read the human situation as a call beyond vicarious suffering to 'vicarious penitence'?[12] This would mean a deliberate 'will to atone' – to make inclusive 'apology to God' about humanity at large as a condition of giving to guilt its true proportions and to hope its due measure.

These must surely inter-depend. Hope is trivial and banal if it has not taken the stakes for what they are. This means a full register of the range of evil. It means also an ability to go beyond private guilt into a sense of collective wrongs in which all are anonymously, variously, subtly, involved.[13] Are there those who can undertake penitence on behalf of those who refuse it? If there is anything inter-religious which demands exploring it is surely this, but it needs careful exposition. A strong tradition of Muhammad can help us, by way of a scene from T. S. Eliot.

When what they take to be ultimate sacrilege occurs in *Murder in the Cathedral*, the chorus of the women of Canterbury cry out:

Clear the air! clean the sky! wash the wind! . . . wash the stone, wash the bone, wash the brain, wash the soul, wash them, wash them![14]

Living 'an instant eternity of evil and wrong',they are in line with a reading of the Muslim tradition:

If any among you sees evil things, he should change them with his hand: If he cannot do that he should change them with his tongue: if he cannot do that he should change them in his heart.[15]

There was little that hand or tongue could do when the archbishop lay dead. But the heart remained – the heart that would have to bear all that the deed signified and would entail. It is lesser ills that can be remedied by handy action – escorting a blind man across the road, throwing water on a fire, or kindling one in the cold like the good king in the carol. Other situations, however, call for verbal protest. Voices must be raised against evils that the hand cannot reach because they are distant or because they are intangible. Without oral reproach they may well be condoned or unidentified.

In other situations only the heart can undertake a feasible resistance. The deeper the moral evil, the deeper the level at which it must be faced. Then, if we do not capitulate or acquiesce, we must bear, and bear in a certain kind of way. That way may include sensing and accusing our own part in the causation of the wrong. The true heart will not claim a false innocence. The right way will mean – on behalf of others, if they will not bring it for themselves – a corporate sense of the guilt that is abroad within society. For only where evil is acknowledged for what it is can it begin to have forgiveness from the wronged. Only in being accused can situations be redeemed.

The Muslim tradition concludes with the comment that the third, 'the heart', is 'the weakest of the three'. The case here is that, on the contrary, it is the strongest, though hands and tongues are certainly more quickly deployed. In the Shi'ah community in Islam the tradition was used to justify *taqiyyah*, the attitude by which, when the political order was adverse or unworthy, subjects who could do no other, lay low, in a submission they could not avoid, while continuing to reject the régime at heart.[16] Continuing to resist, but only inwardly, they cherished the ideal they could not, for the present, make succeed. It was this that made it 'the weakest'.

Yet in another perspective – and without the possible element of subterfuge – such painful cherishing of the good that is denied, or even crucified, is the very strength of hope. It is only when we are 'not overcome of evil' that we can 'overcome evil with good'. The penitence here in mind is just this changing of evil situations 'in the heart'. It is acceptance by the self of the wrongs it has committed and the guilt incurred. Or it is the deepening of the outsider's mere 'regret' or 'outrage', or other reaction about the way the world is, into a positive will to have it redeemed both in forgiveness offered and forgiveness found.

The argument is that such attitudes of wanting penitence to happen, or willing to be party in it, are vital areas of the meaning of religions. They have never agreed about how to diagnose the human situation. They all propose in some way to guide and amend it. Taking it, in realism, for what it is, is surely where their meeting begins.

(viii)

It is striking how great denominators of the major faiths are available to underwrite the task of penitence – with the exception of where the basic clue of transience is the key to all else. For, clearly, transience read as definitive disallows realist hope. Nor can it admit any rescue of the past. Other ruling concepts can, such as duty, obligation, compassion, human solidarity, and liability to conscience. Even the theme of self-escape yields motives and requires skills on the way, as the Eightfold Path of Buddhism demonstrates. A certain 'ought' broods over all religious existence concerning 'that which should be'. The sense, therefore, of the 'ought not', the discrepancy from the 'ought' of that which actually is, has to be equally in place. Regret, even despair, if not penitence, must then ensue. Not even secular scepticism is immune. In indicting religion it is asking it to accuse itself, whether as to dishonest doctrine or insincerity of life. To identify hypocrisy is to recommend penitence.

These obvious truths, however, do not of themselves produce great penitents. For these we turn again instinctively to the great Hebrew prophets with their rejection of 'vain oblations' and their call: 'Wash you, make you clean, cease to do evil, learn to do well' (Isaiah 1.13,16–17). These demands derive from the ruling claim of divine holiness and the vocation of a 'kingdom of priests' required to hallow a land occupied by covenant and promise. The constant self-reckoning with those aspects of destiny kindled in the great prophets a passion for righteousness all too often lulled into complacency by the ready rhythm of the priestly sacrifices supposed to symbolize it. It is always easier to be ritually employed than to be spiritually engaged. Where treasured identity, as profoundly in Judaism, is paramount the ease is all the greater. Hence the glory of Amos, of Hosea and Jeremiah in that tradition – a glory always at odds with what their hearers cherished about themselves.

The moral sensitivity of the Islamic Qur'an is of a different order. Its reprobation has to do with 'unbelievers', with the 'paganism' that resists its message. In the face of a hostile world and with the thrust of an imperious word, there was scant occasion for introspection. By the circumstance of Islam's origins and the context of its immediate mission in Mecca, its supreme demand addressed those who did not yet belong.

Even so, given its experience of the obduracy of its first hearers, the Qur'an has a realistic sense of the wrongness of the world. We noted at the outset its stress on the 'seeking of forgiveness'. There is the theme, so eloquent in the last two Surahs, of 'taking refuge with God' from 'the evil of men'.[17] This *ta'widh* or recourse to the

divine mercy, is a deep feature of Muslim devotion.[18] It corresponds
to that descriptive of God as *Al-Tawwab*, 'the cognizant of penitence' (Surahs 2.37,54,128,160; 9.104 and 118; 24.10; 49.12 and
110.3). Here, as with the 'divine Name', *Al-Shakur*, 'the cognizant
of gratitude', the very nature of God is denoted by that which is
reciprocal to man.

However, it is the verb *zalama* and its derivative noun *zulm* which
enshrine most graphically the Qur'an's warning against human evil.
While *shirk* is the cardinal sin of denying to God his sole sovereignty,
power and wisdom, by ascribing these to pseudo-deities, *zulm* is
inclusive wrong, injustice, oppression. It is the denying of that
which is due, any accounting of a thing falsely, any kind of distortion of the true and the right.[19] There is *zulm* against others, against
God and against the self. The last, *zulm al-nafs*, means all that
defiles or depraves the self by its own consent and guilt. It is a
compromise of the self at the very core of self-awareness and self-
possession. It is therefore where penitence belongs in the inwardness
of each.

The sympathy of this root concept with Christian thinking was
the theme of Muhammad Kamil Husain's perceptive Muslim study
of Good Friday in *Qaryah Zalimah*, or 'City of Wrong'. He borrowed
the title from a Quranic phrase about 'a community in the wrong'
and applied it to Jerusalem in the climax of the rejection of Jesus.

For his purposes, it was immaterial whether Jesus actually suffered death by crucifixion (which Islam traditionally denies). It
sufficed that a will to crucify was equally present whether the climax
happened in fact or whether it was divinely thwarted by the intervention, in some sense, of 'illusion about it.[20] Kamil Husain saw
the will to crucify as the guilt of collective expediency allowed to
override the dictates of personal conscience. Perpetrators did, in the
name of security, the nation, tenure of office, or callous indifference,
what they might well not have done if they had 'thought on God'
and trembled. He read the cross of Jesus as a dramatic occasion of
Quranic *zulm* and an inclusive theme for penitence.

His reflections went further into what he saw as the characteristic
pre-occupation of the Christian tradition with culpability. The disciples accused themselves that they had totally failed Jesus in not
rescuing him at Gethsemane and in subsequently deserting him in
the final hours. But that 'crime' was caught up in sheer frustration

through the very unwillingness of Jesus to have them rescue him. How were they to stay loyal to a leader who disallowed the only, the violent, form in which they – thus far – knew how to respond to his evident jeopardy? How could they know, in the very stress of despair, that they were involved in the central enigma of evil, namely how 'the good' should react and, reacting, overcome? That secret they were only to discover in the sequel of the resurrection.

It is illuminating to have this central structure of Christian meaning analysed perceptively from within Islam. We need not go along altogether with Kamil Husain's sense of a guilt-complex, deriving from the first disciples, as the clue to Christianity. But that faith certainly has at its heart an event which will not allow us to romanticize about humanity or issue selective exonerations to these, or those, among them. 'All have . . . come short of the glory of God.' If we will accept it, that is the very crux of hope.

There is in the New Testament Gospels, at their climax, a remarkable passage in which the disciples are warned by Jesus of impending betrayal. The situation at what we call 'the Last Supper' is tense with foreboding. The disciples are uncannily aware of 'doom on the house', and Jesus is under the dark shadow of tragedy. As to treachery, each of the disciples asks in turn, 'Is it I?'[21] They cannot be asking blandly just in order to be cleared. They do not know their own mind. They do know their own bewilderment, their own unpredictable quality, their own ambivalence. There is a climax coming which will shatter them. Each asks the question outwardly because it harbours an inward fear.

> Deep in all is the base collaborator.
> The betrayer is ever oneself, never another.
> All must say: 'Lord is it I?' There is always
> Evil in goodness, lust in love . . .
> And without it . . . the Cross
> Had never been . . .[22]

It is this register of the inclusiveness of evil which makes 'changing it in the heart' the first meaning of faith.

The Irish writer, James Joyce, once remarked to a friend:

In realism you get down to the facts on which the world is

based . . . What makes most people's lives unhappy is some disappointed romanticism, some unrealizable misconceived ideal. In fact you may say that idealism is the ruin of man, and if we lived down to fact . . . we would be better off. That is what we were made for.[23]

'Better off', perhaps in respect of unrealizable day-dreams, denied to us in the maul of circumstance and folly which Joyce so well described. But are those the only 'facts on which the world is based'? Or is there a 'living down to fact' which finds in them a judgment upon ourselves as the condition of our transformation? Then 'idealism' is not 'our ruin', nor romance our self-deceit. They constitute a realism which opens out to hope. Between them is the fact of penitence, refusing in the realization of evil to despair of good.

5

With Mutual Discovery

(i)

The point of greeting is to transact relationship. Perhaps relationship exists. Then greeting is to set to reinforce and deepen it. Or it is only latent and needs to be kindled by anticipation into fact. Or there may be only a conjecture which greeting will be ready to explore in case the venture may succeed. We are always running risks both of hope and failure. Greeting might be defined as a faith in mutuality putting itself to test.

All the foregoing chapters have brought us to this crucial exercise of faith. Given cosmopolis, relatedness between religions is not in doubt. Whether they bring themselves to the depth of mutuality that true greeting must express turns on their willingness for honesty and self-interrogation. Those requisites of sincerity I have reviewed. If we can assume them, the experience of greeting across acknowledged diversity cannot fail of mutual discoveries. Greeting will still have about it those degrees of risk, of potential and uncertainty, which always obtain, even in less exacting fields, when relationships are trusting themselves further and entrusting what needs proving between them to situations of its possible disproof.

Of all the ways in which faiths express themselves, metaphor and symbol are apt for our study now. For it is in these, rather than in the dogmas or cults that employ them, that we can best hope to sense what is made mutual by them in the one world of sense experience and language imagery. Words and images are necessary to all. All are engaged in the art of representation even when they think themselves rigorously exempt from it. Faiths can find each

other even in the idiosyncrasies by which they read and tell the
'icons', the sign-worlds, of their separate convictions and practices.

'Jerusalem' comes at once to mind as a telling example. The city,
the legend, the ideology, the emotion, the dream, which the name
describes are passionately cherished by all Semitic faiths. For Jews,
Jerusalem is 'holy Zion', where 'the Most High' has 'caused his
Name to dwell', 'the city of truth', whose towers and bulwarks are
'the abode of peace'. Muslim tradition celebrates Jerusalem with
fervour, 'the sweetest sound in Paradise being the strains of the
muezzin from the mosques of Jerusalem'.[1] Gethsemane and the
Mount of Olives have for ever hallowed Jerusalem's meaning in the
Christian soul. Abraham, Jesus, Muhammad have each left their
imprint in its story or its legend. In their rivalries concerning it the
Semitic faiths cannot escape each other. It embraces them even in
setting them at odds. What they have at issue transpires in a symbol-
ism they are bound to share.

Jerusalem leaves geography behind and becomes in the devotion
of generations 'the heavenly city', as in the lyrical *O quanta qualia*
of Peter Abelard or the lilting refrain of the Negro spirituals.[2] It
could even be that the Hebrew psalmist, in a bold access of poetic
liberty, joins it with the pagan legends of 'the rivers of God' which
flows where the divinities dwell. For in Psalm 46 he talks elusively
of 'a river which makes glad the city of God' (v.4). He does not
mean the brook Kidron. It would seem that he is echoing old
mythology and linking the Temple site in Jerusalem with a long
pre-history of fabled sanctity before the time of Solomon. Another
psalm (48.2) hints at Mount Zaphon, in 'the farthest reaches of the
north', where the gods convened, as somehow fellow to Zion.[3]

Such readings by modern scholars may dismay Hebrew orthodox.
If we can allow them they may give the severely Semitic imagery
of Jerusalem some distant translation into Asian faiths which prefer
to cities the imagery of rivers rising in the far vaster majesty of the
Himalayas. Either way, the meaning is not impaired. It would be
impossible to agree or find one single geographical or physical sign
to avail for each and all in the wide diversity of human believing
about life and time, mystery and God. But all alike are one in the
vital role of language and image in the feasibility of faiths. To meet
and greet is to be on a thoroughfare with features all can recognize
and none monopolize.

That it should be so is consistent with all I have said about cosmopolis. Languages, to be sure, are legion. The range of metaphor on which they can draw is bounded by the single earth, the human senses and the yield of nature. Whatever meaning they intend, the terms that languages employ are from the same limited field of perception and awareness. 'Light', 'fire', 'water', 'shore', 'seed', 'well', 'tree', 'breath', 'door' – all form a common stock of religious imagery taken from shared experience of human life on earth. Dialogue between faiths can savour the kinships of imagery even while it grapples with the differing meanings. It is one earth and one humanity. There is a latency of greeting in that very situation.

Nor is it only the sources of metaphor that are shared. Common to all religious discourse is the way in which its themes necessarily engage the imagination in the interpretation of experience. The facts on which it proceeds are never 'bare', or 'plain'. To ask, religiously, for facts in their 'bareness' is to ask for facts in their vacuity. Only in their significance are they possessed. Indeed, it might be said that the whole point of religion is to require a reconsideration, at least in these modern times, of the whole notion of fact, if the term be confined to the laboratory, the test-tube and calculus. All faith is interpretative of 'givens' that possess their significance only in perception of them. In this perception metaphor plays a crucial part. The cross-reference of language enlists what one realm can convey about another. Meaning then captures what is elusive in words that give it shape in familiars of life. Then there are 'rising tides of hope', and 'all the world's a stage', 'God sets his bow in the cloud', and 'something causes me to tremble'. All faiths have their usages this way in transacting what they mean. They will not cease to debate and differ, but only within devices of language and meaning common to them all.

This does not mean that they have licence for any and every kind of fantasy to which they might be liable. It does mean that the actualities of space and time with which they have to do are woven into a fabric of reception whose patterns come from one human cognizance and the art of language telling it.

(ii)

For some faiths metaphor moves beyond imagery in word and undertakes to tell a story. Metaphor is then transformed into narrative. For others again a history is enacted. The ensuing narration is real and could not suffice if it were fiction. But here too the history is received and told from within perceptions of its meaning. The whole is itself a dramatic metaphor, an event in time and place ascertained and possessed, not as a mere chronicle, but as a confession, and a house, of faith. Religions have parted sharply over the question whether event-status is vital to their truth, with Asian faiths broadly satisfied to enshrine finality in what is visionary, the Semitic faiths urgent for history as the only adequate vehicle of revelation. That issue is a large dimension of dialogue itself. Either way, 'sacred myth' or 'sacred history' are, in their contrast, metaphored meaning. What is given in them is through what is perceived of them.

The biblical faiths turn most decisively on history. 'A Syrian ready to perish' was 'our father Abraham', but ready also to migrate, to be a nomad, and 'to seek a city'. Moses and the Exodus stand definitively within the retrospect of Israel. The fire and fury of Sinai yielded the imagery of divine encounter in the context of a nomad people precariously poised between liberation from slavery and the quest for a home. That 'history' is not reducible to bare facts – unattainable anyway. It is seen through the prism of its own interpreters in the long retrospect of an awakening to themselves that the retrospect itself aroused. It is history mythicized. Exodus and Exile are metaphors in which the faithful explained themselves in the act of perceiving their story.

The Christian Gospels stand in the same tradition. Events in Galilee and Jerusalem around the person of Jesus of Nazareth are their theme. They are history recorded out of a faith that can only explain itself by telling the events. They are full of vivid metaphor. Jesus speaks of 'doing God's will' as 'meat and drink'. He tells of 'those who hunger and thirst for righteousness. The whole is lived drama, theological metaphor, where 'the Word is made flesh' and pitches a tent, a tent of divine encounter, the rendezvous of the divine with the world. Meaning is, as it were, biographized.[4] The resulting doctrine of the Incarnation is the most crucial form of religious imagery, in that significance and sign are one. It follows that, in biblical faith, document in scripture comprises both happening and meaning in the form of their interaction.

Islam and the Qur'an are historical, but differently. The *Sirah*, or career, of Muhammad is the sphere of a scripture mediated into his 'illiteracy' within the final twenty-three years of his life. The biography becomes important as a realm of divine guidance with the Tradition, or *Hadith*, yielding *Sunnah*, or Law. But, in respect of the Qur'an it is simply the context of a given text from heaven. That text is woven into the texture of Muhammad's experience among his contemporaries, but there is no thought of his being himself divine disclosure, except in ardent mystical devotion.[5] There are, however, episodes in his story, especially the *Mi'raj*, or 'Night Journey and heavenly Ascent', which some understand as factual and others as a vision. But, throughout, in Islam, there is a living historical personality with whom revelatory processes have to do in legislating for humanity.

There was, in the saga of the Buddha, a decisive 'exodus' from the regal palace into the discovery of human mortality. Sakyamuni, the Buddha-to-be, took his way into the rawness of the world of human privation, sickness, decrepitude and death. The telling is parabolic. The history matters for the lesson it enforces. Elsewhere in Mahayana Buddhism the stories of the *bodhisattvas*, their progression into deities, have no vital need of history since the whole meaning is their mysterious ministry to their devotees. With Hinduism, for the most part, we pass beyond any necessity for historicity in the legends of the gods or the perceptions of religious meaning. Indeed, to be enmeshed in time and place, to come within the confines of the karmic law – where deities may be no less prisoners than humans – would be to fail the nature of transcendence.

The issue here is often the first of mutual discoveries when faith encounters begin. Those with vital histories are bewildered to find elsewhere the supremacy of myth, the devotees of which are confused to understand the necessity of time and place to God or meaning. Yet the happenedness so crucial to the Christian mind *is* crucial not as some magic, nor as an arbitrary construct, but as bearing a character which translates into spiritual truth only apprehended because of it. The same could be true of legend also in the

Asian context, but only in so far as the lack of historical reality does not evacuate the imagery itself.

It will always be right for the Christian to hold that the 'givens' of faith are given in history, since it cannot be in neglect of history that they avail. There was nothing dream-like about 'the crown of thorns': it fits the shape of the world only too well. Yet such realism, holding to its own perception of the human and the divine in Christ, need not fail of sympathy with those who exclude the historical and opt for the mythical, provided that in doing so they stay honest with the world. Either way, the language in which the meaning is told will still be sharing the role of metaphor and imagery.

(iii)

'Discovering' is not 'uncovering', except in archaic usage, but it could well be. To have it so will be useful in moving from imagery in religious language to image-ing in religious art. Here the path of religious encounter is strewn with recrimination having to do with the enigmas of idolatry. If we can uncover here something of what is at issue around the symbols of faith the effort will discover much.

The question 'What is an idol'? would normally be answered very readily by Jew, Christian and Muslim as 'a material object of worship', a thing of wood, or stone, or other craftsmanship, to which a worshipper prays, bows, ascribes praise, or otherwise supplicates and adores. Hebraic rubric required that idols be rigorously abjured as belonging to pagan peoples. Moreover, in Jewry, altars were not to be of hewn stone, for 'tooling' would 'defile'.

The New Testament shares this abhorrence and describes its converts from the Gentiles as having 'turned from idols' to 'the living God' (I Thessalonians 1.9). Paul at Athens had some perception of a pagan altar as the text for a Christian sermon. He had nothing but hostility for the city's being 'full of idols' (Acts 17. 16 and 23). We know that Christians in the first three centuries were averse to quoting street names in planning rendezvous when Roman gods had to be taken on their lips in the pagan nomenclature of Greek and Roman towns.

The anathema of Islam on all *shirk*, or alleging 'associates' with God, is its most insistent witness. For only God is God. Though the Qur'an is not entirely explicit in its reference to 'idols' and 'images',[6] the making, possessing, invoking, adoring of them is totally excluded as violating the unity of God. It is evident from the long story of Islamic art that calligraphy is supreme piety and, with geometrical and floral design, defines the bounds of artistry at least in respect of mosques and public places.[7] Representation of living forms connived with the chronic proneness of the pagan mind to worship what is visually present.

Reading for Athens Varanasi or Bangkok, we may assume that Paul would have been equally adamant about the seeming idolatry of Asian religion. For Hindu and Buddhist shrines are, likewise, 'full of idols'. Western assumptions about Asia have long been comparably reproachful or, at least, perplexed and ill at ease at the sight of endless images, multi-armed and limbed, in fantastic, often seemingly erotic postures, and too numerous on temple walls to do other than bewilder and amaze. At least the Greek pagans had something legible, if not to reconcile Paul, at least to afford a clue from which to argue his better case. What clues can possibly exist in the plethora of forms and shapes and devices by which the Hindu tells the faith? The vast face of the Buddha image is a unity. But how should its enigmatic serenity be read? What is it inviting, what receiving, when beheld?

When we move beyond instinctive reactions, East or West, we discover that ambiguities are shared. Not indeed the same ones, but ambiguities no less. A Hindu teenager asks his Christian tutor, *à propos* of the third commandment in the Decalogue, 'Why take the name of any god in vain?'[8] May not reverence anywhere approve reverence everywhere? An Indian Christian queries a Christian priest apparently in prayer-posture before a wooden cross and is given to understand the object is in no sense worshipped but belongs with certain historical 'givens' about the eternal God who is. The incident served indirectly to stimulate recovery in churches of an ancient tradition now known as 'the westward position' which faces towards the people present.[9]

It becomes clear that we can have the arts without idolatry. For we live in a visual, sensuous world of sight and sound, of form and shape, of colour and design. All these can take their due place in representation of things unseen. Man himself is said to be an 'icon' of the divine, 'made in the image of God'. Islam can be rigorous in banning three-dimensional shape, but will cherish flowing script and arabesque – no less visual and celebratory on wall and tile, dome and minaret. The association of beauty with meaning, of art with mystery, can never be under ban in every realm, if significantly excluded in some. Books, carpets, lamps, doors, will carry the insignia of faith, merely in being wrought the way they are.

Muslim tradition disapproves of the Christian iconostasis which bears the sacred figures of Madonna and apostles with faces open to salutation with candle and prostration, and hands to the kisses of the Christian devout. But these will not be worshipping: they will be venerating, letting the visuals kindle and direct a love which intends what is figured through them – the grace of redemption in the compassion of God understood to avail through Christ and the saints. May not the Buddha-image claim similar efficacy, turning on the same distinction between worship and veneration? Should it not be conceded also in the case of Shiva, Krishna and the innumerable representations of Hindu piety?[10]

Ambiguities indeed abound and demand to be explored. But the immediate truth is that art has no inevitable equivalence with idolatry. The Qur'an was right and wise in its first Meccan-Medinan context, in requiring that the prohibition on images and statuary be total. To be cautionary about them is permanently necessary. Nevertheless, the potential innocence of art cannot be denied in a universe that is God's and entrusted divinely into the human care of artisan and tool-maker, designer and pro-creator. Encounter across religions discovers this will to represent and visualize, in which – it may be said – iconography is calligraphy and calligraphy is iconography. The devotion that fingers the sacred page is kin to the piety that kisses the icon. The Muslim taxi-driver will hang the written *Allah* below his driving mirror, his Hindu counterpart a bust of Shiva, his Catholic equal the image of Mary and the Christ-child. All may be comparably superstitious, each similarly wistful for protection, grace and sacred association.

(iv)

If the 'idolatry' is not in enlisting the arts, we are driven to search its meaning more thoroughly. In what does it consist? If representation is inseparable from the expression of faiths, should it be reproached as idolatrous only when it occurs in other than ourselves?

If none are innocent of the arts, should any be found guilty with them? Hebraic tradition vetoed 'hewn stones', yet nevertheless drew skilled craftsmen to the adornment of the Solomonic Temple – the sons of pagan Tyre, Hiram, and his aids with their cunning arts. (II Chronicles 4. 11). Even the wilderness tabernacle had need of Bezaliel, the master-workman on the cherubim (Exodus 36). Should counterparts in Asia be despised and dismissed? It is not in their skills that they are idolaters, if idolaters they be. It must be in the intention that we have to search.

That art may be a snare we must concede. The sign can be mistaken for the thing signified and receive an adulation it should be denied. The distinction between worship and veneration can be subtle and elusive. It is always liable to be lost in ignorance, fervour or self-deceit. Some forms of art are more susceptible than others to such misuse, because of either their exotic appeal or the lure they have for the undiscerning and the gullible. Usage and familiarity also erode the necessary vigilance. The fruits of the arts are blighted with the mildew of superstition, just as superstition is the besetting sin, the persistent hazard, of faith.

On this score iconoclasm has had its recurrent fascination in the history of religion. Zealots within Christendom, especially in the eighth and ninth centuries under the impact of Islam,[11] repudiated and destroyed the icons. The urge to ban statuary, pictures, even texts and music, from the churches has been recurrent in Christian history. Yet, chastened perhaps and alerted, the arts have always somehow outdone the iconoclasts and renewed themselves, proving confidence in their legitimacy. Islam is no exception in somehow combining the most rigorous unitarianism with a capacity for exquisite beauty.

What robust iconoclasts did not appreciate was that an icon was itself art in the act of worship, a consecration of hand and mind, a hallowing of chalk and pigment and wood, a quest for sanctity through quality. The same can well be true of Qur'an scribes and engravers with their gold-leaf and pen, like their fellows elsewhere in Psalter and Gospel, abjuring imperfection as a scandal to the holy. Artists in Buddhism and the other faiths of Asia conceive their artistry as association with ultimacy, not only in the themes they portray but in the worth of their portrayal. Thus far, in most radically dividing the religions, the arts unite them.

But still we have not identified idolatry, except as what happens when arts are perverted and usurp what they should signify. This, we must say, is aberration. That apart, is there more of which arts must be suspected or accused?

The answer is bound to turn on how we ought to think of unity. Islam here has the merit of the utmost simplicity. God is One. 'There is none but He.' 'None but He' must be the verdict of our whole experience in respect of what we trust and whom we perceive. Power, authority, sovereignty, disposal are his alone. To think otherwise is to have idolatrous thoughts, idolatrous trust, idolatrous worships.

Yet experience is undeniably plural. There is that which lives and that which dies, that which wanes and that which grows, that which gives and that which withholds. There are endless inequalities in the incidence of life, vast inconsistencies in the workings of time and destiny. If we 'unify' these categorically we incur sharp issues which refuse to be ignored. Hinduism certainly refuses to deny them. Let there be deities to ensure that their multiplicity, their very incidence upon us, is acknowledged. So Shiva co-exists with Indra and Rama and Krishna, idols perhaps, but beings within the truth of things. Or the omnipresence of the One, the Buddha, diversifies into a progeny of *bodhisattvas* or an eschatology of Buddhas yet to be, so that the limitless can somehow be accommodated within the conceptual and we have no need to think of 'a jealous God'.

Will these multiple deities, or grounds of worship, be idolatrous? The answer inexorably divides us. To all true Semites, 'Yes!', for they impugn that single sovereignty of God, of Yahweh, of Allah, who is God alone. 'No!', say the Asians, so long as we revere what non-uniform experience requires of us while holding somehow a transcendental unity which eludes our comprehension and must allow, in parallel, the plural acknowledgments our concepts cannot help but make when we read our fate and know ourselves. For the Semites the proper 'jealousy' of the unitary Lord must surely reckon squarely with the impulses – superstition apart – that lead Asians where they do. To do so honestly means undertaking the theodicy which has confronted us in earlier chapters, lest we hold the 'unity' of God only by ignoring the challenge of all those evils and puzzles which bring Asian faiths to plural gods. What this means for Christians will come in chapter 9. The onus is equally on Judaism and Islam. Not to be open to what such faith in final unity entails will be to forfeit all right to call other faiths 'idolatrous'. For refusal of it means that those who, by Semitic terms, are 'not letting God be God' in Asia, or wherever, are denied sufficient reason why they should. If plural worships simply manifest plural fears, or plural gratitudes, then divine unity remains at stake until these also are unified, not by harsh assertion that 'God is One', but by a sovereignty that undertakes the fears and has the gratitudes, a unity that persuades and pervades the soul.

(v)

Does this mean that the ancient command 'Thou shalt not make to thyself any graven image . . .' no longer obtains? If experience between faiths makes it clear that this can be no simplistic order, inasmuch as imagery has due place within divine acknowledgment, inasmuch as imagery is plural with gods only because experience seems to be, where does this leave idolatry? Is the concept obsolete? Is it even fond and foolish, as some anthropologists allege, musing on the superiority of theists who misread 'heathen' folk?

Perhaps so, in times and places. But idolatry, precisely because we let the arts have their place and probe the complexities that wait on worships, is more clearly identified for what it is. The clue may be read in the very phrase 'Thou shalt not make . . .' 'Thou shalt not have . . .'. Idolatry is a false construct, a wrong absolute willed, or erected, or 'graven' on the imagination, a priority given where it does not belong. To find it only in stocks and stones is to miss how it exists in institutions, in power-structures and the vested interests of states and nations, creeds and systems. These are far more damnable idols than the crafted items of pagan invocation which can be demolished with axes and hammers after the manner of that iconoclast Abraham in the Qur'an.[12] To be sure, that may not of itself dethrone them in the heathen heart which, confused, may well spring to their defence. But their hold is far less subtle than the sway the false absolutes exercise over the human realm. The pseudo-deities of race, commerce, wealth, techniques or power *can* be beneficent if they consent to be relative, subservient to what is more ultimate than they. Their significance is turned to menace,

even to damnation, when they usurp the ultimacy that belongs to
God alone. For divine sovereignty is the only right absolute, the
only lordship deserving the subordination of all else.

This truth is at the heart of the insistence of Islam on the sole
sovereignty of God. The *shirk* it denounces is precisely that rivalry
to God which structures of human pretension indulge. Crude pagan
idol-making and idol-having may have been its characteristic form
in the time of Muhammad, but the *shirk* he accused as the cardinal
sin, the root of all other wrong, was 'the exclusion of God'. This
takes its most heinous form in the wilful reading of the human
autonomy in the material world as having no reference outside its
own ambitions, its own pursuits and its own logic. *Shirk* is more
than the denial that God exists. It is the alienation of a single
worship from God by the setting up of other worships, whether
of nation, state, trade or ideology, which then receive our total
commitment, allowing nothing, ethical, material or spiritual, to call
in question what promotes or serves them. The imperious Islamic
call, 'Let God be God', means more than the banishment of figments
of ignorant imagination. It means the dethroning of what the New
Testament called 'principalities and powers' that defy the claim of
divine reality.

Islam sets this theme in its starkest form, being dissatisfied with
what it saw as the Hebraic complication of it by the 'chosen people'
concept, and with Christian sophistication of it by a reading of
divine reality that made room for the significance of Jesus. Deep as
those differences are, they do not affect the radical consensus of the
three monotheisms that idolatry is deliberate human repudiation of
the reality of God in multiple forms of *hybris* and self-will, 'having'
– and not merely conceiving or chiselling – 'other gods'.

When each of the theisms meets the faiths of Asia, either this
entire reading of the human situation is doubted for lack of any
perceived significance in history, or the unity it presupposes is not
of this moral order where there can be any challenge to it such as
idolatry could constitute. Rather, if any unity exists, it so transcends
distinctions that no dualisms of true or false, or good and evil,
finally matter. Therefore, no God reigns in a sense that any idol
could flout. What might move us to think otherwise must be
assigned to illusoriness and itself needs to be transcended.

On this score, it would seem that the common subject of idolatry between us only yields a discovery of how incompatible we are. There is some merit in that conclusion or, rather, in realizing that we have no option but to reach it.

None of us, on either side of that futility, can well be content with it. For when we turn back from our abstraction, to politics and power, to multi-national structures of commerce, to the passions of nationalism and the tragedies of minorities, to the unbridled applications of technology, we find idolatries real and rampant around us in society. Forces of the market, or of race, or of passion, or of creed, demand and enjoy the kind of allegiance which does not stay, or pause, or query, or repent, but readily goes on its way in worship of itself. As we have seen in earlier chapters, religion is among them. Even if we will not accuse them as 'idolatries', we detect the liabilities they flout in being so. For these are evident in human tragedy, in nature-devastation, in exploitation and violence, in the perversion of human dignity and the tyranny of means over ends. Were we to think there is no divine lordship to be violated we would be disproved by the evident violations of the human order. We discover idolatry in the very dis-ordering of the world we know. We learn to see that the sovereignty of God is pledged to the autonomy of man and that is why idolatry is at once our option, our menace and our shame.

(vi)

Faiths meet in the discovery of metaphor, language and imagery, in the issues of art and representation. They also discover each other in the patterns of liturgy. Among the most striking of these is Muslim *salat*, the performance of Islamic worship.[13] Reflection here will usefully carry us forward from things of faith expressed in the art of words or signs to things of faith expressed in acts and doings, the more properly because *salat* is the most graphic of acts denoting that acknowledgement of God which idolatry perverts.

With the preliminary ablutions, *salat* is a highly personal ritual which gains remarkably from the communal action in the mosque, especially at congregational prayer on Fridays, but does not *need* this benefit. Without priestly aegis, and with the Imam only to give the prayer-direction – which the mosque's orientation would provide anyway – each individual is self-sufficient in the act. The sequences of posture and recitation are familiar and personally enacted and uttered. Unison in congregation is full of significance, not least in the final greeting,[14] yet to fulfil and not displace the personal.

The *qiblah*, or direction to Mecca, on which all Muslims pray, converges the focus of all on the central point of Muhammad's birth and of Qur'anic revelation. The invisible radii of countless concentric circles which imagination visualizes as formed by Muslims in their multitudes with the *Ka'bah* in Mecca as their hub are in turn the lines of travel – at least symbolically – when Muslims converge in *hajj*, or pilgrimage, upon the same centre. Thus two physical rituals combine within one pattern. This character in Muslim liturgical obligation makes a discipline, an enlistment of action on behalf of meaning, which is unique among religions. Prayer and pilgrimage are, of course, universal, but nowhere else do they have the same symbolic 'map' of act and meaning on so inclusive a scale.

What is significant *from* those within Islam *for* those credally outside it in the Islamic liturgy of *salat*, its words and postures, is what it tells of *homo erectus*, of the double meaning of being human. Our erect posture – not grovelling on all fours, but taking in the heavens in our sweep of vision and having upper limbs free for dexterity – has long been the symbol of our intelligent *imperium*. That is how Muslims are at the outset and in the conclusion of each *raka'ah*, or sequence, in the prayer act. Between the up-standing come the several bodily movements, through bending to complete prostration, with the brow, the proudest 'crown' of man, touching the earth, or the carpet, or the clay tablet upon it.[15] Thus repeatedly within each time of *salat* is the rhythm of being erect and being prostrate, of affirming human status both in its empire and in its due subservience. Divine Lordship and human meaning are visibly expressed as inter-related. We are 'both-and', having a mastery that worships and a worship that empowers. *Salat* begins in responsible existence typified by that erect stance. It proceeds in self-humbling in confession: *Allahu akbar*, 'greater is God'. It concludes where it began in acknowledged liability to live within what has been confessed. The sandals that have been doffed in reverence are resumed to walk the world responsibly.

Does the exposition idealize? Hardly so. Does it tend to 'Christianize'? Again, No.[16] To account of *salat* this way is simply to appreciate it for what it is. The truth of it is not altered by the fact that masses of Muslims would not have stated it, or may never have seen it, this way. Meanings are often known to be possessed by dint of what they register when outsiders to their form of expression come alive to them. Such discoveries only happen by being mutual, presented and perceived.

It is not suggested that non-Muslims should forthwith reproduce *salat*, or borrow its postures to coincide with other words. As we must note in Chapter 7, there is something necessarily 'copyright' about long-possessed rituals and forms of worship. The *gurdwara* would not long be itself if Sikhs began to set a 'holy table' at its heart as if to emulate the Christian ritual of divine hospitality within the cross of Jesus. They may adjourn, however, from what Sikh worship comprises in order to conclude with a communal meal within the precincts. No faith, however, need ignore, or assign to total irrelevance, the meaning passing over to it from what Islam enshrines in *salat*. It is part of relationship across faiths to appreciate whatever we loyally can while respecting the identity we do not share. How grossly imperceptive the seventeenth-century arrivals in New England were in misreading and despising the pow-wows and smoking pipes of the Amerindians! Rituals of community, of ripe counsel and age-veneration, of diffidence in exploiting nature, of reverence for life and perceptions of time, were construed as sloth, evasion and futility. The settlers had come over a vast ocean. Their purposes reinforced their self-sufficiency. It should not be so today, though congenital insensitivity dies hard.

(vii)

The techniques of Hindu and, more readily, of Buddhist meditation hold significant discoveries for faiths even in dispute with the philo-sophies that underwrite them. Indeed what finds systematic and rigorous formulation in those techniques has often been present without the remotest knowledge of them. The Arab ethicist Al-Muhasibi (781–857 CE) of Baghdad derived his very name ('the accountant') from his painstaking self-scrutiny of motive, conduct and performance. Of a more whimsical sort was the ledger of moral assessment the youthful Benjamin Franklin drew up for himself in Philadelphia around a millennium later. 'For ever in my great

taskmaster's eye' meant, for the poet John Milton, a liability to be
the Lord's own mentor of John Milton. The genius of Buddhism
sets all such introspection within a discipline that turns self-percep-
tion and – if we may so speak – self-management into explicit
'skills' acquired and maintained by constant alertness and honesty.
Outsiders may find it a strange paradox that a religion so essentially
sceptical about self-legitimacy should have so far developed confident strategies of self-interpretation in practice.

Buddhists, however, would say that it is precisely because of the
disavowal of selfhood in the reading of necessary renunciation that
it is able to establish its active formula of control. Only in knowing
the self as finally illusory, fated by the fact of transience and the
'suffering' it imposes, do we fortify the will to undertake what
this logic demands. Nevertheless, what avails from the patterns of
discipline can be appreciated and emulated by those who deny the
logic.

All, especially in its extreme Theravada form, is sharply personal.
The *Dharma*, or Teaching, only shows the way. Achievement has
to be individually attained. There are no alibis, no substitutes. The
elements of the Eightfold Path – right understanding, right thought,
right speech, right action, right livelihood, right effort, right mindfulness and right concentration – are often understood as, in effect,
threefold. The first three have to do with insight, the next two with
social morality, the final three with meditation. All are calculated
to offset, or better, to atrophy, what damages both the self and the
other in the thoughts one harbours, the malice of one's tongue, the
anti-social effects of one's economic livelihood, the musings of the
soul, the contagion of one's example, the kindling within or around
of false appetites. These are all, in Buddhist terminology, actual or
potential 'cankers' in the soul and mind. In order that the senses
may no longer beguile and misguide, they must be steadily curbed
and constrained into abnegation of their appeal.

Any reverent external discovery of Buddhism can register a significance no less apposite to non-Buddhists than the meaning for
non-Muslims of Islamic *salat*. Selfhood remains in crisis everywhere
and there are no exemptions from the need of right introspection
at its heart. Again, this does not mean yielding to the distrust of
selfhood which motivates the Buddhist, who must, in fact, be suspected of 'wrong mindfulness' in that regard. That quarrel, never-

theless, does not diminish what can be transacted between us. Discoveries may occur on either side. Must not 'right livelihood', for example, and 'right action', extend beyond the sphere of individual activity in doing a job or earning a wage, into the whole realm of social economies? Can the bank cashier scrutinize the vast ethical ramifications of the cheques he processes? Or the personal investor ensure the 'cleanness' of the dividends accruing? The 'right mind' must surely take shape in active concern about the structures which serve only their own institutionalized, unethical autonomy.

(viii)

Nowhere, as stressed earlier, is reverent discovery of other faith more to be desired on the part of outsiders than the faith of Judaism by non-Jews. I do not mean some patronizing interest that stems from a sympathy that compensates for persecution, nor an ardent relation born of the guilt of it. Rather, I mean a solicitude that senses what it owes and what it needs to discern through all the tensions and confusions of long history. Admittedly, all such ventures will need to surmount the emotions that belong with their classification as 'Gentile'. For Judaism has always cherished and enforced an exceptionality built into its very essence. It is, therefore, sharply different from the distinctiveness which attaches everywhere else to identities that belief, history, memory, race and culture have sealed into corporate consciousness. Hebraic 'election' and 'covenant' are not of that order,[17] though undoubtedly Jewishness shares them with all peoples as the elements in its own self-reading.

Just as there is an explicit doctrine of all human meaning in Islamic *salat*, so there is a paradigm of people-community in Judaism's perception of Jewry. If the one invites us to an economy of man as tenant-steward under God, the other presents us with a model of corporate nationhood-in-vocation, a nationhood of 'priesthood'. The fact that this incorporation into peoplehood of being 'on behalf of God' in the world has not been widely open to recruitment historically,[18] and is thought inalienable and irrepeatable, does not invalidate the lesson all may perceive in it for themselves and their identity. The sense of having a progenitor of whom it could be said 'In thee shall all the nations of the earth congratulate themselves' is surely a sentiment worthy of emulation. To visualize the identity one experiences corporately as intended for universal service, to study one's corporate history as designed with that intent, is surely to illuminate a possibility capable of imitation.

For the ingredients are manifestly possessed by all who know a birthright, occupy a territory, cherish a history and anticipate a future. Tribe, land and story belong comparably with all human awareness, answering the questions: who, where, and whence we are. They determine the continuity of all community. How to interpret and possess them in nations is a perennial theme of the human story. For that reason the mystique of Jewry has fascinated peoples and places far removed from them. Jerusalem, as we saw at the outset of this chapter, has passed into the lore of distant continents and times.

The inter-acting terms of 'son' and 'servant' – 'Out of Egypt have I called my son' (Hosea 11. 1) and 'Behold my servant whom I uphold, my elect in whom my soul delights' (Isaiah 42. 1) – first applied to the Hebrew nation, come together again in the evangelists' account of the baptism of Jesus. They underlie the entire Christian theology of the Incarnation, in which 'sonship' and 'servanthood' are mutual. Thence, in turn, came the concept of the church, with its writ to 'become the children of God' through faith and, as such, the 'servants of the Word'. Though Jewry, in general, demurs about those translations of its destiny, at least they bring the tribute of strong indebtedness. This Christian inheritance apart, is there not a tuition latent in Judaism from which all nations may learn that their *raison d'être* can be understood as self-possession *for* the wider whole?

Indeed, it has often happened, but sadly the imitation has been perverted. For all religions harbour inner pitfalls. 'God and his Englishmen', 'God and his Russians', 'God and his Afrikaaners', 'God and his Americans', have avidly coveted a Jewish role without the Jewish mystery. But distortions do not cancel out the potential truth. A sense of vocation can mean a care for justice, a right ecology, a trust with nature, a generous compassion, a national ideology capable of 'the dream' of Martin Luther King. That there is enormous ambivalence here and the capacity for self-delusion need not invalidate what genuine contemplation of Judaism discloses for outsiders. Doubtless Jewry has contributed to the ambivalence. Diaspora in Jewish experience might be assumed to under-score the lesson by bringing the Judaic into the midst of other societies so that its significance might register. Zionism intended to reverse that. Even so, the aspirations of initial Zionism in the nineteenth century saw an innocent nationhood which would exemplify vocation and redeem nationhood itself by dint of the example. This ideal failed to be fulfilled, since the exigencies of *Realpolitik* denied exceptionality to the ventures intending it by engrossing them in thoroughly 'Gentile' patterns of power, militarism and diplomacy.

Perhaps the lesson is that there are no exceptional nations. Yet even so the struggle to disprove it will always be open – and open to all. There is always national vocation, if only as something to refuse.

(ix)

Discoveries of, and about, each other which await when faiths meet and greet are many and enriching. The foregoing only illustrates how attentive we need to be and how the grounds we have for differing are themselves a stimulus to what we need to share. Issues of controversy need not conceal areas of reciprocal awareness that are positive. What outsiders might stand to discover to advantage in Christian faith and liturgy should be evident from the *confessio* in Chapter 9. Meanwhile, in the chapter to follow, we must take up the environment of concrete obligations and liabilities with which the world of politics and society confronts all faiths. For any cognizance between them of the sort we have been noting would be insincere if it neglected the world from which we took our clue at the start – cosmopolis here and now.

6

Towards Joint Liabilities

The young Vincent Van Gogh had not yet made art his passionate witness to mankind. In imitation of the father he still held in awe, he wanted to be a preacher. At Richmond, by the Thames, he delivered his first sermon. Exhorting his hearers, he was exploring his own soul, preaching of and to himself. His text was Psalm 119.19: 'I am a stranger in the earth: hide not thy commandments from me.' Deeply religious by instinct and upbringing, he wrestled with a sense of vocation he did not know how to attain. 'Commandments' – dimensions of hope and duty crucial to it – were hard to comprehend. That to live was to be liable he felt with a rare intensity. But why was liability so often left groping for its meaning? Why was destiny so enigmatic? 'Hide not thy commandments from me.'

His plea and his perplexity, whatever the unrecorded reception of the sermon, took his listeners with him to the very heart of religion – the obedience of the ethical in the love of the divine, and both within the reverent bewilderment of existence. The text and the preacher spoke the nature of religion.

Yet how are the faiths 'strangers', having been around so long? How are their 'commandments' hidden when they have supposedly been in trust with them for generations? Are not the faiths their due custodians whether the *Dharma*, or the Vedas, or Torah or Qur'an? They certainly presume to be. But there has always been a place within them for perplexity and the urge to questioning prayer. My argument is that cosmopolis has greatly increased that need. Exclusive religious assurance has to give way, at least at times and points, to an inclusive religious sense of question and enquiry. There are many staunch traditionalists who complain that they no longer recognize the world they live in, its patterns and habits dramatically changed. Can the old codes and customs suffice the new technologies, intruding, as these do, into the innermost recesses of the human psyche as well as the intimacies of human relations? 'Hide not thy commandments from me' becomes a pressing plea in the new environment of technologically induced change, with issues for mind and spirit on which there are no precedents.

Those who do not pray in terms of divine 'commandments' being no longer 'hidden' are at least aware of imperatives on which human well-being has to turn. Whatever our doctrinal language about norms of guidance, the global scene that calls for them makes us jointly liable. That being so, we cannot be isolated from one another in our perceptions of what the times require.

There was an occasion in London when the former Chief Rabbi, now Lord Jacobovits, called on Jews and Christians to 'proclaim a Geo-spiritual Year' in which 'nations and governments' would co-operate in massive research and moral rehabilitation. He had in mind 'the Geo-physical Year' in which there had been what he called 'exciting corporate study of the world's physical features'. His logic was not confined to the two Semitic theisms that made up his immediate audience, but the elaboration of his ideas made the problematics at once apparent. His programme was 'to devise effective means for the elimination of vice and crime' and 'of marital faithlessness and immorality'. In that cause he was strongly in favour of homosexuality and adultery being made criminal offences – even though the law would be unenforceable – in order to underline social repudiation of evils 'gnawing at the roots of our common civilization'.[1]

It was wise, then, to have the word 'towards' in this chapter's title. For this one instance, from the scores that could be cited, makes clear what reservations we have to bring to 'geo-spiritual years' we might jointly 'proclaim'. We all have geo-spiritual centuries behind us and, for the most part, it has been the sciences that have presided over what they brought forth. Lord Jacobovits had his own prescripts about what was evil and what was remedy. Others have theirs. Joint liabilities are entangled in analyses and conceptions which are sadly unjointed. That paradox, however, does not make them less urgent: it makes them the more exacting.

Assuming the will to realism about our histories for which the case was made in Chapters 3 and 4, and taking as read the fact that we meet and greet in cosmopolis, it is clear that our business in this chapter is broadly the politics and economics of human societies in the context of national sovereignty and their relationship with the order of nature. These are the dimensions of our common birth and central to the responsibility of all religions. They comprise a complex of issues belonging to territorial statehood and material dominion. In both spheres, religions have to take honest stock of the authority they exercise, the interpretations they bring and the practices by which they are fulfilled.

Our anxiety must be to keep a lively positive ambition in all the themes here in question, lest the religious way with them seem negative, arrogant, insensitive or banal. Denigration is all too easy, whether of faith by faith, or of them by the world. Jacques, in Shakespeare's *As You Like It*, was no doubt a reflective soul such as the human comedy needs, but his pledge,

> I will through and through
> Cleanse the foul body of the infected world,
> If it will patiently receive my medicine,[2]

was not the wisest model for religious custodians. Medicine, too, readily suggests the warning 'Physician, heal thyself'. Of this we have been well aware in Chapter 3. Moreover, the world is not 'patient', nor likely to warm to those who see only its 'foul infection'. There is no doubt a need to be radical: evils only mock the sanguine. The truest realism is that which lives by hope. Only thanks to the sovereignty of good does wrong require to be confronted and disowned.

(ii)

The nation-state is a salient feature of the modern world. It prevails across the diversity of race, creed and culture adopting it. The grand empires of history have given way to the principle of nationhood. The Ottoman and the British Empires were the last in the sequence.

A unitary 'Christendom' receded centuries ago in the nation-state principle. Islamic purists may still call for the inclusive *ummah* of Islam which, on their view, the separate Muslim nations violate. Yet even in the Arab realm their protest makes no headway against the fascination of separate statehood, albeit in frontiers often designed by retreating empire.

In the sub-continent of India, Muslim insistence on separatism for majority areas of Muslims could only eventuate by the principle which denied that religions were only 'communities' and saw them essentially as 'nations'. The cost, which was enormous, committed both Hindus and Muslims to separate nationality, leaving to the former the bold experiment in 'secular' statehood which could otherwise have been the appropriate and happy destiny for an undivided sub-continent. When created, Islamic statehood for Pakistani Islam enclosed, proportionately, a greater fraction of minorities than all Muslims would have been in an undivided India. That formal illogicality, however, did not halt the powerful factors making for partition. The story is a clear index to the attraction of the *regio/religio* principle in Asia as in Europe. South and eastern Asia have followed nation-state instincts on the retreat of the West, and Africa comparably. 'Seek ye first the political kingdom and other things will be added unto you', was the slogan of Kwame Nkrumah and the Ghana Convention People's Party in becoming the first independent, post-imperial African state in 1957.[3] The flags that flutter impressively outside the United Nations Headquarters in New York, proudly distinct as they are, nevertheless share a single device as symbol. It indicates the sameness in otherness inside. All are *nations*, however their territorial bounds have been contrived and their cultural identities attained.

Few if any of them are fully homogeneous. All contain minority elements, ethnically, religiously, or culturally described. This means that there are actual or potential 'hostages' everywhere. A large element, therefore, in the inter-religious responsibility has to do with the religious factor in the incidence of majority advantage and minority jeopardy – if such it be.

We have first to note that international law finds acute difficulty in reconciling the principle of state sovereignty with that of human rights. States insistently shelter behind their 'private affairs' and strongly resist what they – and they alone – identify as 'interference' in what is 'internal'. All, or most, pay lip-service to conventions and safeguards but reserve these to their own interpretation. All are to some degree alert to 'the international community', but remain arbiters of their own liability to it. It follows that where state sovereignty is seen as inviolate, immune from all but its own criteria, minorities everywhere live with insecurity.

To be sure, these may be majorities elsewhere with the possibility of reciprocal threats or pledges. But a mutual hostage situation would be a cynical and precarious way of resolving the human problems. Short of some kind of world-state – an elusive and utopian idea – states will insist on being their own sufficient mentors or refrain from overmuch intervention on behalf of minorities elsewhere for embarrassment about their own. As is the case with Israel, inter-state criticism may well be affected, if not muted, for ideological or political reasons, just as such reasons may also passionately evoke it. Either way, state-sovereignty emerges as a volatile and uncertain arbiter of human destinies where minorities are jeopardized.

(iii)

The logic to which this leads must be the crucial liability of religion within statehood as, on the worst analysis, the gross conniver with the injustices of power, or hopefully, the careful monitor of its right exercise. Either way, the onus on state sovereignty for the concepts and practices by which it fulfils or frustrates the human meaning, is an onus also on the faith, or faiths, within it. The dominant party in that religious onus is likely to be one particular faith, unless the onset of secularity has partially neutralized them all. The argument here is that, however diversified the population, a dominant faith-culture is likely to be in league with state-sovereignty for reasons of history, tradition and language.

There are notions current in the West of the feasibility of multi-cultural identity – a dubious, if not contradictory, idea. It implies a relativity, if not an irrelevance, in religious beliefs which, broadly speaking, does not ride with religious reality and, outside Western assumptions of secularity, is uncongenial or suspect. It would be rash to speculate about the patterns in the future of the will to faith or to unfaith,[4] but the historical ingredients of corporate existence and cultural identity are not likely to be dissolved or displaced in any viable society. We only know ourselves in possession of our past.

Given such continuity in identity, it follows that the religious denominator that belongs to it must, for good or ill, undertake the major liability as the decisive factor in its ethos. It is this fact of place and time which mission finds it hard to concede, since it seems to question the role of conversion. How to discriminate here I defer to Chapter 8. The due care of truths to take in mission cannot refuse to realize that those to whom they are taken or who are otherwise 'informed', nevertheless hold centre-stage and stand in the primary role in what obtains concerning society, peace, war, law, the role of women, justice and the rest. Mission itself is not realistic if it cannot see a ministry *within* existing establishments as well as, or other than, a recruiting of individuals from out of them.

To realize that the world is plural is to live with a map on which religious realms, though variously infiltrated by secularity, are nevertheless characterized by faiths broadly intrinsic to them and carrying main responsibility for the shape of society. These main traditions of faith are not likely to be significantly displaced where history has long entrenched them. Their tenure being such, the due vocation of all parties becomes clear. Minority faiths must be content to be such. They need not, however, withdraw into sullen privacy or fret under their circumstance. On the contrary, they can positively engage with their condition as occasion for courage and self-searching. They owe majorities appropriate rapport with what shapes them, just as majorities in turn need a lively sense of minority psychology.

Buddhism is the obvious aegis in south Asian nations. By virtue of the religio-political nature of Muhammad's people from their beginning, Islam controls wherever *Dar al-Islam* obtains.[5] Despite growing experience of Muslim minority status, the Islamic instinct for the power-factor remains central and makes that experience uniquely exacting. India's pattern of the 'secular' state, hard pressed as it is, still leaves the central liability for Indian destiny with Hinduism – a fact which the very existence of Pakistan confirms.

The situations vary in Africa where ancient traditions are of African provenance and Islam or Christianity, partly determining nationalities between them, are implanted faiths. They have to relate, in co-operation or competition, in the definition of nation-hoods still in process. African retrospect makes a situation more flexible than that which obtains in Asia. Malaysia is a sharp example of the ability of Islam to identify statehood rigorously with itself. The case of Judaism in Israel is obviously distinctive. A pervasive secularism is paradoxically joined to a will to be homogeneous in the religious terms of 'covenant' and 'land', making the Palestinian presence uniquely inconvenient in both senses of the word.

'Uniquely' is the right word there – given the nature of Zionism.[6] But all majority faith-cultures in national form are liable to be ill at ease about minorities. Oddly, for example, Muslims in Egypt are prone to think of Copts as somehow a menace. They never could be. But sub-conscious resentment of their difference, and their persistence in it against all logic of the 'true' faith, impedes frank and equal relationships. The same paradox of the threat of the powerless lives widely elsewhere. It can degenerate into irrational fear or anger. Dominance that is restive about exemptions from its creed or cult often recruits ethnic warrant also for its suspicions. In such situations, minorities need resilient awareness of where they are. A consent to be minority means the recognition that primacy about the norms of society lies elsewhere.

This, however, need not mean subservience or the ghetto mind. Rather it must be faced with a realism that enlists the inner resources from which identity derives.[7] Majorities, in turn, need to tame the arrogance to which they are prone and concede that in any appropri-ate statehood citizenship must comprise the talents of all faiths and ensure their free participation. The self-searching this entails will be the surest test of the worth of their convictions. How they exercise their dominance will be the measure of their truth.

These imperatives concerning religions within the nation-state may seem more flouted than obeyed in the current scene. Fanati-cism, bigotry and polemic are endemic or the exigencies of politics conspire with prejudices of race and status. In that event, we are the more at the mercy of an order of things we can only resist and not replace. As nation-states remain the order of the day – of the age – the permanent imbalance of the faiths within them will continue to constitute the crucial liability they have to each other and the critical test of their meaning. We inhabit cosmopolis, but cosmopolis is many states where private folk are public citizens and faiths pertain unequally to statehoods.

(iv)

What then, to paraphrase an ancient question, has Varanasi to do with New Delhi, or Mecca with Riyadh, or the Bo-Tree with Rangoon, or Westminster Abbey with the other Westminster? How should the faith that accompanies the history of a nation bear on the statehood which is the nation's political expression? Each faith has to answer for itself. Minority belief-systems in their subordinate standing can only be relevant via their relation with the senior partner – if partner in any sense it concedes to be.

The issues here are written large, and often tragically, across the face of many lands from the Balkans to the South Pacific. Desperate-separatisms arise, as in Yugoslavia, Sri Lanka and East Timur, where the dominant body-politic and/or its religious sanction refuse to accommodate diversity, and minorities in turn invoke the same pattern of state-power by which they find themselves oppressed. Such inter-racial, inter-credal tragedies only underscore what the role of religion ought to be in the politics of identity, namely that of knowing how to transcend inter-human enmity and how to require of the political order the effective priority of inter-human community. That frequently religions fail this test – indeed connive with the abuse of power – only adds to the indictment that had to be made in Chapter 4.

It is sadly evident, from the history of all religions, that their duty in respect of the political order is often deeply at risk from the religions themselves. The reasons are not far to seek. That which it would properly be their duty to discipline they contrive, rather, to unleash. Buddhist society, at least, in modern terms is as politicized as any. The Buddha may have sought the final truth in relinquishment of princely power and in surrender of the rights of office. Nevertheless, power being ineluctable in the affairs of the world, the *sangha*, or core-fraternity of faith, does more than present its example to society of poverty and abnegation. It must exert itself within the structures of politics, by advice, by intrigue, by dissuasion and persuasion, as vigorously as any citizen outside the *sangha*.

There is the obvious paradox here within the ethos of Buddhist society, namely how to apply the skills and virtues of the Eightfold Path to the political and economic order. Essentially addressed to the sphere of individuation and by the logic of a transient reading of time and personality, those criteria of right mindfulness, right occupation, right perception, and the rest, necessarily bear upon the world as market, as government, as power and party. Since they do so bear, the verdict of transience has to be lifted and Buddhism become a public agency as well as a private philosophy. Personal 'undesiring' accommodates – for those monks so minded – to political urgency and activism. Its philosophy remains the strong ethical mentor in so doing but in tension with the final vision. Whether in or outside the *sangha*, political activism applies the undesiring self to the political translation of the same demands of 'rightness' that belong to the Eightfold Path of escape from individuation, the 'skills' by which the 'cankers' may be overcome. There is a fascinating paradox in the political involvement of many a Buddhist monk. The three Semitic faiths might pride themselves on their ability to put political power in its right place by virtue of the theocratic principle. *Al-Mulk li-Llahi*, 'sovereignty is God's', says the Islamic faith. Whatever the due rights of statehood, they are subordinate to the claim of God. The transcendent must be allowed to transcend. The Christian poet, John Donne, said it in congenially Islamic terms:

That thou mayest rightly obey power, her bounds know. Those past, her mature and her name is changed. To be then humble to her is idolatry.[8]

Power has to be understood as serving that which is beyond itself. Its necessary sanctions are only on behalf of its proper ends. All powers, causes, interests, structures, claims and thrones are emphatically subordinate. They are 'under God'. To think otherwise is, for Muslims, the cardinal sin of *shirk*, namely, the alienation from God of that which is God's alone.

In their own idiom, the Judaeo-Christian traditions believe likewise. 'The Lord God omnipotent reigns' is their final doxology (Revelation 19.6). 'Keep yourselves from idols' (I John 5.21) is the final word of the New Testament. On this showing, politics can never be an end in itself. As the only right absolute, God must duly relativize all else. When properly relative to the divine rule, nations, structures, techniques and peoples may feasibly be fulfilled in benefaction, in realizable good. Unsubdued to God, they can only be, or become, demonic and perverse.

Sadly, this truth, central in the religious call to the political order, is itself deeply at risk from the religions themselves. The claim to uphold the sovereignty of God may make its advocates assume supremacy themselves. In being on behalf of God, Jews, Christians and Muslims have proved to be on behalf of themselves. Something like an annexation of God becomes a perennial danger. In the Christian West it has taken large inroads of agnostic secularity to modify political theism and ensure a right tolerance of faiths within the shape of state power. Yet here the non-ultimacy of things political has still, somehow, to be religiously affirmed, otherwise the menace of tyranny, or corruption, or the lethargy of unchallenged party control, persists.

In the Islamic scene the basic Qur'anic concept of *fitnah* makes religious belief and political power synonymous, so that private departure from belief is also personal treason. Religion is wholly God's only when here is no more *fitnah* (Surah 2.193, i.e. sedition/resistance to faith). In this concept, power and state no longer merely adopt faith, they enforce it. According minority status to tolerated minorities within this Islamic form of statehood meant relegating them to apolitical pieties only. From that tradition, as we have seen, some current Muslim states are aiming to free themselves and, so doing, also free their minorities for citizen status. Nevertheless, the old assumptions die hard and the urgency of the danger persists of enthroning what is on behalf of God in place of God himself. It is always urgent to mean *Allahu akbar* and not *Islamu akbar*. They are so readily reversible.

There have been numerous historical examples of Christian unilateralism of power and faith, of a similar temper to that of Islam. Constantine, inaugurating Christian empire, handled deviation from enjoined dogma as politically unacceptable. Since his day the principle of *cuius regio, eius religio* has often prevailed, abetted by inter-religious conflicts taking the form of national threatenings. There is, however, one vital, if often suspended, corrective of these patterns which is in contrast with Islam. It is the fact that Christian

origins, where there was no Islam-style *hijrah* into power, were
innocent of state-reliance. On the contrary, and contra-distinguished
from Judaism, original Christianity lived in catacombs and survived
for three centuries only as a persecuted powerlessness. There was
no faith-power amalgam in the definition of Christianity, a faith
thereby enabled to veto any final idolatry of state or nation. At long
range, this factor has itself contributed to the possibility of modern
secularity by a reluctance to allow to faith any sanction but its own
credentials presented to mind and spirit. The fact that for three
initial centuries the gospel and the church were not a *religio licita*
has fostered the modern understanding of the terms in which *religio*
might rightly think itself *licita*.

Around such terms of openness and uncompulsive credentials,
there is clearly a wide need for inter-faith reflection and common
action. Faiths, as majorities and as minorities, have the task of
attending to individual conscience and to mutual citizenship. Their
sense of finality needs to cope with the shared realities of active
nationhood. Those are interior questions. How, beyond them,
should nationality relate to world community? Across state borders,
the majority/minority situation may be reversed. Where this happens, do the religions aggravate what is political by their perception
of what is communal? Do they connive with the subtle temptations
latent there, or do they moderate the tensions?

At the heart of all these issues of peace and justice, well-being
and freedom, lies the question of ghettoization. What are the factors
inducing or mitigating it? Faiths are differently constituted, whether
in seeking or provoking it. Jewry has been traditionally defined by
the exclusivism of ethnicity, circumcision, dietary laws and fear of
assimilation. Even where secularity reduces the incidence of these
factors, the sense of identity still presides and with it the pain of
historical memory. There remains the instinct to differentiate
between 'righteous' and other Gentiles and to be at a loss how to
surmount the obligation to introversion. Not all Jews appreciate
what 'Gentilizing' others means for all concerned.

For Hindus, Muslims, Sikhs and Jains, in the Western context,
there are all the familiar pressures – social, economic and spiritual
– tending to the neighbourhood enclave and communal separatism.
Some degree of assimilation is proper, but how is it best facilitated
by the host community without minority forfeiture of core-identity?

The will to mutuality, its theology and practice, takes each faith into the policies and attitudes that decide education, nurture and culture in shared tolerance and genuine reciprocal sensitivity. The so-called Rushdie affair demonstrated how obtuse both liberal 'establishment' and minority community could be in reacting to each others' perceived obduracy. For the former the sense of threat could be a matter of disdain and even heartless censure; for the latter it was an occasion of bitter outrage and rash panic. That either – with some exceptions – could be so uncomprehending of the posture of the other in their contrasted pre-possessions remains a sobering measure of the great divide stretching across co-existence. Only a strong will to mutual sympathy and the intelligence to reach it in all parties can begin to bridge it.

(vi)

The faith of Judaism, elsewhere so familiar with life on uneasy sufferance in lack of state power, is uniquely caught in Israel in a tragic form of the state-faith equation. Diaspora Jewry cherished spiritual identity in innocence of political authority or, otherwise, in the will to co-operative citizenship inside so-called 'host nations'. The Zionist demand to rescue Jews and Judaism from these diaspora conditions and to resume Davidic and Maccabean patterns of national statehood bound Jewish faith and Israeli statehood inexorably together in a power structure. The ideals of Zion have inevitably succumbed to the *Realpolitik* of Zionism. In the long history since Theodor Herzl's *Der Judenstaat* (1896), high purpose and the hope of innocence with it have not availed to exempt Jewishness from the compromising normalcies of the power equation. Rather, they have meant a paradoxical experience of how sharply compromising these can be. Judaism has to co-exist in Israel with Zionism, in the conviction that they are proper to each other. So doing, they call in question the other version of the Judaic-in-diaspora, yet arguably confirming it by what being Zionist has entailed on being Jewish. This is why it is possible to read Zionism, for all its logical legitimacy, as nevertheless a tragic decision and one which focusses dramatically the complex of faith and power which we are studying.

Nor is the onus on the Palestinians. Their reactions were justifiable and predictable, given the nature of the Zionist enterprise in its chosen form and place.[9] Being recently contrived, though against a long background of yearning, and aiming to be homogeneous as its own 'host nation', the Zionist state could not enjoy the sort of taken-for-grantedness that attaches to most national identities with long histories and land-tenancies. For it was inherently competitive with the Arab presence invoking comparable right of land for peoplehood and statehood for the tenure of the land. As a result, the Israeli/Judaic equation between power and faith, in the context of territory and politics, compels a compromise of the ideals of both and makes the natural will to secure homogeneity, such as other nations enjoy, necessarily combative and entangles it in injustice and oppression. Divine election, when fulfilled in state power, admits of no exemption from that logic. Faith only properly relates to power when reserving its own concern for the priority of God.

Knowing it so, there are many anxious honest consciences in Israel. No outsider of goodwill can fail to sympathize. The tragedy of frustration and inner compromise runs deep, and the ultimate issue from the impasse is hard to discern and far to seek. The immediate point here is the truth that nation and state, invoking 'the name of the Lord', may also be 'taking his name in vain'. Judaism, albeit in its own form, has the same temptations as Muslims and Christians in presuming upon God. That may well be why many Israelis find it more comfortable to be secular. Yet not to be concerned for absolution is to need it the more. Meanwhile, it is hard to see how non-Jewish faiths represented in Israel can usefully participate in its ethos as long as the tensions between them and its own Jewish definition are so painful to all. 'Towards joint liabilities' is a difficult proposal for Zionism.

(vii)

We turn from mutual liability in the sphere of state sovereignty to how it bears on the religious reading of the natural order and the human relation to the earth as habitat and heritage. What is political about race and culture hinges on what is economic and ecological in daily life. To enquire into ethnic belonging and its nation-state expression is to enquire into the meaning of a cosmos as environment and home. Beyond what politics manage and control is the ultimate mystery of the human scene writ large. Here faiths have their total context and the surest impulse to mutuality in comparing their verdicts and testing their truth. Their readings of the cosmos as a whole, of humanity in present history, will be crucial to any discipline of the wealth of nations, any answering to their poverty and strife.

The confident Semitic instinct here is to start with a doctrine of divine creation and of human dominion, bringing theology and ecology together. However, for Asian faiths there is an urgent prior question deep in the soul. Is the world to be trusted as truly meant in Semitic terms of confidence and exploitation? Is there dependable significance in the experience it yields? Are we not wiser to entertain a genuine distrust of any final meaning inhering in our personhood? May it be that our egocentric situation, as selves in bodies, has deceived us into a misreading of the selves we suppose we are? Have we too readily assumed the right to acquire and exploit? Why not a *caveat viator*, 'Let the wayfarer be cautious', over all existence?[10] Such cautionary philosophy bids us query the positives of being.

Yet positives we instinctively take them to be. The embryo does not distrust the womb which is content to feel pregnant with itself.[11] The newborn do not query the intendedness of their presence. They cry and claim and wonder and belong. They assume a world that ministers and relates. The growing mind deepens into discoveries it takes into possession and finds significance responding. This may simply be our own deceiving, our need to be undeceived. It is the adult mind that suspects and distrusts, worries and denies. The adult temper deserves a hearing. Perhaps we should conclude by denying where we began.

Either way, however, the contrast between trust and distrust, between annunciation and renunciation,[12] *is* an option. There is no decisive proof either way. The theist may be the dupe of faith: the doubter may be the dupe of fear. We may read our life as divinely wanted and humanly worth wanting: we may read life as *dukkha*, the pain of impermanence and no more. We need for each other a lively openness to what decides us so contrastedly, a steady sympathy with its outworking in the humanity common to us both. However, it will only be in the positive context that ecology will be crucially at issue. It is only the theist – or the humanist who in this area is on common ground – who takes full responsibility for the management of nature, in contrast to the diffidence which concepts of *anicca/anatta* tend to bring to it.[13]

That diffidence accuses the vigorous technologist of vulgar exploitation, crude mastery and gross outrage in attitudes to the natural order. A right reverence is thus overborne. This is a charge the West does well to heed. It takes to task the concept of 'dominion' which Judaic, Christian and Islamic faiths understand to belong to humanity in tenancy of the good earth and in the presidency over natural processes amenable to manual control or intelligent contrivance. However, that concept only ratifies authority when schooled to consecration. The mandate may often have been misread as licence to exploit and dominate arbitrarily and violently. In that light Asian reservations have great relevance both to warn and to admonish. Properly understood, however, the Semitic sense of divine 'mandate to man' is conditioned by a vocation to trusteeship that sanctions humanity as 'lords' only in that they are also 'priests'. Islam, to be sure, shuns this second word. But the Qur'an is full of what may truly be called the sacramental principle, an exposition of which, in all three faiths, must be our clue in measure of man and of nature.

The 'image of God' metaphor about man in Semitic religion signifies rulership on behalf of the divine Lord. Ancient rulers had images of themselves erected in the lands of their dominion to signify their presence by that proxy, just as images on coins denote the authority that sustains their value. This is not the whole sense of a rich metaphor, but it captures the truth of the human vocation religiously understood. In the language of Jesus' parable in the New Testament, we are 'husbandmen' in a vineyard we do not own but which we can blatantly usurp (Matt. 21.33–46: Mark 12.1–12; Luke 20.9–19). That analogy stems from the whole Hebraic sense of 'covenant' and 'election', of vocation to belong responsibly under God in a land understood to be entrusted. If that 'glory of Israel' is 'a light to the nations', then its significance must be transferable to all human occupancy of territory, all agrarian, industrial and technological habitation by humanity of the good earth.

Possession, in every case, is very real, concrete and self-perpetuating. There *is* autonomy for human mind and hand. The natural order, it has often been said, makes no statements. It does answer questions. The secrets of science are not shouted aloud: they await the observing eye, the investigating study. Then they yield themselves into structures of conquest. There is a givenness in things – do we not speak of 'data'? – but it responds only to the energy that receives it and turns it into gifts of harvest, of culture, of technique and productivity.

This is the dominion writ large in the biblical account of humanity. It is corroborated entirely in the Qur'anic sense of the human dignity of *khilafah*, or 'deputyship', whereby the first man (Surah 2.20) is set over nature to exercise a mastery, but only on behalf of God.[14] He is only in control by being also under obligation. He exercises a conditional sovereignty. In being master he is to know himself as servant. The technology he will attain is only by a tenancy on sufferance, in a time and place for which he is accountable. Within the Qur'an that accountability is a very dire and solemn thing.

It follows in this biblical/Qur'anic scheme of things that possession is not only material but sacramental. Life in commodity is meant to be life in consecration. Exploitation is only wholesome where there is grateful celebration. There are arts as well as crafts. Sometimes they are one and the same, but always what is skilful to acquire must be skilled to hallow, apt to revere. All that is has this potential 'holiness', because it enwraps mystery, kindles wonder and releases joy. Man, being the register of all these, becomes the poet, the priest, the consecrator, whose utilization of the product is to be disciplined by awareness of its whence and whither.

Then doing and meaning are held together in conscious gratitude – a sentiment which in the Bible and the Qur'an is very close to acknowledgement of God. For thankfulness returns the part to the whole. It does not stop at the visible, or the feasible, or the tangible. It passes with these into a sense of awe and dependence which must induce to reverent acceptance that repudiates all crude acquisitiveness or brash manipulation. Here the theisms come close to the temper of Buddhism, but with the vital difference that the emotions of discipline and reverence are not drawn from abnegation but, contrariwise, from the very fact of possessing and employing.

This sense of things is implicit in the Qur'anic doctrine of 'the signs of God' where a common Judaic, Christian theme of psalmist and apostle can be usefully identified, seeing that many outside Islam are unaware of the emphasis it has there. These *ayat*, as the term goes, are the intimations in sense-experience of phenomena which demand to be read as index to divine mercy and, thereby, to human clue-taking. In a word, the signs signify. To the philosopher they signify what reason can explore, to the artisan what hand can manipulate, to the technologist what science can develop and exploit. But these same signs also kindle the gratitude of the perceptive, the reverence of the religious mind. What yields clues to human dominion, offers clues to divine worship. The world which serves as laboratory is also discerned as a sanctuary.

Since the signs, though differently read, are the same signs we learn the essential harmony of science and religion, or, rather, of a wise science and a true religion. That harmony, studied here from Qur'anic sources, permeates alike the Judaeo-Christian tradition. However, the dominion, or *khilafah*, of which humanity finds itself possessed in a material order responsive to it, is under no duress. It has its option to resist. The secularist takes the option, claiming an autonomy that admits no call to wonder about mystery, no urge to gratitude. Such are they for whom 'everything matters except everything', who are for ever busy with parts that acknowledge no whole, particulars never returned to ultimates. That we can arrogate dominion solely to ourselves in what the Qur'an calls 'the exclusion of God' is simply part of the divine magnanimity bestowing freedom.[15]

(viii)

It may be thought that these criteria of what is truly human are a frail thing to set against the workings of contemporary techniques and the structures of economic and scientific power, or to halt the exploitation of the rain forests, the denudation of the land, the pollution of resources, the disequilibrium of national economies, the vexing of environment, the sovereignty of market interests and the dynamism of applied sciences. But, in the last analysis, they are what alone can avail. For all these evils are violations of the nature of humanity. Their recognition as such is, therefore, crucial to the passion by which they must be resisted. They are not curbed by the kind of 'reverence' for life which must, at least in theory, include avoidance of the sane, sanitary and social steps that must be taken to secure higher life against the threat from lower life. People are different from pests and bacteria. If a necessary discrimination is pressed upon us by the very nature of existence, it is well to grasp liability for the trust of things in the total way proposed to us in the religious doctrine and discipline of dominion. To this liability the religions themselves are bound, since it is at the heart of a religious interpretation of human society.

Responsive shouldering of the human dignity within a faith's sacramental interpretation will always be at odds with what distorts or perverts it. The odds may well seem weighted against its vocation. The instincts of mere empiricism are strong and, with them, the will to untrammelled exploitation. Science and technology have a built-in momentum, an impetus of their own, impatient of ethical control. It is customary to assume that no impediment may be set to their ambition, or their liberty to develop and explore. Knowledge that was not allowed to be open-ended would seem a contradiction in terms. Our dominion, therefore, is prone to exceed itself, in the very act of fulfilling itself, by disallowing a right perception of what transcends it. Then religious curb is dismissed as pious scruple or dogmatic interference. To play its true role of restraint, of hallowing and 'the inclusion of God', living faith needs to be tenacious of its mandate so to do and intelligently alert to all the issues it incurs.

Seeing that vested interests within structures of power are so much a part of the situation that makes the task of affirming a sacramental world so hard, it may be wise to recruit them wherever we can. Other vested interests than those of the exploiter, the profiteer, the desecrator, can be ranged against such – the interests, for them as well as others, of clean environment, conservation, recycling, ecological stewardship and other policies calculated to preserve, to enhance and to retrieve the global habitat. Likewise in the patterns of world economies. There is no final security for wealth in the perpetuation of poverty elsewhere. The arguments from mutual interest on all sides need to be firmly pursued by the religions and must be said to constitute a crucial area of their dialogue. They will need, however, to be resilient and persistent. Some of these factors are long-range and can be offset by pressing immediacies readily blind to them. Or they demand an imagination and an energy that the *status quo* is loathe to allow. Moreover, faiths themselves, by apathy or dogma or perversity, have not seldom been deceivers or deceived concerning them.

The most vital recruits for religions to find in their liability to cosmopolis today will be the scientists themselves, in so far as they are humble enough to be accessible. In contemporary conditions this may well be the case. The pressure and perplexity of many themes in current science – medical, genetic, astrophysical, informational and psychic – tend to a new awareness of dimensions that are beyond techniques. That the exercise of skill and the pursuit of inventiveness are in no way 'irreligious' *per se* but only in their pride and false autonomy, is explicit in all dominion and *khilafah*. Moreover, there is much that is vitally reverential in the scientific enterprise where truth is beyond vulgar manipulation or opinionated handling. There is a spiritual integrity about the quest for meaning and explanation where clues must be followed wherever they lead and former dogmatisms have to be forfeited in the discovery of sounder formulation. Such integrity is not only a religious value: it is a lesson to religions. There is even an element of 'conversion' in the movement of investigative science, not to say also a role for the imagination not wholly alien to the imagery in which faith lives and means.[16]

If the faiths within religions are to fulfil their liability in this climate of technology they will need to merit to be heard. There is much about them in traditional guise that inspires suspicion of their irrelevance or impatience with their mental landscape of metaphor and symbol. They need to show cause why their reading of humanity is not subject to the sort of progressive readjustment to novelty which is necessary to the physical sciences. This, however, will not absolve them from responsibility for the archaisms of language and concept that so often impair their communication or impede its comprehension. They must overcome their temptation to be content with what is doctrinaire and open themselves to strenuous questions about the scriptures within which they house their assurance and conceal their anxieties. This means knowing where their appeal truly lies, to what it is addressed and why it must be heard.[17]

This is a task in which each religion must be responsible for itself. The warrant Buddhists have in their *Dharmapada* is not for Christians to justify. Revelation that is sacrosanct in Torah or Qur'an or Bible is somehow intrinsic to their respective peoples, whereas to others it needs to show credentials. To concede that these are rightly sought by those outside, though assumed by those within (or some of them), is a hard concession for the traditionalist in whatever faith. In so far as the experience is common, it may serve to bring them together. There is obviously something mutual about the fear in fundamentalism. In a world where the factors tending to secularity are more and more pervasive, it may well be necessary for the faiths resisting them to locate the issues first in the context of the human rather than in dogmas about the divine. The conviction in the latter will need to reflect what is legitimate in human competence as well as what is perverse in human pretension. It lies within the privilege of human dominion either to violate it in desecration and wrong or to fulfil it in integrity and truth. A living faith has the trust of that realism and the obligation to interpret and require it in the world.

Such starting from the human end is certainly conducive to interfaith relationships, seeing that the human is the single denominator of them all, whereas the divine, the transcendent, the ultimate, is so diversely understood. It is in the practicalities of the human scene that their co-operation can best proceed and in which their eternal referents of belief are most properly to be tested. Given the current imbalance between 'Third World' privations and 'the North's' techniques, between where needs multiply and means abound, it is evident that the interaction of cultures takes place in down-to-earth things, in engineering, irrigation, food-production, crop-improvement, fighting erosion, conserving resources and monitoring ecosystems wisely. On the one hand, all these concrete activities are indifferent to belief structures and proceed by scientific warrant and human urgency. One might even borrow for them the words in another context of the Christian poet and say: 'The simplicity of the sacrament absolved him from the complexities of the Word.'[18] On the other hand they are steadily interrogating and sifting the concepts by which humanness is measured and the good earth interpreted. To sink a well is to query or confirm a theology. To transplant an organ is to search a dogma. Religious faith is continually being invited into enlivening ethical perplexities which their resources must resolve. It is in fields and hospitals, farms and laboratories, that it happens and only via these in the academies of the faiths, the mosques, temples and synagogues of belief.

(ix)

To think thus of 'the simplicities of the sacrament' absolving us
from 'the complexities of the Word' is to raise the issue whether
the meaning of the former needs to be articulate in the handling
of the latter. If active compassion in its urgent activity is truly
'sacramental' in that it gives material form to spiritual obligation,
do its doctrinal associations matter? If we assume their relevance,
are they not already present implicitly? Need they become vocal
and intrude themselves on action that is pressing, administrative,
skilled and all-engrossing? Are not the Red Crescent, the Red Cross
and Asian counterparts one and the same in any sense that matters?

There are counter-questions. Was the poet right in assigning
'simplicity' and 'complexity' where he did? There are enormous
complexities about the imbalance of world economies: there are
deep simplicities about 'the Word'. Practical response to hunger,
drought, disaster, war and exploitation in global dimensions can
hardly be merely practical if it would be more than palliative. It
reaches into claims upon structures, interests and autocracies which
must be tamed or righted, by criteria which faith alone enshrines,
if mutual humanity is the final goal and the proper measure of the
task. Given the likelihood I have noted earlier of persisting single-
faith state-power systems, where one religion dominates and may
hold itself impervious to other clues but its own, the 'aid' factor
from outside may be the vital, if not the only, leaven to stir within
its mind. Far from neutralizing religious doctrine, the concept of
global responsibility from privilege to privation, from plenty to
poverty, sharply intensifies the self-consciousness of cultures and
therefore also their spiritual insights. There is no authentic giving
and receiving that can be confined to tents and blankets, food and
medicine, clothing and supplies. Since no religion can be exempt
from the community that nature, technology and global economics
create for humanity, none can pretend that the faith within them is
not also at issue.

The form of witness to it will be for each to resolve. The recession
of the various imperialisms of religions liberates the emotions of
identity everywhere, except in so far as nations pursue an interior
imperialism which disallows minority relevance. Each is to that
extent free to tell how 'love of neighbour' is affirmed and sustained.

The Christian sense of its impulse from the 'love of God' and of that love dramatically indexed in Jesus as the Christ will always require 'the simple Word'. Much has happened in recent decades to the theology of Christian mission. In some quarters there has been a marked shift from 'proclamation' to 'aid', with vocations, resources and personnel more forthcoming from the churches within that preference. But, far from laying a silence on theology, the appeal and urgency of aid programmes have refreshed the themes of witness. The next chapter takes this issue further in its bearing on how joint liabilities relate to divergent loyalties.

(x)

Liabilities and loyalties are nowhere more at issue than in the realm of human sexuality. It is a sphere in which the faiths have comparable guilt and in which they subtly affect each other. None can escape the pressures in the contemporary scene from the legitimate aspirations of women, so long thwarted or denied. All are liable for a right discernment of the wonder and mystery of sexuality in the confusions and distortions secularity brings to those aspirations while having also rightly kindled them. It is obvious that religions are in an ambivalent position in this crucial dimension of the human meaning, claiming to be mentor and custodian, yet also so long oppressive or malign. All major faiths, in differing ways, have connived with male supremacy and, despite the enormous significance of the feminine within them, have conspired cunningly to its suppression or its degradation. That paradox only makes the more difficult the onus on religions now to discern aright the authentic interpretation of human sexuality, to liberate themselves from the false and, by such liberation, to serve a true mutuality of the sexes in dignity and delight.

Sexuality is, of course, at the heart of both the spheres with which we have been involved in this chapter – the politics of society and the trust of nature. Sexual partnership is at the core of the one and the most intimate dimension of the other. Procreation, within creation, means that the continuity of humanity is given into the competence of each generation as at once 'freely receiving and freely giving'. That capacity of genesis through the bond of sexuality perpetuates the 'let there be . . .' of biblical creation but leaves it, amazingly, in the provenance of the human creaturehood. The Qur'anic 'sign-theology' sees it as the sign *par excellence* of the *amanah*, or 'trust', made to reside in the human realm. Each incidence of human birth is, therefore, a renewal of the divine mandate to us to be, and – being – to consider, reflect, revere and wonder at the strange replication of ourselves.

Immediately birth entails nurture. The womb gives way to the lap. Its former tenant takes to the breast, and the long jeopardy of infancy makes its dependent way towards maturity and self-reliance. The chief music in that story belongs in the feminine key. Only sperm is physically required of the male. Feminists usually forget how one-sided is the privilege of birth. The natural order allows no alternation or reversal of the roles. Many men would dearly love to shelter the mystery of child-bearing in their own physique, to be house and home to palpitating life within. That utter inequality between the sexes always persists and is not altered by the fact that religious cultures have so often made child-bearing the sad re-iterated slavery of womankind. The primary role of woman in the immediacies of infancy, shared as later needs may be in the family, is by its nature inalienable as long as wombs are wombs and babes are babes.

But, if religions of creation have been necessarily committed to such perspectives, let it not be thought that sexuality is only interpreted as functional to childbirth. Quite the contrary, if the sacramental principle is truly understood as equally the logic of responsible creaturehood and reciprocal personality. Sexual exchange exacts from either partner the most intimate measure of personal surrender given and received.[19] Fleeting, transient, promiscuous it may physically be. Yet, when authentic, it transacts personhood in the most total sense, as the form and token of a spiritual sacrament physically joined. Where sexual exchange is denied that quality, personality in either party is degraded and despised.

Interpretation of sexuality is therefore at the heart of religious faith as the critical sphere of its care for human meaning, its significance as the most religious of human acts. Is it for that very reason that religions, out of fear or prudery or tyranny, have for the most part conspicuously failed in the claim to be its mentor? The study of gender and religions presents a melancholy picture on every side. Maleness and patriarchy loom large, and guiltily, in religious cultures. The destiny of the boy for candidacy as *bhikkhu*, or monk, in the Buddhist tradition marks him off from his sisters. In the same tradition sexual desire with its gravitation into *tanha*, or craving, is seen as threatening to the destiny of monk and nun alike, while the abnegation of these is a steady *caveat* to lay society which, paradoxically, must produce the next generation of ascetics. The strict Theravada Buddhist account of selfhood as illusion insistently queries the instincts which might release and attain desire. Some Buddhist love poetry skilfully transforms the ardours of yearning into the art of renunciation.

Hindu insights know best how to interpret and correct popular views of the ready eroticism of Hindu culture. From its vast lore of myth and poetry one might take random note of the celebration of the dance of Krishna where, in the pastures on the banks of the Jumna, young peasant women, *gopis*, danced with him as he multiplied himself with them in sexual union. However, such access to the deity vetoed any status as married women, *gopis* becoming thereby both low caste and reprobate socially, and a forlorn parable of the relation of the soul to God.[20]

Theistic religions, with the partial exception of Judaism, have been differently derogatory to womankind, in the distortion of the relation between soul and body, the exaltation of virginity and the priority of the celibate state, and in distrust of the will. The urge to control and regulate, the fear of liberty, the weight of tradition, have all played a part. The Judaic mind via the family, the Sabbath and the concept of covenant has been saved from the worst features of female segregation, evident, for example, in some forms of Islamic culture where male relatives exercise total restrictive control over 'the living space and action' of females, and the veil passes its sorry verdict of utter distrust of society in general and males in particular. Yet Jewry has achieved its characteristic womanhood at the price of constraints which its ardent feminists now repudiate.

That all the faiths are now challenged by vigorous movements of female liberation is evident on every hand. What traditionalists see as their excesses is largely prompted by how massively resistant those traditions are. The issues relate the faiths sharply to each other. Feminists seek common cause across frontiers. Their quest provokes charges and comparisons, while traditionalists resist alleged contagion for which they reproach external sources. All are variously challenged by the shift in social patterns, the break-up of static culture, the menace of urbanization, the exigencies of economics and the bewildering incidence of techniques of contraception. All have to cope with the flux inherent in the sequence of the generations. All are in some measure beset by the confusions inherent in mobility, migration and the media. The response of every faith to the entire situation is both an interior interrogation and an external dialogue. Being so crucially human, social and global, it cannot be separately resolved.

Yet the religions have their own sources and sanctions of decision. Vows and homes and families belong where we meet, and the place does not lack for brothels, dens and addicts. What faiths think and say of them must concentrate their mind about each other. To accept to have it concentrated is their first duty, for there is nothing more religious in the whole art of being human. As in every other issue it is for each to search what their perceptions are. To acknowledge that it is so belongs with the recognition of plurality. A brief summary of a Christian perception will have to rely on the convictions to be explored in Chapter 9 below.

It is a perception which lives by the sacramental principle embodied in belief in divine creation of, and intention for, humanity. Sexuality is the most explicit experience of the sanctity of the body, of how hallowing is latent in its very meaning but also entrusted to our recognition and, therefore, subject to our blight. 'Love-making' may often have been sordid or routine, but it was a happier descriptive than the current 'having sex'. When the other party becomes merely functional to appetite, a counter in a commercial exchange, personality itself is forfeited and sexuality is travestied into sheer commodity, transacting only trade in lust. By contrast, to have experienced the authentic exchange of self with self in the total intercourse of 'thou' and 'I', or 'I' and 'thou' is to stand amazed that ever a relating so intense, so properly devout, could ever be had, or read, or grasped, as trivial, perfunctory, callously diversifiable, or mal-intentioned. Such vulgarities have never truly loved. So to think is the awareness of all dimensions in the reality of sex. Of course, it is a way of faith to think it so but a way which coincides with all that the physical knows itself to be. Doubtless there are failures and miscarriages of meaning in the human world. But these are only known as such and overcome by the mystery of the authentic.

'Love,' as the irony of James Joyce has it, 'loves to love love,'[21] and may do so selfishly. But the love that loves to be loved wills to love worthily of being loved in return. The possessiveness which some have detested and deplored in marriage[22] is authentic in the will to deserve the possessed and render again, in the most eager self-dispossession, within the art of marriage.

To believe it so is simply awareness of the sacrament that joins flesh to flesh in binding heart to heart. The spiritual and the physical interact in the one quality of incarnation, where the body finds its hallowing and the soul its meaning. Here is the surest perception of the art of maleness and with it the keenest assurance of the security and dignity of womanhood. The harmony belongs with sexuality *per se*, as do all its fruitions in equality, partnership. integrity and fulfilment. To hold so is the deepest realism.

It is, however, a realism of vocation. Vows may be its public context, its declaration of intent. But it is not a legalism, nor, as I noted at the outset via Lord Jacobovits, can lapses from it be handled by legislation. For, I insist, it is of the nature of a sacrament. There are those who withhold themselves from it out of a differing vocation, who mean their sexuality to be otherwise fulfilled. There are those who read their physicality in ways that disallow the logic of procreation and of the pattern explicit in the body and its organs. Such reading the reverent and the sensitive will hesitate to condemn in every case. It needs, however, to be challenged as surrendering to self-distrust, a persuasion of delusion, or a form of self-interpretation that hope and venture, trust and humour, could have overcome. There are those who read a fate in what, at least initially, was no more than an attitude, who accept as a destiny what was in truth an instinct they lacked the discipline to counter. In so far as this is so, the hopeful sacramentalism of love between man and woman has the task both of honesty and gentleness in perception and response.

In sad retrospect of his former days the stricken nomad, Job the patriarch, recalled how 'the fellowship of God was beside my tent' (Job 29.4).[23] There are feminists with whom he would not pass muster. No more would the Decalogue, where 'wife' is listed between 'house', 'servants, maids, oxen and asses', as that which man *has*. Job's Hebrew word 'fellowship' seems to include 'counsel', 'presence', 'secret' and 'protection.' If so, then perhaps this phrase of the old tragic hero of a patriarchal world, whose wife was no more than a source of advice he did not heed, none the less distils into a word the ultimate meaning of the secret of sexual love. Or as the Hebrew wisdom has it, God himself celebrated the nuptials of the first of humanity and rejoices in the bliss of creaturehood. A Christian's realism has to set that sense of things, and the sacramental principle by which it lives, in the sober light of a history and a world where meanings fail of fulfilment and the divine intention is at odds with human wrong.

Job's 'tent' was not equally shared, but, nevertheless, the patriarchal biblical world yields the clue of divine hallowing in which human sexuality is truly bound and truly free in the benediction of equal personhood. Though so long obscured and neutralized by legacies of that same world, the clue remains the surest charter of a wise and properly impatient feminism variously besieging all religions.

7

By Precincts of Prayer

(i)

The *Sermons* and *Devotions* of John Donne, Dean of St Paul's from 1621–1632, were full of bells. Whether week-long in his study preparing his discourses for the Christian Sabbath, or lying on his bed in sickness, bells sounded through his thoughts. It was as if his mind were a belfry brooding on worship and mortality.

Being learned in the Bible, he had doubtless read of the priests sounding the trumpets at the dedication of Solomon's Temple (I Chronicles 5.12 and 7.6). As for the human voice of the muezzin from the minaret of the Islamic mosque, he knew it only as the summons to the 'Turk', whom his Prayer Book listed with the 'infidel'. The booming of the African drum or the sound of the Buddhist gong were altogether beyond his ken.

Yet he had inklings of a community of worship wider than the precincts of his own. 'All mankind,' he told himself, 'is of one Author and is one volume . . . and His hand shall bind up all our scattered leaves again for that library where every book shall lie open to one another.'[1] He sensed a catholicity which, because it had to do with one mortality, might also attach to mortal liturgies and prayers.

I know Thy Church needed not to have taken in from Jew or Gentile any supplies for the exaltation of Thy glory or our devotion: of absolute necessity I know she needed not. But yet we owe Thee our thanks that Thou hast given her leave to do so and that in making us Christians Thou didst not destroy that which we were before, natural men, so – in the exalting of our religious devotions – now we are Christians Thou hast been pleased to continue to us those assistances which did work upon the affections of natural men before. For Thou lovest a good man as Thou lovest a good Christian, and though grace be merely (i.e. solely) from Thee, yet Thou dost not plant grace but in good natures.[2]

Donne writes thus on Christian ground but, being there, concedes by the very logic of his conversion that there is place for pre-conversion wealth in the celebration of faith. May the same be also true by the different logic of co-existence between faiths? Are there moral unities within differing worships which may be gladly acknowledged beyond – or despite – doctrines in tension or discrepancies at variance, given that 'all mankind is of one Author'?

This is the hard question to which we must pass in this chapter. If we meet and greet can we properly turn into one another's temples? Must converse with each other exclude all but segregated converse with God? Or, if our religion lacks that 'God-dimension', what of a mutual cognizance of some 'single, perfect transcendent non-representable and necessarily real object of attention'?[3] Can we relate only in our concepts and not also in our yearnings? Is there to be nothing between us except debate and witness, discourse and activism? Do we cease to be wistful because we are trying to be articulate? Is there any possibility of 'common prayer' in the context of mutual explanation?

(ii)

The answer, for the most part, seems to be firmly in the negative. 'I will buy with you, sell with you, walk with you, talk with you: but I will not eat with you, drink with you, nor pray with you.'[4] There have been, and remain, such Shylocks everywhere, even if they have less social provocation than he and no niceties of dietary law. At least 'nor pray with you' remains stubbornly insistent, despite perhaps some register of puzzled doubt. The separatisms for most religions seem legitimate and inevitable.

What we are exploring in this chapter is neither an abeyance nor a merging of particular worship, rites and forms of prayer. These, in the strict sense of the word, are *proper* to their peoples, the propriety of religion in its customary properties of symbol and architecture, of ritual and hierarchy. In all contexts, 'the things of God' are 'for the people of God'. Mosque, synagogue, church, gurdwara and temple are embarrassed to 'spy strangers' and vigilant for their immunity from confusion. Their forms and postures cannot be borrowed without arousing suspicion and resentment. Systems of worship are sanctioned by particularities of doctrine, tradition, language, law and culture which continue sacrosanct in the interior psyche and the understanding of those who belong. They are part of the fabric of identity itself.

Yet, for that very reason, can they be denied their exterior relevance, their meaning beyond their custodians? Communities being many, worships also remain so. This is implicit in the very acceptance of the fact of pluralism. Nevertheless, the world they intend to hallow, to consecrate and to interpret becomes ever more mutual both for celebration and for anxiety. Differing shrines do not house an uncommon humanity, full as it is with tragic discrepancies of wealth and tragedy – discrepancies accusing every conscience that truly prays and troubling all transcendent adoration that is honest. Worship has always to answer to its own evasiveness.

There is, therefore, compromise in worship which secretes itself from every other confession of divine omnipotence, every other wistfulness over human finitude, every conscious silence before mystery. Only 'the grave', as Andrew Marvell observed, 'is a private place'. Our corporate privacies before God necessarily belong in an open world with which their intentions have to do. Yet reluctance to have it so is instinctive, even mandatory, for the various patterns of worship to which religions belong and by which they are bound, preserved as these are by the pride and prejudice of history and by fear of what is alien. Sanctuaries, for us all, are somehow only safe with us.

All faiths afford examples of this inveterate separatism in the wills that pray. When they are farthest into their shrines they are farthest from each other. Some even allow their innermost sanctities only to the élite of their own allegiance. The Temple at Jerusalem had the forbiddingly delineated 'Court of the *Goyim*', and 'the Holy of Holies' itself was for the high priest alone once a year. Christian faith promptly opened its doors to the *goyim* on the sole condition of faith at the price, for some, of being 'cast out of the synagogue' (cf. John 9.22; 12.42; 16.2). The faith-condition, in due course,

confined Christian liturgies to those confessing it. Catechumens were
welcome to 'the preaching of the Word' without limit of race or
place, but were excluded from the inner 'mysteries' of the sacrament
until they were fully pledged. That guardedness of the eucharist
came slowly to be reinforced by the development of ordered ministry
presiding over its celebration. Believing and belonging coincided in
careful self-possession.

The long Christian encounter with Islam served only to reinforce
the mutual rejectionism implicit in all that was at stake between
them in respect of Jesus and christology, of the doctrine of God
and the nature of holy scriptures. Their separate worships were
effectively sealed from each other despite the factors that associated
either inextricably with the other, via the common faith in creation
and prophethood. A passing incident in the *Travels of Ibn Battuta*
(1304–1369) tells the situation with a simple pathos. That inveterate
Muslim traveller from his native Tangier into far Asia came to
Constantinople where he met the former Emperor, Jirjis (or
George), who had become a monk. Ibn Battuta writes:

He was walking on foot, wearing haircloth garments and a bonnet
of felt, and he had a long white beard and a fine face, which bore
traces of his austerities. Behind him and before him was a body
of monks, and he had a staff in his hand and a rosary on his
neck . . . When my guide saluted him the King asked him about
me, then stopped and sent for me. He took my hand and said to
the Greek (who knew the Arabic tongue): 'Say to this Saracen
(meaning Muslim), I clasp the hand which has entered Jerusalem
and the foot which has walked within the Dome of the Rock and
the great Church of the Holy Sepulchre and Bethlehem', and he
laid his hand upon my feet and passed it over his face. I was
astonished at their good opinion of one who, though not of their
religion, had entered these places. Then he took my hand and as
I walked with him asked me about Jerusalem and the Christians
who were there, and questioned me at length. I entered with him
the sacred enclosure of the church . . . When he approached the
principal gate, a party of priests and monks came out to salute
him, for he is one of their chief men in monasticism. On seeing
them, he let go my hand.

I said to him: 'I should like to enter the church with you.'

Then he said to the interpreter: 'Say to him, "He who enters it must needs prostrate himself before the great cross, for this is a rule which the ancients laid down and which cannot be contravened." '

So I left him and he entered alone and I did not see him again.[5]

Might it be different today? The pathos of the veto on Muslim presence at the Christian crux of worship is undeniable. All that we have studied in earlier chapters deepens it. Curiosity is aroused only to be thwarted. Jerusalem mediates between a Muslim pilgrim and a Christian ascetic. A *hajji* is briefly at one with an emperor. Due propriety intervenes to cancel a magnetic field of sympathy between them. The 'rule' of those hampering 'ancients' tells against the meaning of 'the bread and wine'.

Roles reversed, the conclusion would be the same with caliph as with emperor. Not for Jew or Christian the clauses and postures of Islamic *salat*, still less the hallowed precincts of the sacred *ka'bah* in Mecca. It is likewise with the *sangha* of the Buddha.

(iii)

Given such fixed categories in acknowledgment of the transcendent imposed by the ministrants, the mechanics and the minutiae of religious diversity, can there, nevertheless, be authentic acts of devotion each and all may share? What factors might move us to have it so? What criteria would have to be applied in the venture? What misgivings would require to be faced and sifted? It is clear that these are the questions with which we must engage in any such dubious and exacting enterprise.

Several urgent positive factors were evident in the survey of Chapter 1. Whatever it is which worship undertakes and enshrines, it has to do with a world that binds each with all, a world of no escape from common themes of hope and menace. The case need not be made again. When John Donne toiled over those *Devotions* he wrote of them as belonging to 'emergent occasions'. There have never been more such than in today's global experience.

Occasions 'emerge' all around us of human needs and crises, local, national and terrestrial, which call for supplication, for the perspectives that only the intention to pray can satisfy. They 'emerge' in the obduracy of racial enmity, the vulgarity of sex-ploitation, the iniquity of economic imbalance and the plight of refugees, in the tragedy of blighted landscapes and deprived communities, in the anxiety which asks with the poet 'where this vast human procession is going'.

Unless we are to exonerate the powers that be, to absolve structures of greed and oppression, to ignore 'the cry of a heartless world', then the will to pray must be keen and true. Does it always have to await a right theology before it can identify itself with the work of love, and the task of justice, in the world? A right reverence for reverence, a sense of effective penitence, a search for the due perspectives of transcendence, will translate whatever doctrine can inform and sustain them, or – otherwise – will search one out. Need a true theologian be alien to any realism that sincerely engages with the world? It may sometimes be better to conclude with what we can believe rather than to preimpose it. We may reach 'the worship-pable' through our anxieties and our shame more surely than from the past of loyalty.[6]

Nor are the factors arguably conducing to a shared spirituality only large and global. They are numerous and urgent in daily local situations and in personal life. Communities where faiths interpenetrate need awareness of each other's festivals and celebrations. Birth and death call for neighbourhood participation. Puberty rites and marriage ceremonies may separate cults, but they relate people. For they concern human emotions in proximities – social, commercial and civic. Thus the ideas that belong with congratulation and greeting become part of an implicit exchange via beliefs around the family, sex, youth, age and dying. The social factor entails, in some measure, the sacramental nature of sympathy, salutation and commiseration. Behind all these is our ultimate interpretation of human existence and how we discern its significance in the puzzle of time, transience and 'the sense of an ending'. Worships are thus invited into some sort of negotiation on the periphery of day-to-day, cult-to-cult, incidents within common life. Festivals associate us: they can hardly do so in neglect of what we signify within them. This means, already, a degree of religious exchange. It argues the necessary 'emergent' elements of a deeper communication of ourselves.

Furthermore, as well as rites of passage differently transacted, and festivals differently calendared, there are busy institutions in which personnel are drawn from variant faiths. Schools, colleges, hospitals and other structures of life may well be staffed by Hindus, Muslims, Sikhs, Jews and Christians, entrusted with a common profession and committed to a common activity towards a common good. Must it be that reference of these to God, or to the transcendent, will be always communally segregated and the togetherness in the action be always isolated in the praying? Healing and medicine, surgery and counselling, are ministries whoever fulfills them. The claims of the Hippocratic – or other – oath about disinterested care, the repudiation of abuse of power or skill, in the service of the sick and dying, as well as the multiple problems of medical ethics, are uniform and consistent whatever the worship-community of those involved.

The sciences themselves by which all practitioners operate admit no frontiers of creeds or rituals of faith. On the contrary, they press identically on the conscience and the convictions of the qualified professionals. Shared tasks suggest at least the possibility of shared search for needed reverence, wisdom and compassion. To find and sustain these will certainly take them into doctrine and belief, though they may well not start there. Will it never be appropriate for those concerned to unite in supplication even as they unite in techniques? Should the operating table have no counterpart in the sanctuary? Can either be a faith-monopoly? It would seem strange to exclude prayer for the 'emergent' occasions of healing or insist on an isolationism in the one which is impossible in the other.

(iv)

It is equally clear that there are 'emergent' occasions for the praying that might engage different faiths together in the entire field of education. They are obviously present in those countries where state education allows, or requires, some form of school worship. Worship in that corporate situation may reduce some to mere auditors or passengers in the others' tradition, if it is unilaterally conceived. Elsewhere, when schools or colleges provide no religious expression, the ethical themes in education cannot, in practice, be reserved from the relevance – or otherwise – of diverse religions present in the school or college community. There are also numerous problems of public order, welfare, housing, employment and environment, race and citizenship, which turn for their resolution significantly on the principles and motives within faith-allegiance.

When these take their due place in educational perspectives, as well as in practical local handling, they can hardly be insulated from what varied faiths mean, symbolize and transact when they are at their devotions. Praying, however separated in communal possession and currency, is caught up in common, human denominators of circumstance and responsibility to life itself. They point to its being, in some sense, conjoined by the shared quality of that to which it relates. Where school worship is devised for a multi-faith school population there is the added factor of *ésprit de corps* and its administrative practice within the school as a single unit. The staff, or faculty, also, however varied, have a unifying *raison d'être* in their very status.

Where, as in Britain, different religious communities have 'state-aided' schools of their own vintage, equal treatment requires that the pattern be available impartially. This, in turn, means that all faiths enjoying this status should conform to agreed national criteria of communal harmony, objectivity in teaching and the nurture of a truly participant society. In disloyal hands the privilege could ghettoize youthful minds and set back both genuine, free integration and due communal continuity. If suspicions are to be allayed and honest faith served, is there not a case for organizing schools and faiths in tandem? Is, for example, a Christian-Muslim school conceivable in which teaching could be planned so as to educate constructively for both communities by having the study of either set within the themes, the characteristics of both? This would offset introverted attitudes and the menace of sheer indoctrination, while developing a healthy awareness of mysteries at stake and issues in common even though differently resolved. It would take education into the very nature of faith as the proper context of instruction into any belief-system. The quality of teaching which this would demand could be a benediction in itself.

There are, of course, elemental themes such as earth, fire, water, climate, health, family, landscape, environment, trees, times, change, cities, farms, and endless other topics, which are the *materia* of religious education across all faiths. It is also possible, for example, to study the career of Muhammad and the story of Jesus, so as at once to inform and transmit a heritage *and* also to identify what needs to be thought on within it, such as the role of power and suffering, or the relation of person to message. Examples are many. The techniques of Buddhist discipline belong well with the practice of Semitic prayer. Both confront the learning process with the question 'Who and why am I?'. Education need not be unilateral in order to serve nurture, nor serve nurture by being exclusive in its sources. In the right hands and with the right intention, nurture and openness can serve each other. Any such concept would certainly require for its implementation a degree of unison in the art of prayer and praise. Hopefully it might also inspire it. Whether or not this is attainable, the concern that it become so points away from the timid assumption that worship can only and always be in *apartheid*.

(v)

There is a further consideration, noted already in Chapter 5, to which this leads. It is that the vocabulary available in any and all language for religious expression is not unlimited. Most readers of St John's Gospel are at once impressed with a small stock of words running like a refrain through its pages. Qur'an users know well the steady reiteration of its verbal frequencies. So it is everywhere. From time immemorial there has been a sort of verbal map of the territory of worship. The world that yields the terms is shared: so also is the imagination that kindles to them. What religion is there that does not draw analogy from 'light', or significance from 'water', 'rivers' and the 'ocean'? 'Speech' and 'silence', 'hunger', 'journey', 'sky', 'day', 'night', 'bread', 'wine', 'birth', 'union', 'death', things natal, nuptial and funereal – all have their place in the currency of beliefs and rituals.

To be sure, the import varies endlessly according to distinctive factors in the story or the ideology of the faiths. But, if there is to be discernment in what perhaps we may call neighbourhoods of metaphor, there cannot not also be opportunity. Shared vocabulary in no way ensures shared meanings: it does indicate proximate ones for exploration. There is a similar situation about the necessary 'techniques' of silence, gesture and posture which religions practise. These indeed divide Buddhist monk from Jewish *hasid*, and Sikh from Muslim. But within the radical diversity there is a common need to bring the body and the psyche into one purpose. Faiths are handling the same necessity differently. To that extent they are never wholly alien to each other. It follows that some sympathy between their forms and patterns must be feasible.

(vi)

The foregoing factors, arguably tending towards hope of some common sensibility, may be discounted by some as being sanguine, visionary, and too docile for the tense nature of religious existence in the contemporary world. I may be accused of losing sight of things reviewed in Chapters 3 and 4. If indeed I need a realism about the capacity of religions for tolerance and humility, that fact, in itself, must be seen as the strongest case for the plea I am making. We have to reckon patiently with what confronts them all, tests their quality and exposes their pretensions. This brings us to the significance of secularity.

It would be a poor response to see the secularizing world merely as a common enemy arousing a common resistance, as if the fact of it made a bond of common interest between religious faiths. Shared enmities seldom make for sound judgments. Moreover, there is much in secularity that religions do well to heed. There is honesty in some forms of scepticism. There are virtues of reticence and realism, or just reluctance to decide, which believing minds might learn to acknowledge.

That apart, Christian, Jew, Muslim, Sikh are all bound in duty towards the malaise of present time and place, as their criteria see it. Buddhists and Hindus, by and large, will not see proud or puzzled secularity in the same terms and must come to their own conclusions. There is little doubt that the issues belong to all. They are evident in the disvaluation of all things human as literature, and the media disclose it on many hands. The Buddhist may find the symptoms only confirming the basic doctrine of the futility of desire. For theists, with their conviction of a purposeful world where perceptive desire is crucial to the receiving of it, the contemporary scene spells an urgent test of such convictions and of their capacity to prove them. Faith in God, however formulated, is committed to trusting life's significance, responding to its meaning as accessible and dependable. For it has the world of life and time within an intention of response and destiny.

It is precisely these which are distrusted and discounted in the current forms of secularity which see only 'questions in the empty air', and the verdict of the absurd. Writing, East and West, 'deconstructs' the traditional assurance of the nineteenth-century novel, where plot, sequence and character could be reliable, where narrators were in control of trusted actuality. Present literature is all too often 'unbelieving in belief', caught in perpetual enigma, the sign of which is boredom, where religious 'meaning' is the most boring illusion of all. For Alain Robbe-Grillet, 'lucid consciousness is incapable of rendering an external world'.[7] Anti-heroes like Samuel Beckett's *dramatis personae* (if they deserve the term) never aspire, so that they may be said never to have failed. Expectations are both nil and frustrated: readers are left wondering why there should be any writing at all. A literature of despair is a contradiction in terms. Yet total 'dis-intention' is somehow conveyed.

Not all secularity, to be sure, is as hope-deprived as this. Some of it has its own honourable quality of courage and positive protest. Yet all such forfeiture of confidence in being human, vocal or merely latent is the very antithesis of prayer. Therefore, the art of prayer is the only antidote. For prayer registers the world as calling both to mind and will. It answers that entrustment. It intends participation in the ultimacy with which it knows itself involved. It takes responsibility for being human into its full dimensions as penitence, gratitude, commitment and engagement. Wherever this existential significance of prayer is realized, however imperfectly achieved, it constitutes a degree of community within the several patterns and forms that undertake it. Previous chapters have reviewed those dimensions of acknowledgment which liturgies and rituals imply, express and, perhaps, abuse and disserve. Their formal and official diversity need not deny to minds that use them a sense of sharing in their goal.

(vii)

Such reflection on the factors that argue the possibility of inter-devotion among the faiths must be alive to due criteria and ready for the misgivings that are aroused. Otherwise its will to venture

will lack integrity. It will need to ask how far worship can be untied
from theology. The Semitic faiths pray 'in the name of God'. They
call *upon* God only because they believe they can legitimately 'call',
i.e. 'name' him, and by 'name' denote him. 'Invocation' is in some
sense 'description', certainly 'affirmation'. If praise and prayer are
ever to 'address', there must needs be 'the addressee'. Worship and
faith, in that way, inter-depend. Doctrine is explicit in all piety.
That situation is perfectly captured by the use of 'the divine names'
in the Qur'an and Islam.[8] In their inner debate Muslims were very
close to the Hebraic, biblical 'mention' of the divine name.[9] Silence
does not escape the issue, for silence needs content unless it is to
be vacuous.

The vocative, with pronoun 'O THOU . . .', must have an
implied 'predicate'. Otherwise there will be no 'subject' within
adoration, no ground of pleading and petition. Doctrine which
somehow 'predicates', however diffidently, seems central to spiritual
realism about 'the Real'. Doctrine, however – not least in the Judaic
tradition – is infused with memory, and is perceived as corporate
identity: 'God and his people' reverses into 'people and their God'.[10]
Other faiths have their version of this equation. It is a cardinal
insistence of Islam that what is ascribed falsely to God makes *shirk*,
or idolatry, of the worship which is guilty of it. This finds right
believing essential to right praying. Christian liturgy since the fourth
century (thanks to the Monophysites) has made recital of the Nicene
Creed standard practice in Christian liturgical worship. Many
Christian churches see ordered and uniform manuals of prayer as a
necessary safeguard of sound belief. *Lex orandi lex credendi.*

Furthermore, it is traditional in Semitic worship and liturgy to
make scriptures and their recital central to public devotion. The
Qur'an is essentially vocal as well as inscribed. The opening of the
Torah and lections from the Bible likewise control the thought-
world of the faiths at prayer with them. So it is also with Hindu,
Sikh and Buddhist. The spirituality of the *sangha* is no less firmly
tied to the *dharma*, or teaching, of the Buddha. The imprint of
sacred scriptures is deeply in the soul of all, however diverse the
content of the page and the concept of the revelation.

What, then, of the will to spiritual commonality, given these
hallowed custodians of the authentic predicates of prayer firmly in
control? Can it happen with them or, if need be, despite them? The

answer must surely be 'Yes'. Are we to suppose that God is heedless unless he is properly addressed or that our human introspection can only happen within prescripts from the ancients and from Asia? Will our predicates, doubted or cherished, carry only what *they* have endorsed? Doctrinal theologies, it is true, have a habit of vigilance with the careful *Imprimaturs* of the scrutineers. *Supplicaturs* are different, belonging in the heart where sincerity is not for censorship. *Nihil obstats* of divine compassion may be granted without reference to verbal test. According to Isaiah it was the prayers of selfish and corrupt religion which remained unheard (Isaiah 1.13–17). 'The readiness is all,' the inwardly genuine, not the conceptually correct.

Yet such confidence must concede that sincerity needs to know how far false assurance can attend it. All religions, as I noted earlier in Chapter 3, have been plagued with self-deceit. Then doctrine, too, is implicated if it has exonerated where it needed to accuse. Either way, the final test of worship is 'intention': 'Create in me a clean heart, O God . . .' is the only right first petition, though it may well be gropingly addressed.[11]

Because of our human personhood, prayer is always inwardly derived. As an invocation of reality it is responsive to reality conceived, feared, revered, loved, or only conjectured. Through all those possible responses as faith, tradition, or ignorance attain them, it is an impulse capable of a unison of all. The unison may be tenuous and elusive, full of unresolved issues. These, though legitimate, need have no final veto over what is shared and meant. Perhaps 'You' or 'Thou' may be the only word that impulse knows: perhaps there is no word at all. The possible wordlessness of prayer is itself an index to how far it may lack a confident theology yet not cease thereby to be authentic. Therefore, even divided, or absent, theologies may admit of mutuality where mortals pray. C. S. Lewis makes even an asset of this condition:

> From all my proofs of Thy divinity
> Thou, who would'st give no sign, deliver me . . .
> Thoughts are but coins. Let me not trust, instead
> Of Thee, their thin worn image of Thy head.
> From all my thoughts, even from my thoughts of Thee,
> O Thou fair silence, fall and set me free.[12]

To be sure, he could pray elsewhere in passionately Christian language to the 'three person'd God', owning himself, in John Donne's words,

> . . . betroth'd unto your enemy.
> Divorce me. . . . for I,
> Except You enthrall me, never shall be free,
> Nor ever chaste except You ravish me.[13]

Such urgent Christian paradox Muslim, Hindu or Buddhist would find repugnant. Yet our return to the ardently Christian does not disqualify the other mind and mood.

(viii)

The case for mutual prayer may best be made by noting how some liturgies are truly between faiths. The Islamic *credo* or *shahadah* insists that 'there is no god except God'. Even ill-taught prayer cannot violate that principle. The unity of God ensures that the goal of 'intention', however misdirected, is also one. Were that not so, there would be no point in the better education of misconceived prayer, no call to remonstrate about the guilt of *shirk*, or false associations of the pseudo with the true. For these only matter because they are awry about the God they seek, than whom 'there is none but He'[14] (Surah 2. 163 et al.).

The Qur'an, like the Hebrew Psalms, can well supply a liturgy of thanksgiving for the mercies to be recognized in the natural order. Surah 55 yields a litany-refrain: 'These, one and all we reverently acknowledge.'[15]

> He raised the heaven above and laid down the scale in which all things are weighed . . .

> And the earth He established for all living creatures, with its fruits, its palm-trees and fruiting dates, the grain in the blade and herbs of fragrance . . .
>
> These one and all we . . .

> He is the Lord of the points of the sunrise and Lord of the setting suns . . .

He made the confluence of the two waters and the bound between them which they may not pass . . .

From these come the pearl and the coral . . .

His also are the ships which stand out on the face of the waters like banners..

All that is on earth is passing away. Only the face of your Lord abides in majesty and glory all His own . . .

All beings in the heavens and the earth are suppliants to Him. Every day He is at work . . .

Thirty times in all Surah 55 uses the refrain when it passes from the natural order into its concern with history and concludes with the words: 'Blessed be the Name of your Lord, whose is all majesty and honour.'

Or, without the litany form of cognizance of God's creating grace, there are numerous Quranic recitals of cumulative praise, as Surah 15:

We have set in the heavens constellations making them glorious to behold . . . and the earth We have stretched out, whereon are borne the great mountains, and where We have caused everything to grow accordingly, providing there a livelihood for you and for those for whom you take no liability. There is nothing whose treasure resources are not Ours and all are constituted from above in their appointed measure. We send the fertilizing winds and bring down the rain from heaven, giving you to drink of reservoirs that are not yours.[16]

Such passages cannot not be apposite for echo beyond Islam. The Qur'an's rehearsal of 'vines and olives, dates and pomegranates' may be outside the ecology of others and may seem remote from the fearsome technology of present time. But so too are the 'sheep and oxen' of Psalm 8 as instances of human 'dominion'. What matters is the theme of entire indebtedness and entrustment, made all the more urgent by our sophisticated productivity both for good and ill. As for war's rape of the natural world, the Qur'an has its cry of reproach, no less anguished for its being only about cavalry, not bombs, the raid by dawn, not the missile by night:

> By the snorting of war-horses that strike fire with their hoofs as they storm forward at dawn, a single host in the mist of their dust-cloud.
> Man is indeed ungrateful to his Lord: witness what he does. Violent is he in his passion for wealth. Is he not aware that their Lord is cognizant of everything about them on the day when the tombs yield up their dead and what is in men's hearts is altogether told?[17]

Wherever the sense of inward reproach arises, faiths at prayer may be said to be on partially common ground. Within *meditatio*, as Luther had it, comes *tentatio*, the penitence which must precede *oratio*, or 'plea'. Would it be improper for any seekers of these three to find tuition of them in the Eightfold Path of Buddhism? Meditation there is crucial, in its Buddhist sense, to those 'skills' (as the Buddhist term goes) towards which, as I noted earlier, 'right thought, speech, action, livelihood, effort, mindfulness and concentration' must conduce. It is true that the philosophy behind them is entirely incompatible with the Semitic sense of the legitimacy of right desire and of the vocation to participate gratefully and purposefully in the life of the world. It is also true that the Buddhist path intends an abnegation of the self where other faiths intend its fulfilment. It is true again that the Theravada Buddhist ethic springs from no conviction as to divine law, Torah, or Qur'an given in revelatory divine authority to a world of creaturehood. All these contrasts are deep and radical. Need they impede a recognition of how far the counsel of the *Dharma* tallies with Christian, Muslim, Jewish self-scrutiny and discipline?

Right livelihood, for example, requires that we set our gainful pursuits within the claims of social well-being. Right speech rides with James' warning of 'the tongue' as 'a world of iniquity' (James 3.6). Right mindfulness has some kinship with the prayer: 'Cleanse the thoughts of our hearts.' Buddhists will hardly allow themselves to continue . . . 'That we may perfectly love Thee . . .', yet the knowledge of our failures in these 'rightness-es' is not far from the meaning of penitence and what old Christian writers called 'comprecation'.[18]

Much in Hindu *bhakti* may coincide with Semitic vocabulary in the love of God, whether in the glow of peoplehood, land and Torah, or in the thrill of Qur'an-possession, or in 'the constraint of God in Christ'. In no way are these doctrinally commensurate, but need that abiding state of things forbid a limited and cautious willingness for what is, or might be, common? To think we are not forbidden may be a surer way to prove, or disprove, the hope than formal argument identifying the incompatible.

These examples of how praise, penitence and petition may partially coincide across religious frontiers must suffice in the present context. There are many more.[19] It remains to face the hesitancies and misgivings which traditions and loyalties involve on what may seem to these a dubious, if not a compromising, road. This can only be done by and for each faith itself. What follows makes no case from within Islam, Jewry, Sikhdom, *Brahma* or *Dharma* or elsewhere. The only demurs here are those of Christians – as vigorous as any.

(ix)

It is feared that any mutual spirituality 'marginalizes' Christ and runs counter to plain and categorical texts, such as John 14.6 and Acts 4.12. But these must be read in their full import in their immediate context. Peter, in Acts 4.12, is not passing a considered verdict on Buddhism, which was never in his ken. The category of 'salvation' to which he appeals belongs with the Messianic hope in which all his hearers, 'devout Jews', share. He is telling them that this hope is forever realized in Jesus crucified and risen. 'The love that bears' what is identifiable at the cross as 'the sin of the world' is the awaited Christ-reality, than whom, in the integrity of God, there is no other. That biblical view of things human and divine, entailing creation, real history, authentic personhood, and redeeming love, has to be mediated into the world of Buddhism that suspects them all. Buddhism is to be gathered into Acts 4.12 not in terms of sharp anathema but only of patient interpretation of whether and how there can be 'salvation' at all and how it can be located in a suffering love. The 'neither any other' refers to the truth that only so, in the cross, is evil forgiven and man remade. It is against false Messianisms, not questing faiths which know 'suffering' well enough but have never brought themselves to any confidence in a positive clue to it except that of abnegation. It would be the height of Christian folly to have only negation for them, for their wistfulness and their compassion. We do not serve the distinctiveness of Christ by culling proof-texts.

There is something comparable about John 14.12: '. . . no man comes to the Father but by me'. The meaning is that there is in the 'Sonship' of Jesus that which is reciprocal to the 'Fatherhood' of God. The one derives from, fulfils and expresses the other. As other verses insist: 'He that has the Son has the Father also', since it is because the Father is 'who he is' that we have the Christ-reality, achieved via 'Sonship' to him (John 5.26, 36 et al.). John 14.6 is not rightly read to mean that 'no one comes to God', as Creator, as Lord, as Ruler, as mystery. That would rule out Job and Abraham and the psalmists, all of whom 'felt after him and found him', but in ways that did not enjoy the sense of forgiving grace explicit. e.g., in the parables of Jesus and warranted only in 'the cup his Father gave him'. 'Coming' in those terms is by the Son only.

To understand such verses rightly is in no way to forego the distinctive faith of 'God in Christ'. Nor is it to elide the challenge that faith presents to all else. 'The wind' must be allowed to 'blow where it lists'. Paul, commenting on the 'altar to the unknown God' in Athens, identifies the God intended by it with the God of the gospel he brings. 'Whom you worship in ignorance, him I declare to you' (Acts 17.23). By Christian predicates God is far from 'unknown' or 'indifferent' (if that is what the legend meant). It is precisely for that reason that the worshippers must be disabused of what, in their ignorance or fear, they have in mind. We do not commend the God known in the gospel by an impatience he does not share at gropings after him. That does not 'marginalize' Jesus which seeks to bring him closer. It was disciples, not he, who repelled superstitious mothers with their ill-conceived ideas.[20] For his part, he does not 'quench the smoking flax' (Isaiah 42.3).

We retain the issues at stake between the Christian and the rest of faiths more fully – not to say more hopefully – by *not* squaring up to maximize antagonism but rather by searching out their potential to recognize the issues for what they are. As I insisted in earlier chapters, we acknowledge where people are in their believing and their doubting. That is the plural situation. It is not one rightly left to silence. Nor is it met by unilateral assertion. The witness we owe moves only from and with the questions which invite it, the answers which pre-empt it. Such witness centralizes Christ.

Christian loyalties are perhaps ill at ease here about how to relate inter-faith ventures to biblical authority. For many 'the Bible and other faiths' is of paramount importance as a duty to be followed. There are many more implications than those of the few texts we have noted and discussed. They are there, some think, in the story of Balaam, the significance of Melchizedek and Jonah, the universalism – and the particularism – of the prophets. More obviously they are present in the Prologue of the Fourth Gospel and in some facets of the Epistle to the Hebrews. Yet the will to find textual biblical guidance in reckoning with pluralism as we now face it is complicated by the limits Holy Scripture exhibits in its geographical, cultural and ethnic range. 'The land of Sinim', China, finds a mention in Isaiah (49.12), but there is no encounter with Confucius. From Midian and Sheba to Tarshish and the isles is the range of 'the Old Testament'. The New Testament is all around the Mediterranean. The recorded early church moves, like the superscription at Calvary, in 'Hebrew, Greek and Latin'. Henry Martyn in nineteenth-century India was right to query, fruitlessly, 'what Paul would do in my condition'. Paul's beloved letters gave Martyn no answer.[21]

Despair might well ask what explicit counsel the scriptures can afford us now. Hebraic notions of 'the Gentiles' will not suffice, for they impugn God's equal grace. The New Testament, incorporating Jews and Gentiles in 'one communion and fellowship', does not tell us how to do so when 'the Gentiles' live by the *dharma* or prostrate themselves in the mosque. There are no letters of Paul to the Meccans, no 'acts of modern apostles' canonized as 'holy writ'.

This limitation of our canonical frame of reference has to be taken seriously and is not made good by isolated quotation, whether 'exclusivist' or 'inclusivist'. It may be that the meaning of the Holy Spirit is that we have to take extra-canonical liberties. Who is to decide them? We must make creative use of the precedents we can identify in Paul and John and others and try to do with our own situation what they did in theirs.[22] But it is vastly more exacting.

It will not suffice to offer subtleties about Melchizedek. To know the task for what it is will be the first condition of fulfilling it.

(x)

If some shared spirituality is our vocation within unfailing witness and there is no ultimate bar to it, in whose name do we pray? Is not Christian prayer 'through Jesus Christ our Lord'? It will seem a sort of treachery to have it otherwise. Will it necessarily be 'otherwise' if the words are not verbally said? Jesus is *not* Lord, to others, in the sense we mean. We cannot yet ask them to share that sense with us, be they Jew, Muslim, Sikh, Hindu, Buddhist or Jain. It is pain that we cannot. Would Christ have us accept it? Is there *equivalent* language which still includes us and does not exclude others?

We are sure, in any event, that the clause is not a talisman, not a magic key. We come to God within the intercession of Jesus as the Christ and on the ground of what 'through' him we believe God to be. He is for us the drama of 'the name of the Lord'.

Will that clause then be a due equivalent, as one already familiar and congenial at least to Jewish psalmist and Muslim pray-er, and perhaps, more tenuously, to others also? Will we be justified in its substitution for their sake? They may be meaning the less: we will be meaning the Christian more. But we shall be together – given themes earlier suggested – albeit in ambiguous intention. Is, or is not, that togetherness an enterprise he might approve? Christians will differ in reply to the question. Such difference in obedience must be honoured without constraint. But there will be those who would say with Paul (in another context): 'We think that we have the mind of Christ.' In any event, phrases like 'for thy name's sake,' and 'for thy glory's sake' have long been part of Christian currency when there has been no question of mediation. For John of Patmos, 'Amen', too, was one of the Christ's names.

(xi)

There remains the difficult question of the location of any inter-faith spirituality. What is, or is not, appropriate about the use of consecrated buildings when people meet who are not one in faith?

It has been stressed that no 'merger' of separate rites and liturgies was argued. The continuing exclusiveness of these would broadly indicate the sanctity to them and for them of their normal 'houses of prayer', synagogues, mosques, churches, temples, gurdwaras and the rest. The Qur'an, for its part, validates 'buildings' which it says 'God has permitted' where lamps of piety burn (Surah 24.36–37). To each their edifices would seem to be due and right (cf. Surah 22.40). Consecration of places of worship has long been a firm tradition of Christian practice. All faiths know and cherish where they belong: they have 'grounds', physical as well as credal. As in all inter-faith ventures, there is an important pastoral obligation towards 'insiders' who may be confused or disconcerted. Their misgivings are not to be overriden but carefully reassured as part of the integrity involved. It is clear that other than Christian prayer in churches, abbeys and chapels proves a major source of disquiet.

This suggests that homes and private dwellings, or neutral venues, or annexes within church precincts, are best chosen for ventures in shared devotion. Homes, in any event, are a true symbol of hospitality and 'house pro church' is already a frequent *locus orandi* in Christian circles. There are, however, public, civic and national occasions when larger, consecrated buildings are proper. Demur in some circles should not then be allowed to constitute a veto, given that due circumspection and careful interpretation are followed. Then the 'hospitality' dimension extends from 'official' community itself when there is sufficient reason, via the shared intention, for the opened rendezvous.

On all such occasions of an 'unbarred temple' there will be significant silences, not merely in respect of the deliberate use of silence but of unsaid things within the familiars of each. Yet, unless our senses are in formulae alone, such silences need mean no curtailing of intention or sincerity. If they are on behalf of mutual discovery, learning and searching, in undiluted loyalties, they can be positive, communicative and authentic. Error may be present by *our* criteria. But we are not conniving with it because we are committed to Christ, with a commitment – however – which we believe would have us greet rather than spurn, venture rather than repudiate.

In a poem for a boy at Christian confirmation, Alan Paton wrote in words any user of the Book of Common Prayer will well understand:

This kneeling, this singing . . .
This 'burden that is intolerable' . . .
This 'humble access', this putting out of hands,
This taking of the bread and wine . . .
This dedication and my apostasy . . .
Take and accept them all, O Lord.

They are a net of holes to capture essence . . .
A shell to house the thunder of the ocean,
A discipline of simple acts to catch Creation,
A rune of words to hold One living Word.[23]

The central Christian sacrament gives mind and heart a home of truth which relates them vitally to all human supplication. As Dietrich Bonhoeffer wrote in a letter from prison:

It is only when one knows the unutterability of the name of God that one can utter the name of Jesus Christ.[24]

8

To the Self in Question

When we meet and greet, do we have designs on each others'
loyalties? Are occasions of conversation strategies of recruitment?
If so, what of their integrity as friendship? If not so, what of
their sincerity within discipleship? Is an inward perception of truth
properly indifferent about its reception elsewhere? Is that real hospitality which only engages out of doors? If others are unwanted in
the dwelling-places of the soul, is not the very will to meet betrayed?
To unstring the bow is to forfeit the music. Faith is somehow
neutralized without community. Yet community obtrudes
uncomfortably into the interests faiths have in each other. It turns
witnesses into proprietors and respondents into partisans. How do
we associate conviction with allegiance, and what should a sharing
of the one mean for a concern with the other? What of faith and
the 'me' everyone is?

Clearly dialogue becomes dialogue about mission, just as mission
requires debate about dialogue. If they are not mutually exclusive,
how do they interact? What, in the conversation of faiths, is the
place of conversion? If we have truly conceded pluralism in the
reality of cosmopolis what can, or should, conversion mean? The
more consciously faiths co-exist, the more arguably parallel, not
mobile, their allegiance. Yet can such implied neutrality about each
other be reconciled with their discordant verdicts on the human
scene, its meaning and its hope? Is there any point or urgency in
dialogue between them if there is no mission from them either to
the world at large or to each other? In such mission can they be

themselves in neutrality and without an identity that makes and holds disciples?

It is easier to pose the questions than to resolve them. Faiths differ sharply, as we must see, in the instincts with which they approach them. We do well to go beneath them all and ask initially about convertibility itself. How convertible are we? The term is a financial one, having to do with currencies and values. It is certainly applicable to the human realm. We must first realize that personality is a continuum in which new bearings, new mintings, can obtain. Conversion, all too often, acquires an external meaning, a shift in adherence from A to B – these being labels of communal identity to which, and their problematics, we must return. Immediately here, the point to be stressed is that inwardness is crucial and that whatever is critical within it has to do with conviction and character.

If we use the familiar analogy of John 3.1–10 and the sense of being 'born again', we must realize the reach of the metaphor. Nicodemus' own incomprehension itself can help us. 'How can a man be born when he is old?' was a right puzzlement. He cannot. Birth is irreversible. We have seen in chapter 3 how birth so far determines religious faith. There is no 'entering the womb' again. Jesus' meaning had to do with the bringing to birth within the self of a new perception, and reception, of it. It would be like 'birth' in its newness and in its potential into life, but it would happen, if at all, within the Nicodemus who already was. Otherwise, there could have been no meaning to the dialogue. 'Born of the flesh' and 'born of the Spirit' were not antitheses but correlatives, not an 'undoing' but a 're-doing' of the self.

(ii)

This fact of the continuum of given selfhood is central to any and all conversion, whose meanings cannot happen in a vacuum. Change cannot be total without cancelling itself out in being denied any abiding locale. 'Peter' was a name Jesus attached to 'Simon' to denote a given destiny. 'Simon-Peter', with the eloquent hyphen, remained his designation in the Gospel. Paul, in all his life-span, never ceased to be the man who 'sat at the feet of Gamaliel'. So it is with all exemplars of 'new birth'. The acquisitions of parental nurture, the milk of the breast, the lie of the land, the lilt of the language, the sense of the place, the memory of the time – all these are irreversible. Biography, like the rings within the tree, is the register at once of the becoming that is being.

It must follow that there is no conversion that leaves original faith to pass without a trace. It finds a residual presence within whatever is discovered. There is a persistence of culture that carries with it a perpetuation, in measure, of the beliefs a culture mediated and enshrined. It is this truth which makes total repudiation of a past faith incompatible with viable embrace of a new one. In the first ardour of something new found, neophytes may disown a whole past, may even disdain that by which they may feel themselves betrayed. But, in due time, psychic dichotomy may overtake them in a nemesis, or their sense of sobered continuity will discern their crisis more truly.

Sadly it does not follow that this continuing presence of the old within the new at all reconciles the communities involved. To the burden of this we will return in assessing the tenacity with which all disciplineships cling to their human tenants of their tenets and resent departures to other allegiances. That has to do with the pride and prejudice attending on establishments and institutions. Our present concern is with the inward dynamics of truth recognition.

Such recognition is best studied under the theme of inward crisis, the crisis which takes us to the heart of conversion. From it, we must add, there comes the need for what we might describe as 'the conversion of conversion', away, that is, from some shift in labels or classifyings to discernments of meaning and commitment.

What might inward crisis be? It may be instructive to begin from a tradition which Luke the evangelist records about an exchange between Jesus and Simon-Peter in the night of the climax Jesus reached in Gethsemane (Luke 22.31–32). It seems odd that the translators into English in 1611 should have had Jesus say to his leading disciple: '..when you are converted . . .' Had Peter not already been far initiated into what discipleship should mean? No, for the very crux of discipleship was still impending, when all asked 'Is it I?' who will betray.

And the Lord said: Simon, Simon, Satan has demanded to have you (all) that he may winnow you like wheat. But I have prayed from you (all) that your faith may not give out and when you (sing.) are turned around (AV converted) make your brothers firm . . .'

The incident is dramatic, the language cryptic. Simon is urgently addressed by name, but the sense intends them all. There is danger that his entire faith may be 'eclipsed'. They are all to be 'winnowed' with the roughest wind. When his personal crisis is survived he is liable for community with all the others.

Much of what convertibility entails is here. The word 'converted' has to do here with 'turning round', 'rallying' after defeat, 'coming out' at some point (as the Greek implies) from a collapse. The sense may not serve what, now, conversion is normally taken to mean. For that very reason, with its accent on crisis and awareness of all it signifies, it is the more right for the case I am making.

The elements of that crisis, we may say, are the self one is and one's part in redemptiveness. Let us study convertibility in these terms and from them explore its meaning for allegiance in the usual sense. If we find ourselves 'converting' what may generally be understood as 'conversion', so be it. The implications for mission will soon become apparent.

(iii)

Why should religions want to be immune from perceptions of the self which others have? For the egocentric situation is where they all belong, with which they have all to do. All faiths are, in some sense, verdicts on the self. Theorists may wish to posit some 'transcendental unity of all religions', but, be that what it may, is there not a mundane unity of all existence in the inclusive mystery of individuation, the 'me-ness' in which all must start and end? Those who shrink from dialogue often talk apprehensively of being left with 'the lowest common denominator'. They mean some reductionism which leaves no faith with anything distinctive. Selfhood does not fit that description. For it is the surest common factor, the likeliest common interrogator of what faiths make bold to claim. It is certainly where we must look for the proving and the proof of conversion. Whatever their doctrines of revelation, the self is where all faiths have to start, the theme those doctrines must concern.

Religious language is full of personal pronouns: 'I' and 'Thou' –

'me' and 'mine'. We need them even when we are trying to escape them. Their use in faiths is more than the Socratic 'Know thyself', more than Descartes' 'I think and so I am'. Search goes deeper in asking: 'Who am I and why?' 'I suffer and so I am', 'I am and so I think', 'being doubts itself' are all part of its language. All faiths have to do, in their own way, with the tenure of the self, its identity, its immersion in society, its mortal brevity, its being intelligible to itself. All these are the elements of consciousness.

It is true that the incubus of traditional faiths may often mean that unexamined answers prevail and become, for multitudes of humanity, simply the assumptions that obtain. Conversion may then mean that, for the first time, these are queried and probed. Not all consciousness is, so to speak, undogmatically self-conscious. We can only hold in a warm compassion those for whom the call to be a self is largely muted by privation or grimly answered by crippling adversity. Where there is hope that entrenching or imprisoning habits of mind may be penetrated by a sense of other options, witness and dialogue must certainly engage them.

All such necessary realism returns us to what we may understand as a ministry to human consciousness, to the ego-centric situation of every human 'neighbour' as society and mortality enclose it. In that ministry both the Asian way of negation and the Semitic way of affirmation can come together. For together they shape the paradox that we have to lose in order to find. There has to be a conversion from self-centredness which is itself the nature of self-fulfilment. In both religious streams 'desire' is seen as the common, and the vital, term. The 'undesiring' which Buddhism proposes as a proper goal belongs squarely with Christian 'unselfing', but only as the way to self-renewing or new possessing such as Buddhism denies. The latter's formula, 'Desire not to desire', does not emancipate us from a self-concern, since it has to be desired. There persists a self-seeking in every self-renouncing, as all honest ascetics, martyrs and saints have discovered. Yet authentic 'undesiring' is present in any Christian bidding to 'desire a right desiring'. For the 'unright' desires have to be denied. Since they are insistent and ubiquitous within the self, the negation of them has to be sustained and vigilant – indeed, thoroughly Buddhist in its scruple and its rigour. But this way of negation serves the way of affirmation. The self is invited to believe and receive itself as divinely meant and intended, with an intention made to turn upon a free acceptance to be mastered by the love that so devised it.

In seeing conversion in these inter-Buddhist, Christian terms, I have made large assumptions about creation, creaturehood and the world of time and place which Buddhists do not accept. That is where the witness in dialogue belongs, but it belongs within perception of a single theme on which all are embarked. It does not make conversion an issue between competitors. It sees it as a crisis, common to both. They are one in reckoning with selfhood: they part in where the reckoning leads. To the one, the ego-centric situation, as we experience it, can only be taken as an illusion from which to be freed. To the other it is a vocation by which to be fulfilled. But there are vital aspects of the fulfilment which require that we discern the deceptions of illusion. Fulfilment, in turn, can well enlist the 'skills,' as Buddhists call them, by which the illusions are discerned.

A full Christian reading of personhood will come in Chapter 9. The immediate point here is to see conversion as the abiding crisis of selfhood and to appreciate that it can associate faiths with each other when its nature is fully explored. Seen only in terms of allegiance, conversion makes for mutual alienation. Taken as what is at stake in being a self, it brings them into a territory they are bound to share, where dialogue and witness have to merge.

(iv)

How appropriate it is for all to keep close to the crisis within selfhood will be clear from the perspectives we had on religion in Chapters 3 and 4. Faiths have been traditionally busy about their own heresies, keeping themselves dogmatically right or fragmenting in the process. They have seldom been so busy about their own hypocrisies. 'Physician, heal thyself' has been of them a very proper gibe. So much about their outward manifestation raises inward questions. We have to see that situation as confirming how crucial is the selfhood question on which we are concentrating. If the religions which purport to answer it can be their own worst enemies, the individual within them is the more at risk. The will to self-criticism will be the sharply critical thing. Persons will need to start on it from within their familiar heritage.

It follows that every thought of convertibility does well to begin with self-accusation. Pride, prestige and preservation tend to be the first instincts of allegiance. Conversion may even be seen as treachery.[1] Then a whole tangle of motives and resentments result and all is externalized. Inward self-reproach is beyond such charges and sees its reasons as the proper loyalty. It starts in a sense of disquiet, which is a very positive thing. It is the yearning to be a different self, not in envy of others or in day-dreaming about circumstance, but in deliberate aspiration which doubts what, thus far, has been. 'O that a me would arise in me that the one I am might cease to be.' Here is the starting-point of convertibility, the will for a difference.

The Christian sense of this is prompted by measure of the need for it implicit in the central event of Christian story, the passion of Jesus. How other faiths originate it they must say. How far also all deter it by self-congratulation and establishment complacence is plain to see. Jewry has the Day of Atonement and all the implications of covenant status. The Qur'an has the insistent demand of the totality of the divine claim. Idolatry then makes a concept within which all violation of the divine good can be inclusively arraigned.[2] Surahs 12.53 and 79.2 tell of 'the soul under compulsion to evil', and the soul 'aware of self-reproach'.[3] Both are powerful pointers to our need to be unmade and remade. There is in Hinduism the basic theme of cleansing whereby 'purity' is to be recovered.[4] A vast range of ideas exist about the liability of the self for the self among the several faiths.

Christian dialogue and witness at this point are rooted in the Christ-event. Let us return to Simon-Peter. The drama of Jesus' passion into which he was to be drawn would be the supreme trial of his convertibility. He would be taken into radical self-discovery as a bewildered, frustrated, broken Simon with all illusions shattered. Out of that intense bereavement, both of self and meaning, he would be remade into an apostle by finding the invitation he was given into the perception of tragedy and the experience of new conviction and new life. He witnessed an inclusive measure of the wrongness of the world and beyond it a summons into alignment with the future of the love that surmounted the evil in 'the power of resurrection'. The sifting foretold of him indeed occurred, winnowing the chaff in his nature from the pure grain of his personality.

His future would be in the resulting discipleship, but it would need to be constantly sustained by present memory of its vital past.

In some form, if only by the proxy of a perceived history, the same is true of the Christian tradition. What the poet called 'Easter in us' only happens in the realism which has true measure of our ego-hood as that which both needs and can receive such transformation. The needing and the receiving belong together, and both are met in the meaning of what was done to Christ and what, by Christ, was done with it.

It is in these terms that Christians are invited into convertibility as at once urgent and feasible. There is a realism about the wrong which belongs in our human-ness: there is an ideology of the cross into which, that realism acknowledged, we are called as a programme of life, a being on the side of this costly love in the world.

It follows that convertibility is not simply *from* a self-enclosure but *into* a self-fulfilment. The self that is fulfilled has to see itself bound into the ongoing redemptiveness which is the divine policy in the world. If that policy has been once for all inclusively exemplified and transacted in the Christ, then it has to be steadily re-enacted in redeeming community. Conversion is not, then, some privacy of experience but a commission to life and to the world. The ego-centric situation is both widened into humanness and also confined into Christ's purposes. These rescue it from 'unchartered freedoms' which only 'tire' and stress the soul.[5] The focus it thereby receives relates it in a chartered freedom to belong and to become within 'the law of Christ'. As such it is a convertibility which is reproductive. It is a prescript for appropriate selfhood.

(v)

The urgent question we have now to ask is whether this reading of selfhood can happen apart from the history with which, for Christians, it is essentially linked. The thought here is not about that problematic notion of 'anonymous Christians'.[6] Instead, it is about synonymous Christ-bearers. Is the secret of the self that is truly dispossessed of itself, by being possessed by love, known and attained without the faith-possession of this history with which Christians will always associate it? The answer surely must be 'Yes'. For would the God active in the one Christ exclude the secret from those who did not share the history? The grace which ordained its where and when must reach, because of them, beyond their expressive history. There remains 'the one name whereby we must be saved'. In every evil situation only love redeems. There is no saving except by means of suffering. This is the exclusivity of the logic that belongs to wrong and right, to sin and grace. But 'the name' may be effectively shared without being historically confessed. Or, better, the ultimate confession will be present in the imitation.

If we can perceive redemptiveness out of love at work in the selves it has fashioned to its own shape, shall we not be reading a formula *infra ecclesiam salus est* in which *ecclesia* has the wider reach of action while still requiring the classic test of origin? Any such conclusion will not make the Christ and the church any less crucial, any less necessary. On the contrary, the necessity sharpens, as the indispensable realm of reference of the secret.

Before pondering that bearing of *imitatio* on *confessio*, it will be well to search further into the thought of vicarious community, reaching in grace into the bearing of sin and, so doing, finding both emancipation from, and fulfilment for, the human selfhood. Aspects of being vicarious were with us in Chapter 4 where I asked how far there could be a volunteer penitence about the world. Can it make sense to want to 'wash the wind and clean the sky'? Certainly, as we saw, the consequences of evil are in no way limited to the perpetrators. Birth and death, competition and strife, markets and means, goings and comings, all occur within the mutual vulnerability which they entail upon us. Connections are everywhere in the web of affairs, and many of them are noxious. It follows that consequence-bearing is a fact of life, a tale of injustice, a threat to security. In the contemporary world even our pleasures tend to be vicariously sought and found. We gaze at film-stars and admire celebrities, and for most of us the grandeur is always vicarious.

Imagination, at this thought, at once opens out the possibility of being positively vicarious on behalf of good, as people of the vicarious Christ. Was not this the very genius of the gospel – to set the reality of love's vicariate at the very heart of the divine nature and so of the human calling? Certainly it is inconsistent with love to seek immunity or to evade what is needed. Christian faith has always seen that principle realized in the faith about 'God in Christ', the faith that finds in incarnation and redemption the self-expression of

God as love. It further takes that principle as eminently reproducible within the will of those who comprehend it.

Such reproduction was at the centre of pastoral nurture in the churches of the New Testament. Repeatedly in the letters of Paul and Peter, 'the mind that was in Christ', as they wrote of it, was to become 'the mind of the community of faith'. The redeemed had, in turn, to become redeemers. They were to interpret what came to them in the enmities they encountered as a liability to respond as Christ had done. So doing, the meaning of the cross would be achieved in them, releasing the same forgiveness and serving the same reconciliation. In this way 'the mind of Christ' was not only the theme of their education, it was also the motive of their will. They had a living role to play in 'taking away the sin of the world'.

They did not understand this as some arbitrary transference to them of the guilt of others. Guilt remained where it belonged and where the sense of it could become a factor in any new beginning. What they did believe was that wrongdoers could be retrieved for righteousness, for hope and truth, by the response to them made by those who suffered at their hands or who undertook the resulting situation. Holding the future open, they did not need to subscribe to the inevitability of evil or its sequel, nor were they preoccupied with their own private world of immunity from some illusory ego-hood. On the contrary, their whole selfhood found fulfilment in the part they played in the opening of the future to grace and joy. There was in their quality a double liberation, their own and those for whom they cared.

This returns us to the question about being synonymous with Christ. The inclusive paradigm is not to be held as an exclusive copyright. If Christians when greeting witness to the Christ-event as making concrete this vision of redemptiveness, they will discover its incidence outside their house of faith. To be sure, there are aspects of all religions that militate powerfully against it, just as there are long stretches of Christian history and practice which have grossly betrayed it. It will not ride easily with some aspects of Buddhist teaching in respect of transience and the stress on individuation. Nor will it accommodate to notions of inexorable *karma* and the irreversibility of time. Nor will it pass muster with those aspects of Islam which demand the eternal invulnerability of God. Nor again will it find entry among those who cling urgently to the dignity of the self-righteous. There are attitudes across the faiths which exclude all vicarious ways and the implications of human solidarity.

All such disowners must be patiently disproved. But they are not the whole, either between or within their faiths. The sense of selves meant for the connections of redemption can be awaited within any faith. The church in Christ was indebted for its interpretation of the Christ-event to the precedent it believed Jesus to have followed in his encounter with the wrong of the world. That precedent came from the heart of the Judaic tradition in the figure of 'the suffering servant' whose travail was so movingly identified by the writer in Isaiah 53.[7] We may believe that the church read Jesus that way because he himself had been minded to read his own unfolding ministry in its light. The Christian, then, is not the sole trustee, the exclusive source, of the clue by which the gospel proceeds. The Christian cross of Jesus is, for the church, the consummation of the truth in the economy of God which interprets and enshrines universally human awareness of what wrong does to love and love does with wrong. If it was a consummation anticipated by the suffering of prophets, it need not fail of kinships with its meaning in the world into which its servants take it. Discerning study can locate them in the capacities of compassion, patience and long-suffering present where its mentorship, in creed and liturgy, is absent or denied. Such absence or denial may be due, in part, to the compromises and betrayals in the history of that mentorship. For the trustees of the gospel are seldom worthy of the trust.

(vi)

Convertibility, then, has to do with knowing the crisis of selfhood in which all are involved, in finding its resolution in forgiven self-investment in the will to love within the human world – the will to love which knows itself committed to the redemptive principle by which wrong is righted and love's travail justified. Since wrong is within, as well as beyond, the self, conversion consists in contrition, the first condition of forgiveness, and in vocation into ministry in its meaning in the outer world, the world of kin and society, of time and place. It is to be part of Christ's redemptive meaning and party to its interpretation and fulfilment in the world. In these the remaking of the self consists. It is a remaking which happens within the givens of birth, of culture and of personality. As such, it is at once decisive and continual. The selfhood in which it has to happen is never static, always in flow, never made but always in making.

For the Christian, as in our earlier framework of the Simon-Peter crisis, this event of the self – as it may well be described – happens by virtue of the significance of Jesus. It is a significance believed to be expressive of the nature of God understood as its source and its ground. Yet, in its eventfulness in place and time, it required – by being what it was – to be recognized by those who were immediately parties to it. Not a construct of their minds as disciples, but in itself the divine disclosure, it nevertheless awaited and received the cognizance of its community's experience. Their gospels were the end-product of the career Jesus had. Witness was, therefore, insep-arable from his whole significance and, with witness, community. So it is still. The disciples who became apostles had, as it were, in their 'report',[8] the conversion of the world in trust. Chapter 9 to follow will aim to develop this mutuality of faith and community.

It does not mean that the church is, somehow, itself the gospel or that its 'order' can rightly be said to be its crux. Its crux is the Christ alone. What it does mean is that the Christ by his very nature had his credentials via 'brothers and sisters' whom his meaning made such, both to him and between themselves. In commending their faith about him they were taking their fellowship in him. They did so universally. They intended the world. As Jews, they over-leaped the fence between 'the chosen' and 'the pagans', between the folk of Moses and the citizens of Caesar. They understood their faith and fellowship as inclusive, by consent, of all humanity.

There can therefore be no question of some abeyance, still less repudiation, of mission. To think so would be to disqualify the very origin of discipleship. Christians from the beginning had to be 'made', to 'become', by 'hearing the word' and 'receiving the bap-tism'. Not to anticipate conversion, in the sense we have explored it, would be to evacuate the faith itself. It would be to abandon the kind of realism about the world on which the faith proceeds. It would disavow the generations who found their way to faith only from where they had not known it. There is no place on earth to which faith was not commended as something hitherto unknown. That truth of things cannot now be reversed by some conclusion that the Christ only belongs to those who have not needed telling. Even these often need mission as much as any do. For, by definition, being 'born again' is not by 'being born'. Nor is conversion a natural legacy.

But, being clear about open faith and offered fellowship, we have also to welcome the presence of what is 'synonymous with Christ'.[9] Outside the Christian frame of reference, it has about it, of Christ, what is 'adjectival', but not 'nounal'. It 'confesses' only by reading selfhood and the world in the way we have studied. It lacks, or even disallows, the 'confession' of which the Christ-event is theme and sum. Into the explicit confession it can always be invited. But the invitation will acknowledge that its logic is already there.

However, the recognition that a 'Christ-mindedness' may well obtain outside the parameters of the corporate care of it the church was called to be, will not make that historical care of it less necessary. On the contrary, the secret of self-giving into redemptiveness as that for which, in the evil of the world, the self was meant, will always need embodiment in a formal faith and in a living society. Rooted as it is in a specific history, a history written by interpreters who owed themselves to it, it obtains only by that history's leave and warrant. The faith-fellowship it generated will be the vital condition of its perpetuation. Or, in credal terms, 'the Holy Spirit proceeding from the Father and, or through, the Son' 'abides with the church for ever'. The gospel was never an abstraction, a philosophic insight, a point of view. It was, and is, a doing on the part of 'God in Christ' which became 'a deed' in time and place designed to fulfil itself in men and women, or – as Jesus prayed – 'I in them and thou in me, that the world may know' (John 17.23).[10] Such is the pledge and point of all humanity's convertibility, a convertibility orientated into a selfhood by which each and all could belong with humanity in the claim and communion of redemptive love.

If community, then, is inseparable from the meaning, it must always be open to recruits. Nobody can well be unwanted in its vision. It cannot allow proprietors who confine it to themselves. There can be no privatization of its commendation. It does not have to see its existing custodians as the only ones there can be. They do not constitute a 'born society' who, for reasons of that status, are precluded from new partners in their obligation. The New Testament is evidence enough that 'whosoever will may come', not

only as invitees into faith but also as apostles for it. It was part of
Paul's calling, as he saw it, to overcome Jewish scruples he once
had shared about risking with 'Gentiles' the treasures of faith. His
pastoral nurture of them via his epistles gave full proof of his belief
in their convertibility, their capacity for holiness. As long as 'Christ
was in them', there was 'the hope of glory', whether in Corinth of
proverbial depravity or among the sophisticates of Colossae. For
him, to narrow the access to faith would be to doubt the resources
of grace. Only the open church could bear the open word or suffice
the open world.

But if such world currency authenticates mission, there are two
sides to the coin. The witnesses must be open to the invitees. They
are not bestowing what is theirs by some patent of their own: they
are bearing what is inherently meant elsewhere. They proceed in a
world of cultural diversity. Their own immediacies of language,
usage, race and time have to mediate what transcends them. There
is in the act of taking faith a de-monopolizing which works also in
its reception. The receivers must transcribe its meaning into their
own expressiveness. Mission, when it is right, is making tribute to
difference in the worlds of humanity precisely in moving by relevance to them.

That Christian mission has all too often failed in this vocation is
obvious enough. Its circumstances have induced it into exploiting
factors it ought to have scrutinized far more sharply, such as political
advantage, technical resources, inequalities of many kinds. It was
easy enough to make dependents where it was only rightly seeking
colleagues, and prefer a docile to a critical response. But the genius
of what it took was to 'make disciples' of the thing itself, not
crippingly of those who carried it. The church had been obeying
what came to be formulated as 'the great commission' long before
the words themselves. But when it found shape in Matthew 28.19,
it spoke, literally, of 'discipling all nations'. The verb is transitive:
'the nations' are its object, by a baptism of them, not an extraction
from out of them into some other identity. The whole biblical
doctrine of creation and grace underwrites this understanding.[11]

Accordingly, to receive the word is to possess a birthright. All
that birth has moulded and conferred has part in the possessing.
The faith counts nothing human alien. It needs what we have been
as party to what we must become. So participation is at once critical

and positive. Was it not that way in the New Testament? The first apostles confirmed Jewish identity in peoplehood to God as a vital corollary of the gospel. But they saw it accessible to all humanity and out of its first particularism. Something was being perpetuated in being also transformed. That precedent may be said to be relevant to every engagement of Christian mission with the diversity of cultures and their religious understanding of themselves.

The engimatic serenity of those faces of the Buddha may seem to have no place for the wood and nails of Jesus' travail. They contemplate a different world and await a different reward. They lack the crown of thorns. Yet they question all who heed them, about the true nature and the goal of selfhood. They represent a universe of discourse where the nature of compassion can draw Buddhist and Christian together while verdicts about it remain in utter contrast. Sadly, we have inside the Christian scriptures themselves no explicit relating to religious meanings outside the Mediterranean world and the first Christian century. But the instinct we find there to 'go' into the world they did and could reach should suffice us in the same confidence. For the 'going' was never merely geographical. It was a perspective of relevance for which it was natural to speak of 'the world', while still in some ignorance of its width and its diversity. We cannot take Paul out of Philippi or John from Ephesus, nor can we locate Peter in Varanasi. But the world-tradition they exemplified has contemporary fulfilment in a living readiness for all that width and diversity have come to mean for us. The ends of the gospel are 'in the ends of the earth', not as 'the eyes of a fool' (Proverbs 17.24) but by the necessities of truth – necessities which mission must serve and only dialogue can learn.

(vii)

But, it must be asked, is there not some arrogance in thus assuming that Christianity must relate to others in this kind of indebtedness? Will it not seem like a willingness for encounter only on its own terms? Should not other faiths be first assured of immunity from expectation from the Christian side? Does our common humanness not require that all interpretations of it should meet on equal ground? Is not any mission, however sensitive, and from whatever quarter, a kind of spiritual imperialism, something to abjure?

The questions are frequently posed and are often well-intentioned. Certainly all faiths deserve to be exempt from vulgar aggression and crude competitiveness. If not, any and every mission is betrayed. But shall we be relating at all if we are not ourselves? Can dialogue ever begin, still less conclude, in the absence of conviction? It is on every faith to formulate how it wills to see and serve its distinctiveness and why that distinctiveness is essential to the world. Only so doing can faiths significantly meet. There is about them all a certain spiritual self-assurance in maintaining an identity at all. Within necessary co-existence in contemporary cosmopolis all have to be in true sense tolerant of each other. Can that tolerance extend to being – under proper safeguards – susceptible to meanings from each other, meanings seen as fit for recognition? If not thus alert to each other, are they even alive within themselves?

That the answers here are often negative can be variously explained. There are massive historical, political and social factors making for closed minds and systems, multitudes for whom meanings are predetermined by life-situations from which they have no escape. But for some, confinement is deliberate. It is useful to ask how different faiths will their own immunity within dialogue, or dialogue apart. Gandhi felt that there was something almost obscene about converting out of anything. No doubt that stance, for Hindus, had something to do with Indian nationalism, for which Hindu loyalty could be seen as emotional fidelity. It had even more to do with the philosophy of transcendent mystery 'codified' diversely, and appropriately, for the races and cultures of mankind in their religious heritage. Given the transcendent unity, it was pointless, as well as pretentious, to want to migrate to faith elsewhere.

For Islam, there can properly be movement only from outside into it, not from within it to outside. For the final revelation is the one anticipated in the truth of all antecedent ones, the truth synonymous, in Surah 30.30, with all human nature, and into which birth destines all mankind until parents divert them. Within the absolute veto on what is 'idolatrous', Islam has been tolerant of such diverted heritages of faith and practice, but leaves no option for the Muslim to accede to them.

Judaism is uniquely concerned for the separate persistence of faith. For assimilation threatens its very *raison d'être*. Its role has not normally turned on outside recruitment. Preservation of the born community is paramount. Dialogue helps to interpret and commend this necessity. Vis-à-vis Christianity, Jews experience a sharp complex of emotions arising from the travail about Messiah, the desperate history of Christian triumphalism and the anxieties of Jewish identity. While the Christian faith has no mandate to exclude any from its open reach, it has compelling reason to care rightly for how its openness is perceived and how obeyed. In no direction is that obligation more insistent than in the perceptions required of it by the tragic sufferings and the long dignity of Judaism and its people.[12]

(viii)

All in all, convertibility has to be seen, by the Christian in the plural world, not first in institutional terms of adherence and description, but rather in awakening to the crisis in selfhood and to the claims of the human world around it, as these are illuminated and resolved in the 'givens' of 'God in Christ', of the faith and fellowship they constitute. The commendation of these 'givens' is an invitation to know them for what they are. But 'that they are so' is no imposition of mere dogma, no arbitrary assertiveness calculated to override demur or doubt or distrust. These have to be undertaken in converse with the dubious and in discerning of their mind. This means, in turn, a lively sympathy with the mind-sets of the world.

Properly the question about mission is not whether, but how. There is no single aegis within the Christian diversity able to legislate on how. There is only appeal to the Holy Spirit. This, given our waywardness and perversity, will not yield a uniform result. The divine Spirit has his *kenosis*, his stooping into human long-suffering, no less than the divine Son.[13] There will be Christian ventures in the world that try the Holy Spirit deeply. The authentic is only made the more urgent by the unworthy.

If the Christian is properly bringing to others an interpretation of themselves which is also an invitation into faith and a presentation of community, what happens, some may ask, of the commission to baptize? Can we think of convertibility without 'the sign' of faith? Was it not 'baptizing into the Name' to which the church was called? Indeed, but did not Jesus speak of the whole drama of his ministry and of its climax as 'a baptism to be baptized with' (Luke

12.50)? And what is 'the name' if not the storied significance of that
drama? So then, the interpretation, the invitation, the presentation,
for which we plead become – in the receiving – a baptism of the
heart and mind, an initiation into 'the name'. Formal 'sign' may
follow in its own time: perhaps not at all. What happens has,
anyway, to tangle with the complex of misconception and to fulfil
itself in spiritual obedience. It needs to come through this before
engaging with civil and religious law and with communal identity.
The intrusion of these may well obscure the meaning of the continuity within which, as I stressed earlier, all obedience must happen.
Due sense of truth, grasped by mind and will together, is not well
served by the kind of trophy image mission has often attached to
human response. Wherever truth is transacted between reverent
persons, it is well that there be a certain self-abnegation on both
sides. This will best fulfil a ministry called to cherish persons in
their own right and personhood in all its mystery. A vulgar apologist
is a contradiction in terms.

It is sometimes argued that the history of Christian mission has
caused it to forfeit the right to continue, that it should heed a call
to desist. That failures and ignorances have attended its way is not
denied. There are those who propose to write its obituary.[14] For
many dialogue and 'Christian Aid' have displaced it within the
programme of the churches. But the logic of all its trials and temptations, and of how it has succumbed beneath them, is for a surer
grasp of the indebtedness to all which Christ creates in hearts that
love him. It is not that intention for the world should be abandoned,
rather that it should be refined. Dialogue has the potential to achieve
this. Christian faith cannot be itself without the will to discipleship.
It has to see its openness to all as explicit in its reading of
humanity.

Perhaps we can best capture what convertibility means in the
words of Saint Bernard on the Christian Feast of the Annunciation.
They have to do with the conception and the reception which belong
together in all trust with truth. They speak both the taking and the
receiving that conversion means. They are apt to both parties.

Answer the angel speedily . . . Speak the word and receive the
Word: offer what is yours and conceive what is of God: give what

is temporal and embrace what is eternal. . . . Let your humility put on boldness and your modesty be clothed with trust. . . . In this one thing, fear not presumption: open your heart to faith.[15]

9

Where is Home?

(i)

A question all must ask unless their faith is a bastion or a prison. In thoroughfares we meet and greet, but as those who come and go from homes of conviction and communities that house the selves we are. Cosmopolis is our common planetary place, and all our thoroughfares criss-cross it. It is surely into homes, however, that genuine encounter must repair. The deepest exchanges cannot well remain where we cannot accede to be guests or offer to be hosts. Meeting is kin to hospitality.

'Where home is' is what only each occupant can describe, provided they take due responsibility for co-occupants. In relating to others we speak only for ourselves. Witness is best told in personal meanings. Truly there is no such thing as 'a solitary religion', as John Wesley learned.[1] Yet 'Jesus, lover of *my* soul' was the core of his experience. Without the personal pronoun Christianity cannot be stated. 'The Son of God loved me', 'my Lord and my God', 'I am a witness of the sufferings of Christ' – speak, in Paul, Thomas and Peter, the language of the New Testament. It remains so for the contemporary Christian. Without the personal equation there is no faith confession. The only hospitality I can offer is where I have my home. When we turn aside off the street we are hosts with guests, interpreting and savouring habitations of the heart.

The enterprise is necessarily personal. Yet it has to do with what has long endured and taken to itself bewildering diversity. When we come privately inside to meet, Jew and Muslim, Christian and Buddhist, Hindu and Sikh, how do we wrestle with the legacies, the contradictions, the compromises, that go with our identities? Is

'Christian' a descriptive that any *one*, as insider, can categorically define or aspire to represent? Other 'witnesses' may be so far rivals as to count the first one false. All faiths know the problem and only those within can undertake the definition of consistency. What is in hand in this chapter is one Christian attempt to say: 'Here's where I live,' alert to all the other verdicts there could be from those who share the name. Every faith has a personal equation.

One who lived perplexity as painfully as any was the English poet of the First World War, Wilfred Owen. He wrote of himself as 'a primitive Christian becoming more and more Christian as I walk the unchristian ways of Christendom'.[2] His poetry lives in the irony of the will to faith within the evil of the world. He was 'a conscientious objector with a very seared conscience'.[3] He saw the war which he abhorred as, nevertheless, a personal Gethsemane he should not evade. He knew himself required to redeem situations after the manner of the cross of Jesus even though they entirely violated the ethic of the Sermon on the Mount. Life seemed to offer him ethical propriety only at the price of self-exclusion from the real travail of humanity. He decided to belong where the anguish lay. He died within five days of the war's end. 'The unchristian ways of Christendom' set the paradox of his Christianity.

It is clear that being Christian is no easy rule of thumb but has within it a crisis of decision, a need to undertake responsibility for the very obedience we bring. To this point we will return. But there is first a clue in Wilfred Owen's description of his Christianity as 'primitive'. All faiths are aware of development in them, regarded by some of the faithful as distortion needing to be corrected or disowned. That question, in turn, generates much inner debate and contention. No religion is exempt from controversy about what is legitimate and what compromising in its definition. For to endure long, as religions do, and to command obedience, is to make loyalty a crucial issue, setting some against others in argument and passion. The 'primitive' will then often be invoked as an arbiter, without resolving matters. Either development is thereby discredited or is the only form in which the 'primitive' can be had. Christianity is no stranger to this dilemma.

Some Christians will look for original Christianity in the ministry and teaching of Jesus, others in the faith of the first apostles in its documentation in the New Testament, others in the subsequent

formulation of creed and tradition by the ecumenical councils. It is
vital to remember that the first of these can only be had in the shape
the second gave to it. Its originality in Jesus is not in doubt and
demands to be carefully explored. However, he never wrote anything.[4] His teaching was wholly oral. Everything about him, his
parables, the Beatitudes, his education of disciples, his personal
impact – all were retained in the memory of followers. Only second
to what he was to them was what he allowed them to be to him –
repositories of his teaching and legatees of his ministry and meaning.
It was, therefore, through them, and them alone, that he and his
significance are present in history and available to all seekers after
the truth of him. Alternative evidence about Jesus is minimal in
both Jewish and Roman history and scarcely enough for us to
know of him at all. It is either Jesus via the disciples or Jesus by
conjecture.

(ii)

Here is the crux of the matter if we are seeking the 'primitive' in
Christianity. Did they faithfully deliver the Jesus-referent of all they
were and said and did? Or did they somehow miss-present him? I
am not asking if the Gospels are infallible – a foolish request.
Infallibility does not sensibly belong with portraits. Portraits are
interpretations taken from their sitters. If the Gospels did significantly falsify their Jesus-theme the rest is silence. But did they?

The question being central, we had better undertake it radically.
To do so it is necessary to realize the inter-relation of event and
record. Such inter-relation obtains in all historiography. We have
to ask what Jesus must have been to have engendered the docu-
mented faith. His personality and ministry reach us through the
film of the disciples' mind from whom it was printed out in the
literature we have. Complex factors were evidently present in that
process into text – memory, tradition, collection, recollection, edit-
ing, shaping, and redacting, all transpiring within the exigencies of
life and growth, of community deriving from the origins that were
entering into record. There are large tasks of scholarship in rightly
relating the four canonical Gospels to the original disciples and
together to Jesus himself. These tasks, however, have to do with a

vital connection that was always there. It is this reciprocal relation, its credential being its very existence, with which we are concerned.

To hold that the credentials of Jesus stand in the very existence of the church is not to imply that believing makes it so or that sheer assertion is the way of faith. It is to say that the familiar debate about a 'Jesus of history' and a 'Christ of faith' is not about a mutual exclusion. It is about the fact of an inter-relation, an inter-explanation. It was the 'faith' which derived from the 'history', the 'history' which issued into the 'faith'. The two belong together as origin and sequel. Whether the origin was rightly comprehended in the sequel is the question for which scholars and believers are responsible. It cannot be resolved by ignoring either in reckoning with the other.

The Christian saying 'Here's where I live' is setting discipleship in a confidence that the original disciples had it right when they identified Jesus, through cross and resurrection, as the Christ from God. 'Confidence' is the proper word. There is no absolute guarantee. The New Testament itself, in its very character as scripture, is not infallibilizing absolutes. How could it be, when its Gospels have the form they do and its epistles are so obviously occupied with living situations in communal education into meaning and behaving? Like the faith itself, they are scriptures inviting trust. Their witness is open to scrutiny and proper for scholarly assessment, but only finally verified in the personal experience that ventures upon its open credentials. Those who first did so spoke characteristically of 'Our Lord Jesus Christ' – a possessive pronoun plural, a personal name, a fulfilled office and a loving title.

(iii)

The Jesus of that first creed – for such it was – taught and ministered in the world of Judaic belief, worship and Messianic hope. 'Galilee of the nations' was cosmopolitan, and it may well be that Jesus and his disciples knew Greek.[5] His teaching was rooted in the sovereignty of God. Its keynote was always 'the kingdom of heaven' or '. . . of God'. Jesus the Jew, as modern Jewish scholarship is properly eager to insist,[6] frequented the synagogue, cherished the Sabbath and addressed himself to 'the hope of Israel'. Yet there is enough in his story to underwrite the readiness for Gentiles which the church promptly pursued in continuing his mission. When his parables began 'A certain man . . .' there was no limit of tribe or race. The meaning of the Beatitudes was universal. The Sabbath could be over-ridden by the claims of compassion.

It was, however, in his sense of the Fatherhood of God and his own Sonship in its meaning that Jesus was distinctive. The awareness in him of an ever-present, all-embracing divine grace informed his acceptance of vocation. It fulfilled itself in his welcome to the needy and rejected. It was there in his assurance of hope to the anxious. Presumptuous as it seemed to his critics, it inspired him to speak as if he were instrumental to the divine pardon itself. There was, mysteriously, in him a correlation between the divine attributes and his own expression of them in his verdicts about sin and mercy, his way with the guilt-ridden, and his reaction to the authority of priests and scribes. It was from an inner authority of his own that he preached and represented 'the kingdom of God'. It is not surprising that many, down the centuries, should have seen it sufficient to esteem him as superbly a teacher and retrieve him from what they see as the complexity of the creeds.[7] The first Christians had that option, but manifestly they did not take it. When they confessed 'Our Lord Jesus Christ', they gathered the teaching, character and personality of 'the man from Nazareth' into a perception of his identity as 'Son of God', believing that only so could they explain his ministry as they had known it.

The reason belongs with the culmination of that ministry in the climax of tragedy, in Jesus crucified, where the house and home of Christian faith is fully reached. His cross belongs with the whole significance of the Sermon on the Mount. The accents and patterns of his teaching clashed with institutional Jewry in Temple and synagogue. His brief career had the likeness of a gathering storm, despite the eager celebration with which his compassion was popularly crowned. Indeed that very adulation sharpened the antipathy of those who saw their tradition threatened or their authority impugned.

At the heart of the issues was Messiahship. Public acclaim of the teacher could hardly dissociate Messianic possibilities, given the excitable and volatile atmosphere of Palestine under Roman yoke. We must read the ministry of Jesus as locating the Messianic within the theodicy for which Job and psalmist yearned, and within the precedent of suffering prophethood agonizingly exemplified by Jeremiah. Did not the precedent fit the emerging situation of his own ministry? At a critical moment Jesus consulted his disciples with the question: 'Whom do men say that I am? Whom do you say . . . ?' (Matthew 16.13–15). He was searching with them, and beyond them, for the logic of the actual ministry, the tragic climax into which he was plainly heading. His teaching would never be retracted, but nor could it avoid encounter with establishment. Conspiracies of expediency were on foot against him. Should he stay, arguably secure, in Galilee? Should he challenge Jerusalem, citadel of all the stakes? Might Messiahship in fact lie in the very acceptance to suffer – not as some unworthy attempt to precipitate divine intervention and an apocalyptic 'kingdom', but as the very principle of redemptive love 'bearing the sin of the world'?

Reading the impending crisis as 'the cup my Father has given me' Jesus undertook to suffer, to go the way of the cross as the logic of what he faced, the logic of the divine mind, and the logic of who and how Messiah must be. The three logics came together in Gethsemane and made the agony he suffered among uncomprehending and finally deserting followers. The resurrection was his vindication, a vindication that had the form of aligning his community's perception of the drama with his own, their assurance of his being Christ with his antecedent achievement of it.

As we have seen in previous allusions to this climax of history and faith, it is the place where Christians live, the house of Jesus-interpretation into which others are invited. Christianity is not a facile or an optimistic faith. It has at its heart 'the sin of the world'. It reads the cross of Christ as epitome of the wrongness of humanity and the measure of what God does with it, did with it in Jesus, in an answering activity of grace from which forgiveness flows and by which 'the kingdom of God' makes its way in human hearts. As such it stands as the very index to the divine nature, the signature of the divine hand. 'God was in Christ reconciling the world . . .' (II Corinthians 5.19). The evil of the world is not answered only by a law which indicts it, nor an exhortation which deplores it, nor a judgment which condemns it. These leave it, in different senses, untransformed and unreversed. In every evil situation, love suffers and, suffering, overcomes.

Born of such conviction, identified and warranted in 'our Lord

Jesus Christ', Christians, standing in that vicarious achievement, pondered on its sources. Entering into an experience of forgiveness and associating it with this history, they read it as an enterprise 'born of God', or, in credal language, 'begotten of the Father'. It is clear that the doctrine of the incarnation is consonant with the experience that flowed from the reality of Jesus, the fact of the Christ. It is an explanation of experience. Job's sensing 'the fellowship of God about my tent' in an earlier chapter becomes an inclusive perception of the ultimate 'tent of meeting', where, in old Hebraic imagery, 'the tabernacle of God is with men'.[8] The whole significance of Jesus becomes the divine presence, the divine action, in the human world, known as such by its realist engagement with the guidance and salvation of humanity undertaken and achieved in him as Lord and Christ.

This is the meaning of 'only . . .' in the credal faith, inclusively, essentially, one-ly, consistently as being where the unity of God is evident. What eventuates in time is from eternity. The gospel begins historically with birth and baptism: it begins eternally in the nature of God – begins in the later with the sense of 'belongs and issues', as drama and dramatist. The doctrine of the Virgin Birth does not avail as an extraneous wonder. It was never in the forefront of Christian preaching, nor did the first hearers in Galilee ever say, 'Ah, yes, this is the one whose birth was so strange those years ago.' The story was a fitting sign of the divine-human action, retrospectively acknowledged to have happened in all that Jesus proved to be. The brooding 'Holy Spirit' and 'the handmaid of the Lord' expressed the divine intention in the Christ, and the human sphere, from the very womb, of his being so. This is not to say that the birth of Jesus could not have been other than this way, if we were to make that requirement itself the crux of the gospel. For then we would be locating only in mysterious pregnancy the whole design of God, whereas pregnancy itself only served that design. Serving it, it also truly parabalized the vital interplay of human agency and divine purpose.[9] 'Conceived by the Holy Spirit' must never be separated from 'born of the Virgin Mary'. The two clauses belong firmly together. It is clear that 'the conception of the Holy Spirit' embraces all that the entire event of Jesus as the Christ constituted in the economy of God, as symphony does the mind of a composer

– a truth implicit in that most moving of New Testament reporting: 'There stood by the cross of Jesus his mother.'

Some Christian tradition derives a quality of co-redemption in Jesus' mother, but the living history of Messianic decision and action belongs to Jesus alone. It is his cross which alone avails. She once stood uncomprehending on the edges of the crowd when he informed an over-excited admirer of them both that all around who 'heard and kept the word of God' were equally his mothers and his family (Luke 11.27–28). Nevertheless, her dogged loyalty endured the travail of the crucifixion and found its completion in the birthing of the church. By Luke's inspiration we have the haunting paradoxes of the *Magnificat*, the Song of Mary, to capture the pattern of inter-acting wills – divine grace and human means – that characterizes 'the kingdom of heaven'.[10] Such is the secret of the 'highly favoured' – a dignity for which the economy of grace makes ample space in human lives, as that which, however uniquely Mary's, is in measure the vocation of all.[11]

(iv)

'Here, then, is where we live', in these perspectives of what Paul called 'God in Christ'. If Job's desperate plea is being echoed around us, 'O that I knew where I might find him' (Job 23.3), here is the 'where' of our answer. Or, in the loved phrase of the prophets about 'the place of the name . . .', this is 'the place', the making good in history of the ancient Aaronic blessing: 'the Lord lift upon you the light of his face' (Numbers 6.23–26). Paul picks up the allusion and with his characteristic richness of phrase writes of 'the light of the knowledge of the glory of God in the face of Jesus Christ'. 'The face', in Hebraic tradition, meant the divine presence, and 'light' the ability to know it as it would be known, or reality in recognition. That same tradition set great store by event in history, most of all the Exodus from Egypt when – in the meaning of the words to Moses – 'I will be there as he who I there will be'[12] – the liberated people learned Yahweh's 'name' in Yahweh's action. In the New Testament all that occurred in the event of Jesus as the Christ was to the first Christians the self-expression, the self-giving, of God, the history in which he was dependably known.[13] What had been lived through was the clue to what might be believed. 'The word of life' was 'that which they had seen, and heard, and handled' (I John 1.1).

This 'house of faith' is not a fortress made impregnable and, for that reason, scarcely habitable. It is ever ready for interrogation: it invites trust only because it welcomes scrutiny. It is aware that there are those who read its story otherwise, who think it spiritually overloaded or too decisively interpreted. Its alert inhabitants know that their confidence is final faith, not final guarantee. They believe they come to God through Jesus Christ only because God is truly 'come to' in him.[14] We only have Jesus as he was – and is – because we have God as, through Jesus, we believe him to be. The truth of revelation has always to be intrinsic to itself, as must be evident in the double fact of our need of it and capacity for it. The Christian 'house of faith' shares that situation with all truth-claims, but it is distinctive in associating 'need' and 'capacity' with a rational register of the natural order as intending us by creation, with a realist register of human wrong explicit in a single Christ-history, and with a glad register of forgiveness and liberation through inward experience of that history's power to save.

(v)

If this is to be a 'primitive Christian', the 'original' to which it returns is not the ethic and teaching of Jesus without the drama of the passion, nor a cosmic Christ somehow divorced from the human ministry. Rather it is these in one, the integrity of event and interpretation, the interdependence of what happened and what it came to mean, to which the New Testament points and without which no New Testament would exist.

What, however, of the third test of 'the primitive' which we noted earlier – namely the formulation of credal christology in the ecumenical councils up to Chalcedon in 451 which approved the creed of Nicaea (325) and the creed later known as 'Nicene' (381). Here, certainly, was development. Some would regard it as unwarranted, over-subtle and unduly tied to the mental interest of its own time. Coptic and other Eastern Christianity never accepted its formula, though the reasons why – apart from political and provincial tensions – had more to do with a zeal for definition which was in danger of turning meaning into enigma.

There was a resounding confidence about the five hundred and more bishops assembled at Chalcedon:

> We all with one voice confess our Lord Jesus Christ one and the same Son, the same perfect in Godhead, the same perfect in manhood, truly God and truly man, of a rational soul and body, co-essential with the Father according to the Godhead and co-essential with us according to the manhood . . . to be acknowledged in two natures, without confusion, without mutation, without division, without separation, the distinction of natures being by no means taken away by the union, but rather the property of each nature being preserved and concurring in one person and one hypostasis.[15]

The complexity of language at least bears witness to a will to trust words and satisfy reason. Yet there is a sense in which what is being meant is preoccupied with anxiety about what is not being meant. Contemporary Christians are more minded to see 'God in Christ' in terms of deed, of action and event, than in terms of essence, ontology and nature. 'Substance' in the credal vocabulary can at least be read now in the modern sense of how the event of Christ 'substantiates' the reality of God.

There are, however, those Christians today who read the formulations 'in terms of intrinsic rationality' operating 'like a natural law in science which . . . disqualifies any other theoretic construct of the same data'. But that instinct to align religious truth with scientific verifiability nevertheless safeguards itself by the preface *Credo*: 'I believe'. Thus:

> Correlated to the open range of belief which indicates more than can be expressed, the formal statements of the Creed are incomplete and inadequate, but are as such revisable in the light of the inexhaustible intelligibility of God to which they direct us . . . By asserting our doctrinal convictions under the rubric of *belief* we claim that they fall short of their intention.[16]

Most co-occupants of where Christians live would be ready for that conclusion, though with differing measures of what 'revisable' entails and certainly about 'intelligibility' being 'inexhaustible'.

Creeds are for living currency, not for deposit in a bank of static security.

(vi)

In the faith of 'God in Christ' there was, for the 'primitive Christians' of the New Testament, an immediate development that concerned, not the definition of faith but the discovery of fellowship. 'God in Christ' was perceived to be 'reconciling the world'. Cosmic dimension was seen to belong not only to the Christ in glory but to the church in being. It is remarkable how 'world-association' emerges so clearly and quickly, whether about God 'loving it', or sin attaching to it, or commission into it. Faith had not previously talked this way. 'Election' and 'covenant' meant a preserved community, some would say a perpetuated tribalism which, for humanity's own sake, could not belong with it except by separation. That was the old order. From within it, its own heirs broke free of it in proclaiming there were 'no more Gentiles', no more *goyim*. All were to be 'one in Christ Jesus'. This was clearly seen as the logic of the cross itself – a 'lifting up' 'drawing all' to itself. They did not mean a universally successful salvation, but a universally accessible one. The condition of repentance and faith would still obtain, but community would now be constituted, not for some by fact of birth, but for all by dint of pardon and acceptance. The church both defined and created itself in this discovery. It saw itself as heir to the magnificent meaning of 'priesthood to God', of vocation to hallow land and kin and power – that triangle of human identity – which belonged with Israel and Hebrew destiny, but the heritage was now the potential vocation of all peoplehood, all nations 'bringing their glory and honour' into the kingdom of God.

Inevitably the development was painful. Privilege is always reluctant to surrender even in fulfilment, the more so when exceptionality is on behalf of those who cannot share it. Then there are altruistic reasons for being self-sufficient. The strains of the development are evident in the New Testament as those 'primitives' – Jewish for the most part – wrestled with the problems of Gentile inclusion. Were the necessary rigours of Jewish law to be relaxed? Could there be table fellowship? What of the sinister undertow of Gentile depravity, indiscipline, idolatry and promiscuity persisting beneath the surface of unified community? Should not the church only recruit itself through the synagogue?

An issue that ran so deep inevitably meant a clash of personalities and exchanges of reproach and enmity. Paul was in the forefront of these stresses, and the Fourth Gospel is vivid witness to their presence in the very writing of the Jesus record. We have to keep in mind that we do not hear sufficiently from the Jewish element within the churches, and the fall of Jerusalem in AD 70 desperately intensified the need for self-defence, the more so since Christians had refused to share in the revolt against Rome.

The first 'Gentilizing' of the church was joyous and instinctive. Later, by the second century, it had become a sad de-Judaizing as, increasingly, the Jewish dimension diminished and Greek instincts took over theology and Roman patterns Christian structures. But within the New Testament the pastoral teaching of the apostles was shaped precisely by the need to implement the conversion of pagans in a moral education of its meaning, not only to initiate them into a true 'newness of life', but also to reassure Jewish Torah-lovers that Gentiles were truly redeemable. Paul's epistles, for example, consistently move from affirmation of faith to discipline of life: 'I beseech you, therefore . . .' (Romans 12.1), where the appeal finds its logic in the long recital of 'God in Christ' and takes its confidence from the same source. 'The mind of Christ' had to be 'the mind' of the community, formed in them not merely by exposition but by inward sway, as music in musicians.

It is here we must look for an answer to the question 'Did Jesus intend the church?' It is appropriate to ask. For much that the church has been and remains can only be judged far from his intention. Nevertheless, its will for the world could be seen as translating into the human whole the readiness for the reject, the outcast, the prodigal, the tax-gatherer, which had characterized his ministry. The Gospels are unambiguous about the Jewishness of Jesus. His life and ministry were certainly confined to Palestine and southern Lebanon. The Gospels are equivocal about his attitude to non-Jews, and some suspect that the picture is influenced by the subsequent universalism. The ultimate question must be what his geographical confines essentially contained. There is no doubt as to what the 'primitives' understood from them. If they were who and how they were because of him, then his intention for the world must have been latent and fulfilled in theirs. We need to understand again, however, that their sense of world-mission was well under way before they came by its mandate in the form of 'the great commission' with its full baptismal formula in Matthew 28.19–20. The obedience found words long after it had found expression. That is in the very nature of faith-documentation.

So then, to want to say to others when we meet, 'Here is home', is to show a very personal abode which, however, can only be so described because it is one shared, uneasily yet gratefully, with a vast diversity of people and times, of accents and dictions that caution but also hearten the personal equation. 'There are many with me,' as the psalmist said. Being a house of faith and of fellowship, it is effectively a house of worship.

(vii)

When old John of Damascus was asked about Christianity he pointed to the icons – the icons that brought together the piety of art, the personality of faith, the patterns of sanctity and the aura of mystery. Behind the iconostasis where they met the reverent gaze of the devout was the inner sanctuary of the eucharistic celebration from where the consecrated bread and wine would be brought through the iconostasis for the perception and reception of the faithful.

There are many 'shapes of the Christian liturgy', Eastern and Western, staged like drama or done in simplicity, and many emphases of interpretation, varieties of intention, in the common fact of sacramental food. Saying 'Here is home' on the part of a Christian will be a personal account of 'holy communion' – excepting those who find their sacrament in silence or, for reasons critical to them, abstain from sacrament itself. All, with differing accents, will explain themselves by reference to a command they attribute to Jesus himself, saying, as he took bread and wine, 'Do this in remembrance of me.'[17]

The words have a vast and awesome legacy of fulfilment, engaging with great structures of hierarchy, rituals of celebration, theologies of efficacy and forms of architecture, music and language. But the central reality is

. . . of those innumerable millions of entirely obscure faithful men and women, every one with his or her own individual hopes and fears and joys and sorrows and loves – and sins and temptations and prayers – who . . . each worshipped at the Eucharist . . . The sheer stupendous quantity of the love of God which this ever repeated action has drawn from the obscure Christian multitude through the centuries is in itself an overwhelming thought.[18]

How would they all characterize what the central reality was? And what of the great controversies of doctrine which have gathered around it, troubling or bewildering the responses of these private souls?

The task here must be to undertake the onus of history while exploring the private sense, reading what has been contentious as the price of what is always crucial. There are four evident strands in the meaning of Holy Communion. They are the consecration of the created world, the act of living again in the history of redemption, the food analogy of personal faith, and the reality of corporate fellowship. Each element penetrates the other: together they are God and humanity in mutuality through Jesus Christ.

Bread and wine are, manifestly, tokens of the interaction between the potential of the good earth to yield them and the capacity of the human hand and mind to have them yielded. Neither is just 'natural' like rain or weeds. They are products, yet products which hinge on processes. Skills with plough and mill and oven are necessary to bread, yet none could avail were soil not soil, stone not stone and fire not fire. The producing wit and wisdom turn on a chemistry they did not contrive but with which they co-operate, a means they did not originate but can employ. Wine, likewise, stems only from vineyards by the same will to techniques that exist only through their relation to a world where they can function.

In this quality bread and wine are symptomatic of all the economies, the usages, the products of humanity. They are tokens of a physical universe and a dominion-holding creaturehood. In this measure of its meaning, holy communion is close to what we earlier studied in Muslim *salat*, which we saw to be the acknowledgment of accountable *khilafah*, or 'lordship', in the natural order by the status of humanity. Just as prostration symbolizes gratitude and awe, so erectness spells responsible acceptance of control. Comparably the Christian taking of bread and wine hallows the possession of all material things, the manipulation (i.e. the handling) of all that is. It is the recognition of divine mercy in all we are and have. It intends to make all usage reverent, all occasions holy. It is the visible corrective to that despair of meaning, or secular repudiation of obligation, which we studied in Chapter 1. To the doctrine of creaturehood the sacrament adds the practice of its meaning in the reiterated taking and receiving of the sacramental elements. All things, it reminds the scientist, the engineer, the marketeer, all things are yours on trust. Here is the clue to a universe of means.

(viii)

That material significance of eucharist is fused with the history of redemption. The meaning deepens from the gardens of conjured fertility to the garden of Gethsemane, the place of suffering love. 'On the night in which he was betrayed, Jesus took bread.' It was around the Jewish Passover. It enlisted those associations of crisis and liberation. The Exodus which had once been, as we saw, 'the place of the name', was being transposed into the different key of Messianic action where the divine name would have its ultimate 'place'. It was innovative yet within the Jewish discourse of divine event. 'This is my body given for you', 'this is my blood shed for you' meant in the Upper Room on the lips of Jesus present 'in the midst' that bread and wine were charged with the significance: on his part of self-giving – on theirs of participation. 'Take and eat, take and drink.'

As we saw in the conclusion of Chapter 4, the disciples were uncomprehending in bewilderment and an appalling sense of something dire impending. The meaning would only be clear when he drank it 'new with them in the kingdom'.[19] It would be known only in the sequel when the significance of his cross and passion became the open secret of their retrospect. But in that retrospect they would always be guided by the clue he had set at its heart. Without the life given, the blood shed, there could be no 'new order'. Initiation into its meaning would always return to the price, and the nature, of its inauguration.

That returning the church called *anamnesis*. It is a telling word.

It does not mean merely the recollection of that which has become pure past and needs therefore to be called back to thought. It is a re-enacting of what once happened so that its import is for ever present. The third strand of holy communion will bring us back to this point. Reenactment, however, does not make the sacrament a spectacle, a theme of theatre. The event was once for all and irrepeatable. What is renewed is the inward expression of its perpetual reality. 'Saviour of the world who by thy cross and passion hast redeemed us' is prayer into its truth, its truth alive in prayer. The fact that Jesus – as the New Testament believes – instituted it in the immediate prospect of his suffering climax of ministry means that we receive it as his own central commentary on his entire significance and, like the four Gospels, he finds it in his death.

(ix)

The historical in Holy Communion passes, then, into the participatory, into what I called the food-analogy of faith. Eating and drinking are clearly inalienable activities of each of us. There is no vicarious feeding: metabolism is within and digestions are our own. 'Thy words were found and I did eat them', said the prophet (Jeremiah 15.16). It is a very lowly metaphor, yet a vivid enough picture of what it is to digest – as we say – the significance of what we receive. Only in receiving is the nature of the sacrament complete. There is, for most Christian churches, a ministry that 'presides' over the liturgical action, in which 'humble access', confession, lections from the scriptures, credal affirmation and intercession culminate in 'the great oblation', the *anamnesis* in the sacred elements of bread and wine, consecrated for this end by *epiclesis*, or the invocation of the sanctifying Spirit, so that all present may 'present themselves' 'a living sacrifice' in the context of the once for all self-giving of the Lord. That 'giving' is renewed to them in the emblems of his death and risen life.

'Here' is 'where Christians live' – at the exchange of divine grace and personal discipleship. It is here that the personal pronoun, the individual receiving, properly belong. These were the mysteries from which the emperor George excluded the Muslim pilgrim with whom he piously shared the mystique of Jerusalem. 'The things of God', as a very ancient rubric has it, are 'for the people of God'.

Yet, essentially, according to Paul, the holy communion is itself a 'proclaiming', a 'showing' of 'the Lord's death'. An urgent duty of Christian dialogue is to have the central Christian liturgy intelligible to all. It only belongs to intimates in being an intention for all. 'Here is home' is plainly sensitive to curiosity, eager to invite.

By the same token the intimate inwardness which calls to be explained is a crowning dimension of experience. What hallows nature, celebrates grace and transacts faith, also realizes fellowship. The food-analogy belongs to what is communal as well as personal. A shared meal is a truth token. 'We are one body,' says the liturgy, 'because we all share this one bread.' As one, 'we drink the cup of the Lord'. In a significant passage in the life of the early church in Corinth, Paul – ever anxious for a right discipline – had reason to reprove unruly communicants who mistook the nature of the sacrament by turning it into a vulgar bout with hunger. He told them that they were not 'discerning the body' (I Cor.11.29). There was a double meaning. They were not realizing the sacramental 'body', treating the 'bread' as ordinary food, thus negating its significance. But also they were not recognizing community, they were not behaving as 'members one of another'. Those twin meanings of 'the body of Christ' have always belonged together in the meaning of the eucharist. The meal which 'remembers' is the meal that incorporates. This fact of 'the body of Christ' is part of the meaning of the resurrection.

The imagery of 'membership' in Christ may be pondered from another angle, namely by asking the surprising question whether anything 'in memory of Jesus' was necessary. Hardly so, for the disciples to whom the command to 'do this in remembrance' was first given. For them emphatically Jesus was, and remained, unforgettable. Their experiences had been too deep, too despairing, too awesome, to be ever forfeit from their minds. Moreover, there was the fact of his risen presence. Why then any ordinance about 'remembering'? The question is illuminating. The purpose cannot have had to do with any danger of oblivion. In a word, it did not have to do at all with *whether* he would be 'remembered', either then or since. There would be the New Testament scriptures, eloquent of how active memory was. It had to do with *how*. The supper on the night of his betrayal had to do, not with the matter of memory but with the manner.

What else might conceivably have been devised by Jesus? A ceremonial recitation of the Sermon on the Mount? A dramatic rehearsal of his works of healing? A pilgrimage to the Nazareth of his early years? None of these, only 'the breaking of the bread'. Jesus was clearly signalling the centrality of his suffering, the inclusive meaning of Messiah crucified. Not applause for wisdom, not esteem for goodness, but 'make this your own'. Paul called it 'being conformed to his death' (Philippians 3.10), meaning that the principle of redemption which Jesus fulfilled should be the pattern for our own relation to the world, its sufferings and its wrongs, so that those who know themselves redeemed become in some measure, in their turn, redeemers. It is this truth of holy communion which is meant in that other central sacrament of Christian identity, namely baptism. We can well conclude 'Here is home' with baptism, the first and last word in Christian personalism. For death and baptism in the New Testament are strangely found as analogies of each other, and death, for all religions, is the insistent question mark on life.

(x)

Drinking, washing and crossing have all been lively symbols for faiths. In cisterns water serves for ablution, in rivers for passage and transit. According to Mark, the gospel began at the river Jordan where John was baptizing. The wilderness nearby symbolized the stark realism which cities, markets and shrines could well conceal from folk busy with their concerns and entrenched in self-approval. For baptism, in the tokens of washing and of crossing over, had to do with the crisis attaching to all selfhood. Who and what am I? is the question life puts to itself. The fact that we have to die makes it more than academic. Such is existence that it can only be asked and answered in the singular, as Chapter 8 has studied. We face it in our singularity.

Nowhere does Christianity come closer to Buddhism than here, and nowhere do the two so far diverge. I have to decide about me. Can I distinguish, in being a self – the question is what being one entails – between a selfhood which is legitimate and a selfishness which is ruinous, between some 'me' that can be authentic and a 'me' I must read as illusion and so learn to abnegate? That the issue is critical is not in doubt. Buddhism, at least in its bleaker Theravada form, reads the crisis in the second sense. Selfhood is inherently selfish, trapped into acquisitiveness and the illusion of significance based on appetites transience must inevitably frustrate. I must therefore strive, on the Eightfold Path, for an inclusive disinterest in 'me' as the proper response to 'being' in such a world as ours.

The Christian, in the ultimate significance of baptism, accepts that there is indeed this crisis in my selfhood, but – sustained by the doctrine of divine creation as 'intention' for me – believes that it is not about selfhood being unselfed. Rather it is about selfhood finding a way to positive unselfishness, the sort of unselfishness which needs me as its centre and condition. Its call is not to a self-forfeiture but to a self-surrender. There *is* a 'No' I need to say to 'me'. It does not, however, 'cancel' me into disinterest: it sets my interest into co-operation with the work of love in the world. So doing it is the liberation for which the Buddhist yearns, but with the difference that the liberty is the self in true being, not the self in abnegation of the will to be.

This experience of 'conversion' we have explored in part in the previous chapter, where we noted how far definitive of who I am are the determinants of place and time, of nurture and culture. With those givens in their universal acceptability in God's order, Christian faith has always read the transformation of the self by setting it inside the paradigm of Jesus crucified. This is the clear perspective of the epistles. 'If one man died for all, then in him all mankind has died' (II Corinthians 5.14). 'I have been crucified with Christ, nevertheless I live . . .' (Galatians 2.20). 'His own self bore our sins . . . that we being dead to sins should live for righteousness' (I Peter 2.24). In the First Epistle of John our human sense of sinfulness is linked with the dying of Jesus as the shape it has in history. Where we learn that sinful truth of us we find what 'cleanses us from sin'. The whole argument of the Epistle to the Romans is based on this interpretation of the cross as incriminating us all and, in turn, inviting us into an acceptance of forgiveness on terms which require us to become forgivers in our own relationships. That liberation from guilt and from enmity – 'of sin the double cure'[20] – is our 'unselfing', but one which happens inside a self that becomes thereby 'a child of God, an inheritor of the kingdom of heaven'.

What death and resurrection were to Jesus in the very history of our faith, the 'No' to the old self and the 'Yes' of the new self are to be to us. 'Reckon yourselves to be dead to sin and alive to God through our Lord Jesus Christ' (Romans 6.11).

The cleansing and the crossing over of baptism express and sacramentally transact this understanding of who we are and what we must become. Jesus himself likened his impending suffering to 'a baptism to be baptized with . . .' (Luke 12.50). It was natural that 'the sign of the cross' would be the mark of the rite of water initiation into faith – an initiation understood as a present fact and, as grammar has it, 'a present continuous'. The saying 'No' to self on behalf of the 'Yes' to Christ happens as a pledge and promise only in being a pattern and a practice.[21]

(xi)

It will now be clear why the mystery of death and the ritual of baptism have long been seen as parables of each other. Physical death is at the heart of the puzzle of the self. There is for us this ineluctable necessity to concede the forfeiture of being in the only way we have hitherto known it. We may talk evasively about 'If anything happens to me', but we know well to what we refer and the fact that there is no 'if' about it. It is, therefore, an apt analogy of what has to 'happen to me', if I would be a Christian self, namely a 'death to sin' for the sake of a 'new life in righteousness'. Physically, as mortal, we have to forego 'this earthly tent of our habitation' (II Corinthians 5.1), so spiritually we resolve to forego the self as sin has it for the sake of the self as grace and love can make it. Death then can tutor us, in anticipation of its inevitability, in the truth of a surrender which is the secret of authentic life. Both are mirrored for us in how our faith has read the cross of Jesus ever since it happened. In him we can 'die to self' and thereby 'live in him'.

Here then is 'where home is' as Christians meet and greet and relate. What the faiths have to say about self and about death will both unite and divide them. The verdicts differ but the wistfulness is one, since death comes to all equally and makes all equal when it comes.

If Christianity has made death a parable of baptism, how might baptism educate about death? Here we can only speak of faith. If, in the sense now studied, we have been foregoing ourselves in surrender of the false 'version' in order to know the true one, have we not been doing spiritually what physical death requires us finally to do, namely yield ourselves into a certain 'No'? That, to be sure, will be 'the last enemy', but will we not have been knowing its essence all the time? If, then, our moral surrender to the love of Christ by the 'No' to a selfish 'me' leads to finding a strange, glad 'Yes' to my being, may not our final self-surrender give us back ourselves in 'his eternal joy'? But that final dying, you say, is not choice but 'strict arrest',[22] not option, like baptism, but necessity and fate. Indeed, but necessary things can also be occasions of will and attitude: they must be if we would be intelligent about dying. We – most of us – have ample opportunity for reasoning anticipation. Inevitability, therefore, need not deny us a conscious cooperation with necessity, if the practice of self-foregoing has been central to our moral life.

We are all in transit camp. Yet what is 'transit' if there is no beyond, only this mortal whence and no eternal thither? The 'bourne' of 'the undiscovered country' is, for faith, not thereby unknown. 'His servants will serve him and they shall see his face.' 'Here, where we dwell in Christ' neither the serving nor the face are unfamiliar.

Notes

1. Cosmopolis

1. T. S. Eliot, *Murder in the Cathedral*, London 1935, p. 55.
2. In his *Towards a World Theology*, New York & London 1981, the Canadian scholar, Wilfred Cantwell Smith, would have the word 'faith' be a verb, like hope, as well as a noun. The 'faith-ing' can be thought an orientation, a pattern of mind, irrespective of doctrine or dogma. These are customarily plural as 'faiths', but this usage Smith denies. 'Faith' can only be singular. 'Faithful' in the context here, however, intends *both* the 'act' and (if such they be) the 'facts' of faith.
3. 'Starts', here, must be meant in respect of its diagnosis of inner experience. Properly, no doubt, it 'starts' from the given truth of the *dharma*, or 'teaching'.
4. Cf. the intriguing reference in the Qur'an to the Prophet's vision of the figure of revelation at 'two bows' length' away and approaching (Surah 53.9).
5. The expression may startle but is warranted. The verb *ista'mara* in the Qur'ān means to 'be planted as a colonist to wield an empire' over things. It is used of man in Surah 11.61 to denote this human 'dominion' and yields to modern Arabic the word for 'imperialism'. In the order of nature we are all imperialists.
6. Friedrich Nietzsche, *Genealogy of Morals*, I. xi.
7. For example, the Muslim Egyptian surgeon-philosopher, Muhammad Kamil Husain, in *The Hallowed Valley*, Cairo 1977, with its fading hope of the application of scientific principles effectively to society and the individual self.
8. Colin Wilson, *The World of Violence*, London 1965, p. 40.
9. The Palestinian Christian poet Tawfiq Sayigh (1924–1971), and translator of T. S. Eliot, is a case in point. See my *The Arab Christian: A*

History in the Middle East, London 1991, pp. 261–3. He is also strongly reminiscent of Franz Kafka.

10. Najib Mahfuz, *Fountain and Tomb*, ET by S. Sobhy, E. Fattouck & J. Keuneson, London 1990, No. 73, pp. 110–11.

11. Najib Mahfuz, *Thathara fauq-l-Nil*, Cairo 1966.

12. Najib Mahfuz, *Children of Gebalawi*, ET by P. Stewart, London 1981. See also Jareer Abu Haidar, *Awlad Haratina* (the Arabic title), 'An Event in the Arab World', in *Journal of Arabic Literature*, Vol. 16, 1985, and my *The Pen and the Faith*, London 1985, pp. 145–64.

13. This is the figure named 'Arafah, 'the man of knowledge', with whose debacle the novel closes.

14. Paul Davies (ed.), *God and the New Physics*, London 1983, p. 44. The writer is S. Weinberg, quoted without reference.

15. Arnold Toynbee made a neat reversal of the usual stance in his *The Western Question in Greece and Turkey. A Study in Contact of Civilizations*, London 1922, about the bane of the Western factor on local nationalisms. Cf. the remark of Hasan Saab in *Arab Federalists of the Ottoman Empire*, Amsterdam 1958, p. 205, on the Muslim's problematics in relating to the West and the alternative of 'remaining a Muslim or becoming nothing at all'.

16. George Eliot, *Essays*, ed. T. Pinney, Oxford 1968, p. 161. See also pp. 337–8. George Eliot excelled in satirical prose.

17. J. W. Cross, *Life of George Eliot*, London 1884, Vol. ii, p. 343.

18. See A. A. A. Fyzee, *A Modern Approach to Islam*, Bombay 1963; Arnold H. Green (ed.), *In Quest of an Islamic Humanism*, Cairo 1984, on Muhammad al-Nuwaihy; A. B. K. Brohi, *An Adventure in Self-Expression*, Karachi 1955.

19. See her novel, *Daniel Deronda*, 1876.

20. Iris Murdoch, *The Sovereignty of Good*, London 1970, p. 79.

21. Ibid., p. 91.

22. Richard Baxter, *Self Review*, London 1910, p. 6.

23. Ibid., p. 6 and 25.

24. Ibid., pp. xvi-xvii.

25. Ibid., p. 31.

26. Owen Chadwick, *Michael Ramsey. A Life*, London 1990, p. 407.

27. Wilfred Cantwell Smith in the 1950s warned against the designation of faiths by a negative. He thought 'Non-Buddhists' is an odd way of denoting Christians.

2. From Adamant Square and Cavil Row

1. The phrase is frequent throughout the Old Testament; it is absent in the New. This does not mean that gospel and church were indifferent to family and continuity. It indicates that 'faith' and 'faith-nurture' – not birth *per se* – is the crux of ongoing identity and ongoing community.

2. Thomas Merton, *Asian Journal*, ed. by N. Burton, P. Hart and J. Laughlin, London 1973, p. 233. The entry occurs a day or so before his tragic death.

3. *Tribute to Geza Vermes*, ed. P. R. Davies & R. T. White, Sheffield 1990, p. 158.

4. Ibid., pp. 154–5.

5. Surah 22.52 assures Muhammad that there was no messenger sent before him into whose intentions Satan did not cast insinuations. Surah 6.112 says that God appointed for every prophet an enemy. Divine over-ruling ensured that no 'enmity' via speech or thought ever succeeded in corrupting the pure word which reached the hearers and so the earthly text.

6. The distinction is Martin Buber's. See his *Moses*, Oxford 1946, p. 17.

7. For example, Fazlur Rahman in *Major Themes of the Qur'ān*, Minneapolis 1980, and *Islam and Modernity*, Chicago 1982.

8. See discussion of the crucial Qur'an passage (Surah 7.157 and 158) in my *The Event of the Qur'an*, London 1971, pp. 56–62. The word that has been taken to mean 'illiterate' has rather the force of 'unscriptured', denoting a people yet to be 'scriptured' by means of a prophet of their own people, a 'native'. This tallies with the Qur'an's point that no prophet is sent to a people who is not of their tongue (Surah 14.4).

9. None other than the famous Sufi poet, Jalal al-Din Rumi, uses precisely this metaphor of water-piping engineered through a stone lion in a Persian garden to emit a spout of water from the mouth. No one suspects the stone to be more than the channel. See *Discourses of Rumi*, ET by A. J. Arberry, London 1967, pp. 51–2.

10. 'Seem to demand' is necessary for many New Testament verses cited for a rigorous exclusivism. I Corinthians 14.8, for example, 'If the trumpet give an uncertain sound . . .', is not about 'sound doctrine' but the possible mystification in 'speaking with tongues'. See further Chapter 7 below.

11. Newman is a classic example of this dilemma. See *Apologia pro Vita Sua*, London 1864. In his *Grammar of Assent* and other writings he probed deeply and anxiously into what might be the criteria by which

to ascertain 'truth'. But its 'ascertaining' (in the precise sense of the word, i.e. 'certifying') in the sphere of religious faith meant 'ascertaining' the infallible authority and forthwith submitting unequivocally. This was the meaning of his conversion – a meaning which much in his subsequent experience called ever into question. No decision to 'go for the infallible' can escape being a judgment one makes. It does not exonerate us from decision: it short-circuits one. The current of assessment should continue flowing.

12. Martin Buber, *Two Types of Faith. A Study of the Inter-Penetration of Judaism and Christianity*, ET by N. P. Goldhawk, New York 1961.

13. Surah 30.30, where the root verb and kindred noun denote human nature, while also meaning 'religion' understood as proper to mankind. There is an essential affinity between Islam and being human when the latter is duly understood.

14. In the Book of Common Prayer the question to godparents is 'Will you be baptized in this faith?', not 'Will you have the child baptized in this faith?' The baptism is theirs in being a proxy acceptance of faith and, thereby, a pledge to ensure, as far as in them lies, a nurture which leads into it, in terms of the freedom presupposed in the subsequent 'confirmation' by the child, now capable of intelligent reckoning with what faith is and with its own anticipatory initation into it.

15. Surah 42.7 seems to validate human diversity by the observation that had God so willed he could have created mankind 'a single *ummah*, or nation'. So ethnically diverse parentage would seem also to be within the divine will.

16. *The Travels of Ibn Jubayr*, ET by R. J. C. Broadhurst, London 1952, p. 345.

17. Henry David Thoreau, *Walden*, New York 1854, ch. 16, p. 198.

18. Martin Buber, *Two Types of Faith*, (note 12), pp. 9–11.

19. *Tribute to Geza Vermes* (note 3), pp. 258 and 251.

20. Used in verbs of 'creating', 'sending down', etc., where the usage may be a plural of majesty, or interaction of God and the angels. On no count does it countermand the truth of unity.

21. For example, Gunapala Dharmasiri, *A Buddhist Critique of the Christian Concept of God*, Colombo 1974.

22. See Hans Küng in *The Christian Century*, Chicago, 9 October 1985.

23. Surahs 6.164, 17.15, 39.7 and 53.38. Also the emphasis on the fact that 'No soul is chargeable except for its own' (Surahs 6.152, 7.32, 23.62, 2.286, 65.7, 2. 223), which would seem to exclude 'suffering' for another. But see Chapter 6 below.

3. To Common Honesty

1. Noted in the Barbican Centre Exhibition of Jewish Art, 1990.
2. Jonathan Swift, quoted from A. L. Rowse, *Jonathan Swift: Major Prophet*, London 1975, p. 32.
3. William Shakespeare, *The Merchant of Venice*, Act 1, Scene 3, line 112.
4. The Qur'an's antipathy to Jews and Christians occurs in the Surahs which date after the Hijrah from Mecca, for example: 5.18, which chides them for saying 'We are the sons of God and His beloved ones'. However, along with denunciation of Christians for 'taking Jesus and his mother for gods' (5.116), there is praise for their piety and as potential 'friends,' given the circumspection which is aware also of their enmity (5.82 and 5.51).
5. Typically the Mexican José P. Miranda, *Marx and the Bible, A Critique of the Philosophy of Oppression*, ET by John Eagleson, Maryknoll and London 1977.
6. Isaac Pennington, quoted in John Buchan, *Oliver Cromwell*, London 1934, p. 68.
7. By virtue, that is, of participation in the minimal Noachid covenant (Genesis 9.3-7), of 'dominion' in nature and the sanctity of human life, but none of the exclusive privileges covenanted with Israel at Sinai.
8. The interplay of text and context is evident in the reiterated report of what 'they (i.e. Meccans) are saying', therefore 'Say thou (Muhammad)' in reply.
9. The technical term 'ignorance' (*jahiliyyah*) means not only the absence of revelation, which became less so as the Qur'an accumulated under Muhammad's reception, but also a certain wildness or uncouthness, a waywardness, which was not only without discernment but without discipline.
10. See, for example, Isma'il al-Faruqi, *Islam*, Illinois, 1979: 'To convert out of Islam means clearly to abandon its world order which is the Islamic State. That is why Islamic law has treated people who have converted out of Islam as political traitors' (p. 68).
11. By the year 619 CE, after thirteen years of preaching, Muhammad's cause was still oppressed; his protecting uncle, Abu Talib, and his wife, Khadijah, had died. A preaching venture he made uphill from Mecca to Al-Ta'if was rejected. Surah 10.46 even warns him that he may die before the issue with the Meccans is decided.
12. See, for example, Shabbir Akhtar, *Be Careful with Muhammad*, London 1989.

13. Plato, *Politeia, The Republic*, ET by Thomas Taylor, London and New York, n.d., p. 38 (Bk. ii).

14. It is this, in the view of some Jewish theologians, which calls Jewry to 'perpetual futurism'. Messiah does not 'come', Messiah is for ever 'awaited', as a symbol of hope in God. If Messiah is 'identified' and the world remains in evil is hope not discredited? Hence belief in the advent, first, of pre-Messianic tribulation in which evil, by its very apex, would herald Messianic day.

15. It is necessary to say 'chronologically' here since there might be an event, confronting Messiah and requiring what the Messianic takes, not determined as climax on a calendar but as an inclusive epitome of evil at any date – the Christian view of the Cross of Jesus.

16. Albert Camus, *The Fall*, ET by Justin O'Brien, London 1957, pp. 82, 96.

17. Compare the 'lesson' drawn from the Parable of the Two Men in the Temple (Luke 18.9–14): 'We learn to thank God that we are not as this Pharisee.'

18. Camus, op. cit., pp. 52, 102–103.

19. See Ch. 1, note 2 above.

20. Christopher Fry, *Plays: The Dark is Light Enough*, London 1971, p. 90: 'Weep for what you can. 'Tis grateful to our brevity to weep for what is briefer . . . It is not unseemly that man's compassion should begin at the thought of a sparrow's fall.'

4. And Active Penitence

1. The root word *ghafara* and its derivatives are very frequent in the Qur'an. Three of the divine names concerning 'forgiveness' belong with them. The imperative 'Seek forgiveness' (from God understood) occurs in Surahs 4.106; 40.55; 47.19; 110.3.

2. The demand to be *muklisun lahu al-din*, as the phrase goes, is reiterated in the Qur'an. The quality of *ikhlas*, 'entire sincerity', is vital to all religious acts (see, for example Surahs 2.139; 7.29; 10.22; 29.65; 31.32; 40.14 and 98.5).

3. The Qur'an echoes this in accusing the Jews of considering themselves 'God's beloved ones', and asking 'why then He punished them for their transgressions' (Surah 5.18).

4. The poet Edwin Muir, for example, was alive to the antecedents of Hitler's Germany at work in the aftermath of the Treaty of Versailles, 1919–20, when the notorious Hitler Youth were children bred in resentment. See his *Autobiography*, London 1954, p. 262. One cannot well comprehend history by foreshortening perspective.

5. The writings of Elie Wiesel are the most telling documentation of this
   need from within the soul of Jewry, written in Hebrew, French or
   English. Any adequate 'revenge' for the Holocaust would need to
   'burn down the whole world'. A universal nemesis would have to
   include itself.

6. A line not the less ironical for being in the heart of one of Robert
   Frost's most moving poems. See *Complete Poems*, New York 1964, p.
   467.

7. Those, for example, of Maulana Azad (1888–1958), whose political
   career and Qur'an Commentary exemplified a deeply conciliatory,
   sensitive comprehension of Islam for which he suffered much enmity
   on the part of other Muslims. See Ian H. Douglas, *Abul Kalam Azad*,
   ed. C. W. Troll & G. Minault, Oxford 19 and my *The Pen and the
   Faith: Eight Modern Muslim Writers and the Qur'an*, London 1986, pp.
   14–32.

8. At the opening of the classic poem, Arjuna flinches from battle and
   the slaughter of his own kin arrayed on the battelfield. Reluctantly he
   is persuaded to accept the 'warrior' 'duty' and engage, and to do so in
   'disinterest' in personal glory. The question persists whether 'interest'
   should not be taken into the issue itself, i.e. not attitudes *within*
   combat but attitudes about it and whether it needs to be 'fated'.

9. Al-Azhar, the celebrated premier university of Islam in Cairo, and
   Deoband, a well-known centre of studies in Muslim India.

10. In the writings of Karl Rahner and many other Christian practitioners
    of dialogue it is instinctive to pose inter-faith questions within the
    category of 'being saved', or 'the salvific' in other faiths, without
    appreciating how the very notion is liable to impose Christian criteria
    in ways already excluded by what other faiths comprehend.

11. The thought and career of Mahatma Gandhi illustrate both the need
    and the capacity of the Hindu mind to generate and sustain such
    initiatives. The point here is how inter-faith mediation may best serve
    them.

12. The principle under which R. C. Moberly presented his theology of
    Jesus' cross. See *Atonement and Personality*, London 1907, one of the
    major works of Christian theology this century.

13. A telling fictional study of this fact is John Steinbeck's *The Grapes
    of Wrath*, New York 1939, where the evil which dispossesses the
    smallholders and makes them fugitives is vast, impersonal, anonymous
    and inaccessible to their protests. One cannot get avenging from a
    brass plate on a far-away bank and its capitalist profiteers.

14. T. S. Eliot, *Murder in the Cathedral*, London 1935, p. 84.

15. The tradition is frequently quoted. One source is the *Sunan* of Abu

Isa Muhammad ibn Sawrah al-Tirmidhi, Beirut ³1978 (A H 1398), Vol. 3, p. 318.

16. Sometimes translated 'dissembling', *taqiyyah* has a positive intent, when circumstances admit. One may feign quiescence to which one has not really assented. The concept has played a great part in the history of Shî2ah Islam, where it often had to be practised when they were disadvantaged. Its protective aspect has to be balanced by the inwardly defiant non-capitulation.

17. Surahs 113 and 114. Evil in the workings of nature is included, but the sinister *sharr* is the 'whispering' in 'the bosoms of men', i.e. envy, covetousness, bad faith and enmity.

18. On *Ta'widh* and many other aspects of Muslim penitence see Constance E. Padwick, *Muslim Devotions*, London 1961.

19. See *The Mind of the Qur'an*, London 1973, pp. 99f. and Muhammad Kamil Husain, 'The Meaning of Zulm in the Qur'an,' *The Muslim World Quarterly*, Hartford, Vol. 49, No. 3, July 1959.

20. Muhammad Kamil Husain, *City of Wrong*, ET Amsterdam 1958. See also full discussion of the meaning of the 'apparentness' of the death of Jesus and Surah 4.157–58 in my *Jesus and the Muslim*, London 1985, Ch. 6, 'Gethsemane and Beyond'.

21. Matthew 26. 21f; Mark 14. 18f.

22. W. R. Rogers, *Europa and the Bull and Other Poems*, London 1952, p. 60, quoted from N. P. Harvey, *Death's Gift*, London 1985, pp. 30–31.

23. Arthur Power, *Conversations with James Joyce*, ed. Clive Hart, London 1974, p. 98.

5. With Mutual Discovery

1. Muslim *Fada'il*, or Celebrations of the Virtues of Jerusalem, were numerous in the Middle Ages. See the collection by Muhammad ibn Ahmad al-Wasiti, ed. Isaac Hasson, Jerusalem, 1979. See also Henri Sauvaire, *Histoire de Jérusalem*, Paris 1876; also I. I. Levine (ed.) *The Jerusalem Cathedra*, No. 1, Jerusalem 1981.

2. Peter Abelard (1079–1142), 'Truly Jerusalem name we that shore, Vision of peace that brings joy evermore.'

3. See the discussion of the references in the two psalms in R. Davidson, *The Courage to Doubt*, London 1983, pp. 141f. 'Zaphon' in 48.2 is referred to in Canaanite texts of Ras Shamra (fourteenth-century BC) as the traditional abode of the gods, located vaguely in the far north. In the same texts the Canaanite god 'El' sits 'at the source of the rivers'. How far the psalmist intended the associations must be conjec-

tural. But the sidelight on 'inter-religion' is interesting within biblical texts.

4. The four Gospels are, of course, a genre on their own and are not, strictly speaking, 'biographies' of Jesus. But the other sense of the word, i.e. 'writing in a life', is a right way of speaking of 'the Word made flesh', the Christian understanding of what we have in Jesus.

5. On such mystical interpretation of Muhammad as 'beloved of God' and 'axis of the soul', see Annemarie Schimmel, *And Muhammad is His Messenger: The Veneration of the Prophet in Islamic Piety*, Chapel Hill 1985.

6. Surah 5.90 mentions *ansab*, 'idols', in a list of abominations, while Surah 5.3 uses the word *nusub* (pl.) in reference to what is sacrificed to idols. Abraham and others repudiate 'idolatry' in five passages where the word used is *asnam*. *Tamathil*, or 'images', occurs only in 21.52 and 34.13 in reference to Abraham and Solomon rejecting 'images'. Explicit prohibition has therefore to be read within the overall anathema on *shirk*, or belief in 'associate deities' with God.

7. On art in Islam in caliphal palaces and private homes see e.g. Carel I. Du Ry, *The Art of Islam*, New York 1970, and Thomas W. Arnold, *Painting in Islam*, New York 1965.

8. The incident is noted in Herbert Birks, *Life of Thomas Valpy French*, Vol. 1, p. 58, London 1885.

9. See Roger Hooker, *Themes in Hinduism and Christianity*, Frankfurt 1989, p. 194, and Hooker's reference to L. W. Brown, *Three Worlds, One Word*, London 1981, p. 68.

10. Al-Biruni (973–1048) was a noted Islamic scholar and geographer. In travel in India he wrestled with the meaning of Hindu imagery. See E. C. Sachau's translation of his writings *Alberuni's India*, London 1888, Vol. 1, Ch. 11.

11. How far Islamic influence was directly responsible for the outbreak of the iconoclastic controversy in those centuries is a matter of debate. See E. J. Martin, *A History of the Iconoclastic Controversy*, London 1930, and my *The Arab Christian*, London 1992, pp. 80–2.

12. On the Qur'anic Abraham as an iconoclast see Surahs 21.51–73 and 37.83–113.

13. 'Performance' is the right word here and in no way derogatory. The command is always, not 'say', but *'perform the salat'* It is something to be done as well as said.

14. The salutation 'Peace be upon you and the mercy of God' is said as the head is turned full left and full right, so that it is 'carried' right around the line, and circle, of praying Muslims on the one focus to Mecca.

15. Inscribed clay tablets two or so inches by one are used in Shîʿah Islam where the brow makes contact in the act of *sujud*, or prostration.

16. Though in a half century or so of study in Islam and travel among Muslims I have not come across this analysis of *salat* explicitly from Muslim sources, this may simply be my limit of reach. But many have attested it when suggested as the right 'reading'.

17. However, secular Jews in the manner of David Ben Gurion tend to read 'chosenness' as 'virility' and to discount 'election' except as a spur to self-fulfilment.

18. There have been times when proselytes were welcome and when Judaism accepted converts. But the vast majority of Jews are not received from outside but 'born into the covenant'. One may note the view of Lord Jacobovits, lately Chief Rabbi of Great Britain: 'Judaism is content to remain for all time a minority faith restricted to those born into it and the few who may spontaneously seek to embrace it' (Chaim Bermant, *Lord Jacobovits*, London 1990, p. 171).

6. *Towards Joint Liabilities*

1. Chaim Bermant, *Lord Jakobovits*, London 1990, p. 174. His full title was 'Chief Rabbi of the United Hebrew Congregations of the British Commonwealth'.

2. William Shakespeare, *As You Like It*, Act 2, Scene 7, lines 59–61.

3. Kwame Nkrumah, *Autobiography*, London 1957, p. 164, where he adds that the adoption of this official 'policy' of the Party was 'met with enthusiastic cheering from the audience'.

4. Arend Van Leeuwen, writing in 1964, in *Christianity in World History*, ET by H. H. Hoskins, London 1964, predicted that the religious view of the world would surrender to secularity, reinforced by technology, within a quarter century. He had not reckoned with the resilience, however 'superstitious', of religious belief (see pp. 410f.).

5. On the *dhimmi* system of minority status in the long centuries of Islam and its Caliphate see my *The Arab Christian: A History in the Middle East*, London 1992.

6. What distinguishes the Judaic/Zionist understanding of the relation of people to land and of both to power is the understanding of special divine warrant and the bond of 'covenant'. This makes the 'national-ism' different from all others, but it is important to realize that the physical and spiritual facts of *all* human tribe and tenancy are one and the same.

7. This should not mean for Christians any neutralizing of the distinctive accents of Christian faith. Some twentieth-century exponents of the

Christian role inside Arab nationalism argued for a kind of 'Christian' adoption of Islam in the interests of national unity. Thus, for example, Michel Aflaq (1912–1989), a Syrian Christian and main theorist of the Ba'th Party, called for a single Arab consciousness which would nourish itself vitally on blood and culture while disallowing the divisiveness of religious doctrine. Similar voices called for a Christian confession of Muhammad's prophethood as the supreme expression of Arab genius. Whether such cultural readiness for Islam on the part of Christians could ever satisfy the canons of Islam only Muslims can decide. It would certainly silence the significance Christian faith should bring to the critique of nationhood. See Sylvia Haim (ed.), *Arab Nationalism, An Anthology*, Berkeley 1979, and my *The Arab Christian*, Ch. 7.

8. John Donne, *The Satires, Epigrams and Verse Letters*, ed. W. Milgate, Oxford 1967, p. 14.

9. Was it the sense of a *de facto* occupancy of Palestine which prompted some pioneer Zionists like Herzl to contemplate, briefly, the notion of a state 'somewhere', say East Africa or Argentina? When all the demands of history and yearning made a Palestinian locale imperative there developed in many Zionist minds the conviction of 'innocence' – on the part of 'a people without a land' taking over 'a land (allegedly) without a people'. That misconception has been the tragic tribulation of the Zionist hope ever since.

10. Echoing the proverbial *caveat emptor*, 'let the buyer beware', to suggest 'Let the traveller, the wayfarer, beware'.

11. A fervent poetical celebration of 'embryonic' meaning is that in Psalm 139. 13–17.

12. Not merely a play on words, for life is sensed in creaturehood as a veritable 'annunciation', an invitation and summons into what is eminently 'greetable'. 'Renunciation', however, must be used with caution. Buddhist *nirvana* is not ultimate extinction prefaced by 'negation'. Properly understood, there was 'no-thing' to extinguish or negate. The true wisdom realizes so. Nevertheless, the practical meaning of such realization is a kind of forfeiture of being that *might* be read, alternatively, as 'annunciation'.

13. *Anatta* and *anicca*, the technical terms by which Buddhism denotes the 'illusion' of selfhood and the fleetingness of life.

14. In the Surah 2 passage the divine announcement of the impending creation and dignity of 'man' draws from the angels in the heavenly conclave a reaction of pained surprise. Why not the angels to preside as deputies over creation rather than frail, fickle, blood-shedding humans? God, in reply, has his own reasons and is not deflected.

When Satan, among the angels, resists further and refuses to 'worship' Adam it is clear that his defiance of God concerns the human meaning. It is in dis-esteeming the human that he flouts the divine. So it is still. Satan is then set to demonstrate to God the divine folly by instigating the proofs of it in the fallibility of man. Thus, in turn, the 'enemy' – the *diabolos* – can only be discredited, and the divine wisdom vindicated, by the genuine fulfilment of humanness. There could hardly be a more powerful 'mythology' of the meaning and dignity of man in creation.

15. The Qur'an's phrase is *min duni-llahi*, lit. 'from . . . without God', where God is excluded from cognizance. This is the ultimate state of 'atheism', since it is about 'the God we ignore' – always a more heinous thing than 'the God we deny'. The latter may be a gesture of despair or vain search, the former is a posture of indifference.

16. See, for example, T. F. Torrance (ed.), *Belief in Science and in Christian Life*, Edinburgh 1980.

17. Being 'content with the doctrinaire' is characteristic of many influential figures in faith-commendation today, a kind of 'it is so' stance about what is 'believed', whether in Asia, or Islam, or Jewry, or the Christian scene. Such believing takes its scriptures, or its institution, or its other grounds, as self-sufficient, properly immune from enquiry, and not obligated to 'show cause' for their status. In some Christian quarters it is the very assertiveness of this attitude of faith which gives it 'cutting edge' in the world and constitutes its thrust in studied contrast to the wistful, tentative or sceptical mentality it aims to overwhelm with certitude. Some Christian thinking understands its witness as categorically challenging and disputing all else, relying exclusively on its inner authority as being under no obligation to associate patiently with what might call it into question or feel an honest disquiet about its claims.

     This contentment to be doctrinaire in no way facilitates understanding. Nor does it dissuade others from being the same; rather, it encourages isolation. But perhaps its greatest fault is simply its impatience.

18. R. S. Thomas, *The Echoes Return Slow*, London 1988, p. 68. He was thinking of liturgy mediating truth more readily than theology. I have argued throughout for the sacramental nature of human activity via the senses and the mind in the natural order.

19. This is not to romanticize the sex act or to say that it is never callous, fickle and culpably insincere ('the night my father got me his mind was not on me'). It is to say that in its utter physical juncture, or coition, it couples selves in the most total fashion. There is that about

it which speaks a sacrament even where the will to know it so is flagrantly absent.

20.. See *Gender and Religion: On the Complexity of Symbols*, ed. C. W. Bynum, S. Harrell and P. Richman, Boston 1986, pp. 232–56.

21. James Joyce, *Ulysses*, Harmondsworth 1960, p. 331. He goes on nonchalantly: 'Nurse loves me new chemist . . .'

22. Shelley, for example, with his notion of marriage as love on condition of 'property rights', 'the longest journey . . . chained to a jealous foe.'

23. There is deliberate irony in this citing of a patriarchal story. Job's marriage plays no visible part in his saga, despite the travail of his mind and spirit. Even in tribulation his wife seems irrelevant. The situation portrays dramatically the assumptions feminism has to overcome. Nevertheless, the 'tent' is a lively symbol in the whole Hebrew tradition. The verse quoted allows us to register the sacred and the intimate, divine nearness and conjugal habitation, as one experience.

7. *By Precincts of Prayer*

1. John Donne, *Devotions upon Emergent Occasions*, ed. John Sparrow, Cambridge 1923, p. 87.

2. Ibid. p. 95.

3. A kind of definition that struggles to define and avoid defining. See Iris Murdoch, *The Sovereignty of Good*, London 1970, p. 55.

4. William Shakespeare, *The Merchant of Venice*, Act 1, Scene 3, lines 32f.

5. Ibn Battuta. *Travels in Asia and Africa: 1325–1354*, ET ed. H. A. R. Gibb, London 1929, pp. 163–4.

6. 'The worshippable' is a term coined by Daud Rahbar to designate that 'worth' which justifies worship and which in some sense the soul must discern and responsively identify. The thought is reciprocal to the Islamic idea of *shirk*, that the 'not-divine' shall on no account be misread as the 'divine'. See his *Memories and Meanings*, Cambridge, Mass. 1985.

7. Alain Robbe-Grillet, *Ghosts in the Mirror*, ET J. Levy, London 1989. The Egyptian Nobel prize-winner, Najib Mahfuz, may be cited from within the Arab world in the same sense.

8. The *asma'* al-husna, or 'excellent names' of God, in Islam have been the theme of long debate as to how they could 'mean', since their connotation derived, necessarily, from the adjectival sense they had as applied to man. Yet when used of God they must be 'totally other'. They were therefore used, by Qur'anic command (see Surah 59. 23–24

and 17.110), in the sense in which they could be true, and 'without asking how'.

9. Since evil and falsehood could not exist in the presence of the divine name, invocation was made for 'a strong tower' of security. Jerusalem and the Temple were 'the place of the name' – a crucial concept in Hebrew religion.

10. Cf. Surah 109.6: 'To you your religion; to me mine,' where Muhammad firmly exempts himself from the Quraish on the ground of their false, and his true, worship. The Hijrah to Medina later fulfilled this new people shaping.

11. The Five Pillars of Islam require the statement of *niyyah*, or 'intention', so that the performance of them is ensured only in a true intent.

12. C. S. Lewis, *Poems*, London 1964, p. 124, 'The Apologist's Evening Prayer'.

13. John Donne, *Poems*, ed. H. J. C. Grierson, Oxford 1933, 'Holy Sonnet' xiv, p. 299.

14. This is an aspect of *shirk* which is often overlooked. Were the doctrine of divine unity (*tawhid*) false, pseudo and plural deities would not matter. There would, in fact, be entities corresponding to them. The cardinal doctrine and the central veto in Islam belong together.

15. Surah 55 is unique in its reiterated refrain, where the verb intriguingly, is in the dual form, as is the possessive pronoun 'your' attaching to 'Lord'. 'You and you' is how it is mostly translated. The root idea in the verb is that of 'denying', 'refusing to acknowledge' with the sense also of 'discounting'. Both the fact of the 'mercy' is belied and also the relationship it should induce, i.e. gratitude and wonder.

16. Surah 15.16 and 19–22, a very typical passage.

17. Surah 100. Some pre-Islamic poetry also bewails the violence of the feud and the raid. See C. J. Lyall, *Translations of Ancient Arabic Poetry*, London 1930, especially the poet Zuhair, and poems Al-Hamāsah.

18. Lancelot Andrewes' *Preces Privatae* use the term to list what out of condemnation, i.e. deprecation, the soul seeks after.

19. Many may be found in my *Alive to God*, Oxford 1970, a working anthology of Muslim/Christian praise, penitence and petition, with an introductory essay dealing with many of the issues more briefly ventured here.

20. It seems clear that the mothers were seeking *barakah*, or blessing, perhaps as a preservative from disease via the touch of the 'holy rabbi' they felt Jesus to be. Was this what prompted the disciples to rebuff

them? Jesus met them on their own ground (see Mark 10.13–16; Matt. 19.13–15 and Luke 18.15–17).

21. *Journals and Letters of Henry Martyn*, London 1837, Vol. 2, p. 252. See also John Sargent. *Memoir of Henry Martyn*, London 1816, p. 107.

22. For example, in making ventures into vocabulary congenial to the world of their witness (logos, mystery, and the like) at some risk of misunderstanding inseparable from creative communication.

23. Alan Paton, *Knocking at the Door*, London 1975.

24. Dietrich Bonhoeffer, *Letters and Papers from Prison*, ed. E. Bethge, London 1971, p. 157.

8. To the Self in Question

1. As for example in Isma'il al-Faruqi's reading of the law of apostasy in Islam. See his *Islam*, Niles, Illinois 1979, p. 68. 'To convert out of Islam means clearly to abandon its world order which is the Islamic State. This is why Islamic law has treated people who have converted out of Islam as political traitors.' Cf. also the comment of Rabbi Julian Jacobs: 'Conversion, from whichever faith, would be apostasy' (*Common Ground*, October 1990).

2. Recalling the discussion in Chapter 5 and the whole nature of the religious interpretation of all experience. Idols may be much more than figures of wood and stone, and such figures may well not be idolatrous. The supreme emphasis – and spiritual issue – within Islam is precisely what divine sovereignty means in the faith as to divine unity.

3. These are *al-nafs al-ammarah* and *al-nafs al-lawwamah*. They are meant to become *al-nafs al-mutma'innah*, 'the soul in peace' (Surah 89.27).

4. See the valuable Hindu/Christian study in R. H. Hooker, *Themes in Hinduism and Christianity*, Frankfurt am Main 1989, pp. 132–91.

5. Echoing William Wordsworth's 'Me this uncharted freedom tires', *Poetical Works*, Vol. 4, ed. E. de Selincourt and H. Darbishire, Oxford 1947, p. 85; 'Ode to Duty', line 37.

6. The concept developed by Karl Rahner, the eminent German Jesuit theologian (1904–1984), of 'anonymous Christians' was intended to express a 'self-gift' of God in grace, outside the church and the gospel, and responsive to the sincerity of believers within other systems in whom 'salvific intention' could be read.

7. See also the comparable description of the disesteemed tragic sufferer for righteousness in Wisdom 2.10–22.

8. In the question that opens Isaiah 53, 'Who has believed our report?', 'report' is a passive – 'the thing that has come to our ears'. Yet what is heard becomes active in their 'amazement' and so in their 'telling'. This is exactly the double sense of the 'tradition' in I Corinthians 15.3, where Paul describes himself as receiving and relaying the *traditio* of the faith.

9. 'Synonymous' means 'of one name with'. Is it, then, a usage which ignores, for example, Acts 4.12, which speaks of 'no other name' than Jesus – the verse used to claim 'exclusivism'? All depends on whether we read 'name' as a mere label, or whether, as in all biblical tradition, it intends an identity, a pattern, a reality. Is not all 'love that suffers and forgives' synonymous with the way Jesus was the Christ? It is that Messianic reality which is 'the name whereby we must be saved'. See further Chapter 9 below, section ix.

10. It is right to understand this inclusive prayer of Jesus as the evangelist's summation of his whole significance as this was grasped from within the retrospect of corporate experience. It is like a testamentary document which even refers to 'the Christ whom thou has sent' in the third person (v. 3), and it breathes the whole realization of meaning. This does not make it less, or other than, Christ's, inasmuch as the lens through which he is here seen was of his making.

11. The commissioning here and in Mark 16.15, with the developed baptismal formula of the threefold name in the church's own charter of its obedience. This does not mean that it mandated itself: it means that it had its sense of mission from its experience of Jesus as the Christ. They were sent only by his sending and moved by his motivating. It was his commission in them.

12. All that properly makes for reticence and patience in Jewish/Christian relationships against the awesome background of the Holocaust should not argue non-Jewish, i.e. 'Gentile', exclusivism in the Christian Gospel. This would be to deny both its origins and its character. There can be no exclusions from Christ, only readiness for all. To think otherwise would be guilty of yet more 'Jewish unwantedness'.

13. Meaning, by 'human long-suffering', of course the suffering humans occasion to the purposes of God. Cf, the warning in I Thessalonians 5.19, 'Quench not the Spirit.' See also Horace Bushnell, *Vicarious Sacrifice*, New York 1866, p. 85.

14. Thus, for example, in the *Scottish Journal of Theology*, Vol. 43, 1991, Professor J. Heywood Thomas quotes Max Warren, eminent exponent of mission and General Secretary of the Church Missionary Society from 1942 to 1967: 'We have marched round alien Jerichos the requisite number of times. We have sounded the trumpets, and the walls

have not collapsed.' He then comments: 'In effect an obituary on traditional missionary policy and practice.'

15. *Homilies of Saint Bernard*, No. 4, 9.

9. *Where is Home?*

1. John Wesley, *Journals*, ed. Nehemiah Curnock, 1938, bicentenary ed., Vol. 1, 469. See also Henry Moore, *Life of John Wesley*, London 1826, Vol. 1, p. 162. It was a remark to him of 'a serious Christian', name unknown.

2. *Wilfred Owen, The Collected Letters*, ed. Harold Owen & John Bell, London 1967, Letter 512 to Susan Owen, May 1917, p. 461. He added: 'Thus you will see how pure Christianity will not fit with pure patriotism.' One might compare R. W. Emerson's question: 'In Christendom where are the Christians?', *Collected Works*, ed. R. E. Spiller et al., Vol. 2, p. 48.

3. *Ibid.*, p. 461. The words are in the form of a question: 'Am I not . . .' 'Christ,' he continued, 'is literally in no man's land.'

4. Saving for the incident in John 8.1–12, when Jesus 'wrote on the ground' and no doubt the shuffling of feet soon erased whatever he may have written.

5. The point is usefully discussed in R. O. P. Taylor, *The Groundwork of the Gospels*, Oxford 1946, pp. 91–5. See also Oscar Wilde's lyrical expression of this conviction about Galilee and Greek in *De Profundis*, Oxford World Classics 1990, p. 119.

6. A notable example is Geza Vermes, *Jesus the Jew*, London 1973; also Samuel Sandmel, *We Jews and Jesus*, London 1965, and an increasing flow of studies reversing a long Jewish avoidance of issues about Jesus, due perhaps to a feeling that he was unduly 'possessed' by Christians, or out of the complexities of the Messianic issue.

7. An important nineteenth-century study of the ethical impact of Jesus, written at a time when dogmatic christology was queried or discarded by many, was John R. Seeley, *Ecce Homo: A Survey of the Life and Work of Jesus Christ*, London 1865.

8. Tents were homes to nomad people, and the prophet Hosea, for example, makes use of the imagery of the wilderness (12.9) and 'dwelling in tents'. The divine presence was also 'tented' in the midst. It was natural for the Gospels and epistles to return to that imagery in expressing the meaning of the Incarnation.

9.   'Each thought of God that would take flesh,
         Needs human handmaid still,

> And all immortal loveliness
> Waits on our mortal will.'

Cf. Paul's words about 'Christ being formed in you . . .' (Galatians 4.19).

10. On the role of Mary in history see Marina Warner, *Alone of All Her Sex. The Myth and Cult of the Virgin Mary*, London 1976. There is scholarly discussion as to whether in fact the *Magnificat* was Mary's hymn or Elizabeth's, mother of John the Baptist. Luke the evangelist was clearly drawing on the song of Hannah (I Samuel 1) and on Maccabean hymns in which 'the mighty' were literally dethroned. It was his genius to apply those legacies to the contrasted celebration of 'the exaltation of the lowly'.

11. It is noteworthy that in Ephesians 1.6 the identical word 'accepted in the beloved' is used of the ordinary believer as of 'the highly favoured' handmaid of the Lord.

12. The meaning of the phrase in Exodus 3.14, not the puzzlingly philosophical 'I am that I am', but 'I am (or 'will be') what there I am', Neither Moses nor the people can have advance knowledge: they can only trust. The event alone will bring the experience which fulfills the name.

13. Hence the expression 'Christ our Passover' (I Corinthians 5.8).

14. This is the circle of Christian truth expressed in John 14.1: 'Believe in God, believe in me . . .' (or both verbs can be indicative, or interchangeably imperative). We can start from Jesus and find that 'necessitates' God, or we can start from God and realize there has to be that which Jesus is, for either approach to be sustained.

15. Quoted from H. R. Mackintosh, *The Doctrine of the Person of Jesus Christ*, Edinburgh 1912, p. 212.

16. T. F. Torrance in id. (ed.), *Belief in Science and Christian Life*, Edinburgh 1980, p. 17.

17. It is only Paul in I Corinthians 11.25–26, not the evangelists, who indicates that the rite should be repeated, by the phrase '. . . as often as you eat this bread, etc.'

18. Dom Gregory Dix, *The Shape of the Liturgy*, London 1945, pp. 744–5.

19. In Mark's account 14.25; cf. Luke 22.16; Matthew 26.29.

20. Echoing A. M. Toplady's hymn 'Rock of ages, cleft for me'.

21. How this belongs with infant baptism is not discussed here.

22. William Shakespeare, *Hamlet*, Act 5, Scene 2, line 342.

Index